THE
1783 TAX LISTS
AND THE
1790 FEDERAL CENSUS
FOR
WASHINGTON COUNTY, PENNSYLVANIA

୬ଡ଼ଡ଼ଞ

COMPILED BY

KATHERINE K. ZINSSER AND RAYMOND M. BELL

Heritage Books
2024

HERITAGE BOOKS

AN IMPRINT OF HERITAGE BOOKS, INC.

Books, CDs, and more—Worldwide

For our listing of thousands of titles see our website
at
www.HeritageBooks.com

Published 2024 by
HERITAGE BOOKS, INC.
Publishing Division
5810 Ruatan Street
Berwyn Heights, MD 20740

International Standard Book Number
Paperbound: 978-1-55613-159-2

TABLE OF CONTENTS

COMPARISON OF RIVAL CLAIMS TO SOUTHWESTERN PENNSYLVANIA BY VIRGINIA AND PENNSYLVANIA

(Boundaries Approximate)

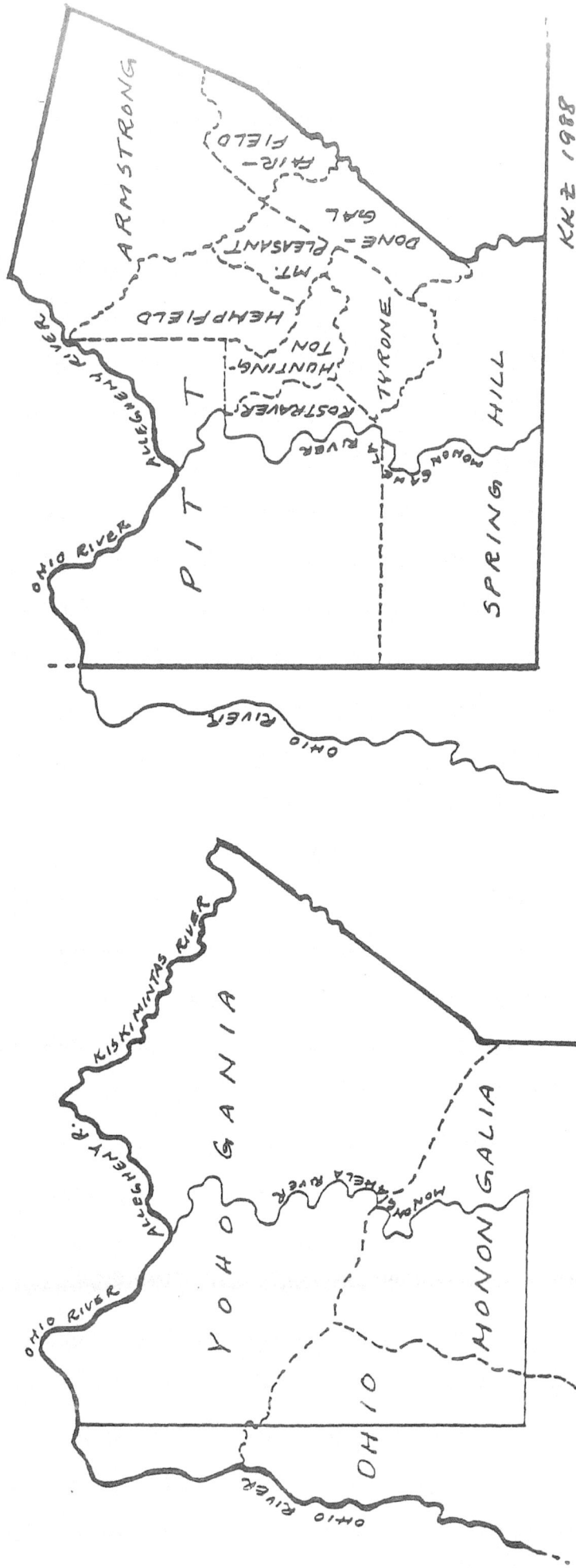

TOWNSHIPS OF
WESTMORELAND CO, PA

1773-1781

COUNTIES OF THE
DISTRICT OF WEST AUGUSTA, VA

1776

SECTION 1

THE 1783 TAX LISTS

OF

WASHINGTON COUNTY, PENNSYLVANIA

by

Katherine Kendall Zinsser

with an introduction by

Raymond Martin Bell

INTRODUCTION

An important source for genealogical searchers in Pennsylvania is the early county tax lists. Taxes were assessed in the fall for the next year, listing all persons within each township who owned land, horses or cows and all single men aged 21 or older ("single freemen"). Persons without property were not on the tax list, but most inhabitants of Washington County had at least a horse or a cow. The 1783 tax list also assessed sheep and slaves - slaves along with livestock. Tax records can be especially useful in providing information (that is difficult to obtain elsewhere) on the residence of individuals. Also, the single freeman list can help in estimating the ages of sons by giving a date when they first appear as freemen.

Washington County was formed in March 1781, and was fully organized by the fall of 1781. Its territory included all of southwestern Pennsylvania west of the Monongahela River and south of the Ohio River (see map p. 11). This area comprised present Washington and Greene Counties and parts of Allegheny and Beaver Counties. The first tax lists, though assembled late in 1781, were for county and state taxes to be levied in 1782. These lists have been published in the Pennsylvania Archives, Series III, Volume 22 with the erroneous heading "Washington County Supply Tax, 1781".

Before 1982 the only known tax lists for the 1780's were those stored in the Washington County courthouse, beginning with 1784. Twenty-four lists for various townships and years were missing from 1784 through 1789. Fortunately, about 1982 a complete set of duplicate tax lists for Washington County (1782 through 1789, except 1784) was found by chance in Harrisburg. These lists fill the gaps left in the original Washington County tax records. Copies of the original tax lists were sent 200 years ago to the state capital at Philadelphia to enable levy of state "supply" taxes. These lists have been reproduced on microfilms RG4-340 and RG4-341 by the Pennsylvania Historical and Museum Commission.

Exoneration lists of persons exempt from state taxes for the years 1782, 1783, 1789 because of Indian attacks are included on these microfilms. An Act of Assembly passed 22 Dec. 1781 exonerated all 1782 state taxes for Washington County inhabitants. In 1783, all but a few Fallowfield residents were exonerated. Again in 1789 the state exonerated a large part of the county by an Act of Assembly dated 3 Oct. 1788. The state's copy of the 1783 tax lists for Washington County was received at Philadelphia on 27 Feb. 1784. The 1783 exoneration list was compiled 4 Oct. 1784 and received by the state on 3 Sept. 1785. The 1789 exoneration list was received 9 December 1789.

The 1783 tax lists are published in this book because the year 1783 is particularly significant. The 1782 Indian attacks in Washington County (especially the western section) were severe between the March attack on Miller's Fort through September when the attack on Rice's Fort occurred. Both forts were in Donegal Township (see map p. 11). Many persons fled from their cabins to safer quarters farther east and the 1783 tax lists reflect this dispersion.

At least ten Donegal Township taxables show up in Strabane Township, (which included the town of Washington) for 1783. The same year, Donegal Township listed the names of twenty-some persons from Ohio County, (West) Virginia, which lay just to the west of Washington County PA. A man taxed in an eastern township of Washington County in 1783 for only horses and cows may well be a refugee from a western township. (There are forty-eight names listed in Donegal Township for 1782 and 1784 that do not appear on the 1783 tax records.)

Three examples from the tax lists show the movement of families during this period: In 1782, Moses Williamson Sr. and sons Jeremiah, Moses Jr. and Thomas lived in Ohio County (West) Virginia. In 1783 the father was listed in Somerset Township, while the three sons were in Donegal Township where their brother Samuel lived.

In 1782 John Williamson Sr, Moses Sr's brother, was in Donegal Township. A year later he was listed in Somerset Twp, but his sons, (Colonel) David, Eleazer and John Jr. remained in Donegal.

In 1782 Samuel Byers Sr. and sons James and Thomas were in Donegal Twp. In 1783 they were listed in Strabane Twp, although they were still taxed for their land in Donegal Twp. By 1784, all of the parties were back home.

Table 1 shows the population shift in 1783. The ratio given in column 3 is the number of taxables for 1783 divided by the number of taxables for 1782 (i.e., Robinson had 60 taxables in 1783, 138 in 1782, 60/138 = 0.42.) Low ratios mean settlers had fled; high ratios show an influx of fleeing settlers, with the exception of Hopewell Township, where those escaping from further west equalled those fleeing to the east. Column 5 shows the number of 1783 taxables divided by the number of houses. The data for columns 2 and 4 comes from Table 2 on p. 10. The data for columns 1 and 6 were obtained by counting the names on the tax lists themselves. Freemen, being more transitory, were not included in the calculations. The map on p. 12 shows how each township was affected by this migration.

TABLE 1   ANALYSIS OF POPULATION SHIFT IN 1783

Townships	COL 1 Married Taxables 1782	COL 2 Married Taxables 1783	COL 3 col 2/ col 1	COL 4 Houses 1783	COL 5 col 2/ col 4	COL 6 Married Taxables 1784
AMWELL	177	212	1.20	139	1.52	180
BETHLEHEM	250	285	1.14	178	1.60	250
CECIL	273	376	1.37	295	1.27	285
CUMBERLAND	185	150	0.81	68	2.20	196
DONEGAL	144	104	0.72	83	1.25	148
FALLOWFIELD	223	360	1.61	228	1.58	257
GREENE	143	112	0.78	71	1.58	141
HOPEWELL	216	230	1.06	174	1.32	287
MORGAN	117	154	1.32	100	1.54	135
NOTTINGHAM	171	258	1.51	182	1.42	186
PETERS	351	460	1.32	225	2.04	405
ROBINSON	138	60	0.42	23	2.61	217
SMITH	139	84	0.60	70	1.20	146
SOMERSET	143	205	1.43	158	1.30	157
STRABANE	170	265	1.56	223	1.19	202

The tax lists show the value of the taxpayer's possessions in Pennsylvania pounds. In 1782, the tax rate was about 5 pence per pound, thus, a man with a property value of £ 48 paid £ 1 ($2.66) in state taxes. £ 30/10 means 30 pounds and 10 shillings or £ 30 1/2; 1 pound = 20 shillings = 240 pence. (A Virginia pound equalled $3.33)

Table 2 on the following page, "Summary of Taxable Possessions in Washington County" was found at the end of the 1783 Supply Tax returns on the microfilm [RG-4 340]. It presents the first clear picture of Washington County inhabitants and their most valuable and taxable possessions.

Raymond Martin Bell
Washington, PA 1988

TABLE 2   SUMMARY OF TAXABLE POSSESSIONS IN WASHINGTON COUNTY FOR 1783

	acres	h	c	sh	sl	gm	sm	di	ty	fe	hou	oth	F	tax	w	B	W+B	W/hou
Amwell	33252	390	511	644	10	4	0	3	0	0	139	192	20	212	1029	17	1046	7.4
Bethlehem	33472	521	678	794	7	2	1	1	0	0	178	192	35	285	1500	7	1507	8.4
Cecil	49413	658	738	948	27	4	1	13	1	0	295	121	80	376	1444	50	1494	4.9
Cumberland	9365	168	230	258	7	2	1	3	0	0	68	30	24	150	543	7	550	8.0
Donegal	34229	175	232	255	12	1	0	3	0	0	83	50	16	104	515	12	527	6.2
Fallowfield	37797	615	710	1035	58	5	3	14	0	½	228	313	46	360	2740	117	2857	12.0
Greene	43497	173	211	170	2	3	1	6	0	1	71	34	21	112	500	7	507	7.7
Hopewell	51826	460	570	930	11	2	2	5	0	0	174	40	33	230	977	11	988	5.6
Morgan	29178	272	390	445	3	0	0	0	0	0	100	100	21	154	782	5	787	7.8
Nottingham	47677	480	520	651	24	3	2	14	1	½	182	221	41	258	1116	28	1144	6.1
Peters	48177	935	940	1090	34	3	1	14	2	0	225	162	62	460	1923	42	1965	8.5
Robinson	47431	106	136	172	17	0	0	1	0	0	23	10	8	60	204	32	236	8.9
Smith	50507	217	259	380	12	1	1	3	0	0	70	70	14	84	484	18	502	6.9
Somerset	21225	380	380	562	14	3	1	4	2	0	158	64	21	205	892	14	906	5.6
Strabane	41394	461	560	920	22	2	0	8	1	0	223	190	40	265	1348	36	1384	6.0
Total	578440	6011	7065	9254	260	35	14	92	7	2	2217	1789	482	3315	15997	402	16399	7.2

LEGEND:

h	horses	gm	gristmills
c	cattle	sm	sawmills
sh	sheep	di	distilleries
sl	slaves	ty	tanyards

fe	ferries
hou	houses
oth	other buildings
F	single freemen

tax	taxables
w	whites
B	blacks
W+B	total population
W/hou	ratio of whites to houses

RMG 1988

10

Beaver County
(1800)

Allegheny County
(1788)

PITTSBURGH

SMITH

ROBINSON

OHIO RIVER

CECIL

PETERS

HOPEWELL

NOTTINGHAM

STRABANE

SOMERSET

DONEGAL

AMWELL

BETHLEHEM

FALLOWFIELD

MORGAN

CUMBERLAND

MONONGAHELA RIVER

VIRGINIA

Greene County
(1796)

GREENE

KKZ 1988

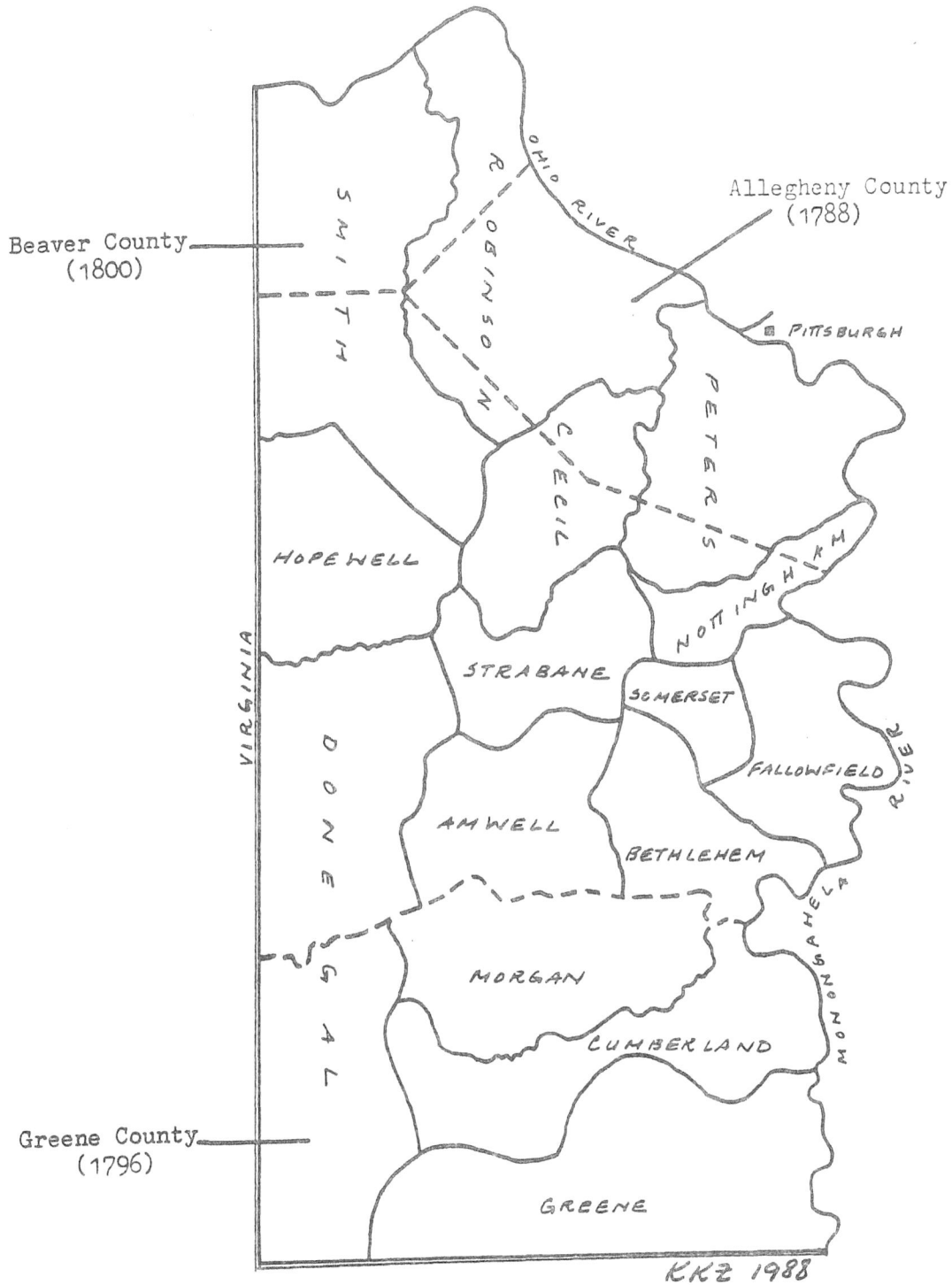

----- indicates present boundaries of Allegheny, Beaver and Greene Counties

STATISTICS FOR WASHINGTON COUNTY, PENNSYLVANIA IN 1783

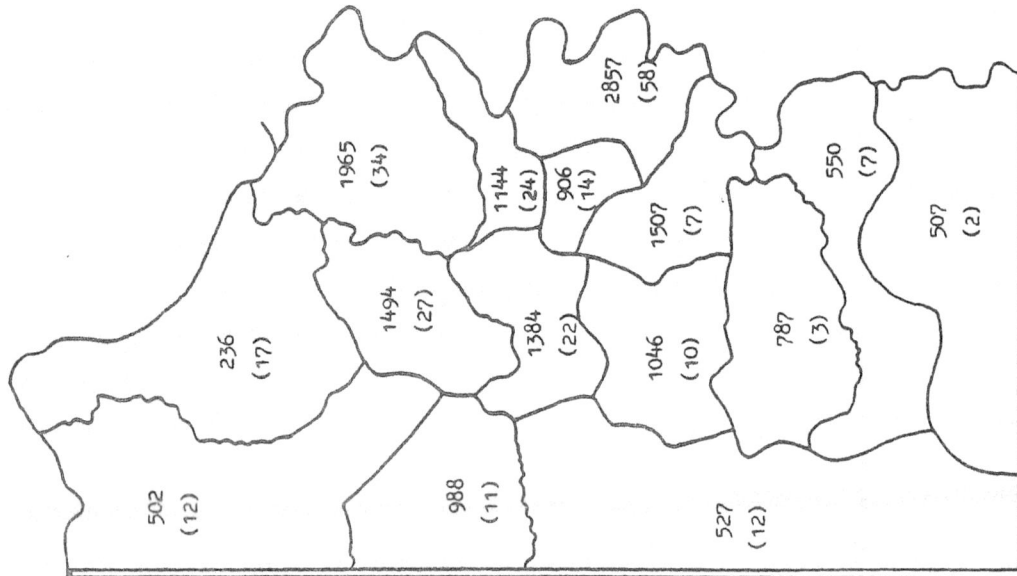

Number of Houses
(1783 Taxables Divided By 1782 Taxables)

70 (0.60)
23 (0.25)
225 (1.32)
228 (1.61)
295 (1.37)
182 (1.51)
158 (1.47)
174 (0.98)
223 (1.56)
178 (1.14)
68 (1.00)
139 (1.24)
100 (1.32)
83 (0.72)
71 (0.75)

KKZ 1988

Number of Inhabitants
(Number of Slaves)

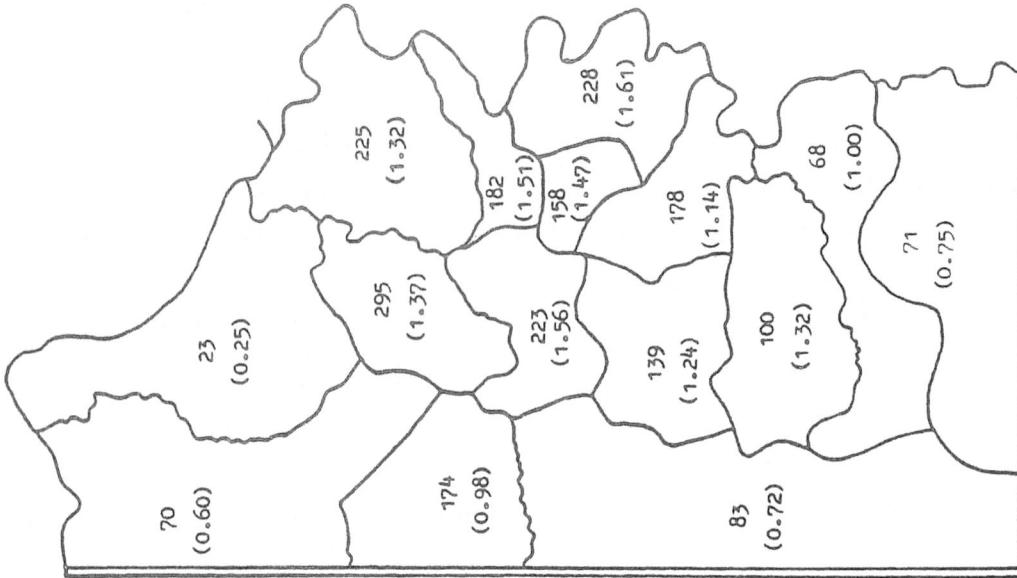

502 (12)
236 (17)
1965 (34)
2857 (58)
1494 (27)
1144 (24)
906 (14)
988 (11)
1384 (22)
1507 (7)
550 (7)
527 (12)
1046 (10)
787 (3)
507 (2)

1783 AMWELL TOWNSHIP TAX LIST

NAME	ACRES	HORSES	COWS	SHEEP	SLAVES	VALUE £/S
Thomas Atkinson	400	4	5			160
George Atkinson	400	3	5			127
Thomas Atkinson Junr	150					30
William Atkinson	500	2	4	3		140
Thomas Axtell	100	2	4	3		31
Patrick Allison	600	4	2	6	3	293
Daniel Axtell	300	3	2	6		67
Charles Boner		3	3	2		36
Jabez Baldwin	100	3	6	7		133
Ellis Bane	170	4	3	4		67
Richard Bilby			1			2
Caleb Baldwin/Blacksmith	300	2	5	7		100
Robert Bennet	20	1	2	6		40
William Bennet		2	2	1		12
Jacob Beck	300	3	4	10		74
William Bryson	200					20
Joseph Bane Junier	400	4	6	7		81
Jesse Bane		1	2			21
Joseph Bane Senior	200	2	2			25
Ephraim Bales	300	3	3	4		39
Isaac Bane	50	3	3	10		29
Nathan Bane	600	3	4	7		121
John Craig Esqr	500	4	6	5		116
Samuel Craig	300	1	2	2		69
Dennis Carrol	50	2	2			23
George Cartar		3	1			15
Charles Crecraft	300	2	6			85
Thomas Craig - Single		1				10
Laurance Craft	400	3	3	3		86
John Craft	400	3	6	8		89
John Carmichael	400	4	2			55
Joseph Coe	200		2			14
Stephen Carter			1			1/10
Stephen Cook	100	2	4	8		47
Moses Cooper	100	2	2	1		38/10
Widow Cooper	100	2	2			27
Zebulun Cooper	40	3	4			37/1
Cheniah Covett	50	3	4			15
Christian Catts	200	2	2	2		31/5
William Corwin	150	2	2	2		24/10
William Carter	80	2	2	2		19
Samuel Coulson	150	1	1			45
John Coulson - Single		1				7/10
James Carter	414	3	6	12		120
Noah Cook	200	2	1			60/10
John Carmichael Junr	300	2	2			35/10
Jacob Cook	600	2	2	12		156
John Dickerson	300	4	6	9	3	189

NAME	ACRES	HORSES	COWS	SHEEP	SLAVES	VALUE
Gidion Dickerson	300	1	1			22/10
Henry Dickerson		2	2			12
Isaac Dille	200	1	3	2		46/10
Patrick Derby	25		1			33/10
John Davis	250	3	4	7		84
John Dickerson Junr	250	2	6	6		103
Daniel Dustman - Single	100	2	1	1		27/7
David Dille	100	3	3	5		64
Israel Dille - Single						
Nathan Davis - Single						
Samuel Dille	80	2	2	2		45/10
Caleb Dille	80	2	2			18/10
John Dille	80	3	5	9		58
Thaddeus Dodd	150	2	3			27
Price Dille		1	2	2		8/10
Daniel Dodd	100	2	2	5		19/10
James Drapper	300	2	1			18
Luke Enlow		1				10
Abraham Enlow						
William Elliot		2	2			13/10
John Eddy	150	3	6	15		75
Abraham Evans	280	3	3	2		76/10
Caleb Evans		1	2	3		7
David Evans /Gristmill	340	3	4	13		116
Abraham Fordice /Millwright	300	2		4		21/10
Benjamin Frazee	120	2	2	4		27
George French	150	2	4	10		69
David Frazee	135	2	2	4		48
Jonathan Frazee	200	2	2	6		40
Matthew Golden		1	1	1		8/7
Ebenezer Goble	400	2	2	2		74/10
John Goble		1	2			6
Daniel Goble	250	2	2	3		46/10
Caleb Goble - Single						
Benjamin Goble		2	1			14
Edward Grandine		2	2	2		15
Amos Gregg	760	3	8	7		146/10
Archibald Greenlie		2	2			15
John Greenlie	100	2	2	2		39
John Gregg	600	4	9	17		130
Israel Gregg	150	1	2	1		41
John Gardner	100	1	3			40/10
John Galloway		1	2	1		20/10
Samuel Hazlep	195	2	2	2		49
Nathan Hatheway	300	3	4	12		38/10
Abraham Hatheway	300	2	2			30
John Hughes /Merchant	300	4				85
Thomas Howell	100	2				30/10
John Hill	150	1	2			30

NAME	ACRES	HORSES	COWS	SHEEP	SLAVES	VALUE
Peter Huwett	70	2	4	3		40
Philip Hawett	150	2	2	6		43
Hardman Horn	225	3	7	7		83/10
Abner Howell	200	2	2			30/10
John Horn	150	2	2	7		53
Jacob Hoosong Sr	300	3	2	5		55
Jacob Hoosong Junr	100	2		1		15/10
Richard Hathaway	400	3	2	4		51/10
Joseph Jennings	130	2	2	4		40/5
Abraham Johnson	300	3	3			52/10
Duncan Kennedy		1	10			35
Thomas Kitton	100	3	4	17		67/10
John Kemble	100	2	3	6		107/10
Zenas Lindsly	100	1	1			18
Joseph Leacock	140	2	2	7		40
Richard Lee		4	2	9		17
Caleb Lindsly	800	3	4	5		92/10
John Lindsly		1				4/10
Demas Lindsly /Gristmill	600	2	5	3		86
Daniel Lindsly - Single	60?					15
Isaac Leacock - Single		1				10
Thomas Lackey	600	3	4	8		106
Thomas Luckes	100	1	2			38/11
Abraham Lynch		3	2	5		22/10
Anthony Lynch		1				10
Leonard Love	150	1	1			18/10
Elisha Lacock	100	2	2	1		28
William Leacock	125	4	5	16		59/10
Joseph Lindsly		1	1	2		6
David McCrackon		1	1			16
Cornelius Miller		1	1			13
Samuel McCollough	100	2	2			25
Robert Morris	100		3			26/10
William Morris		1				3
Archibald Morris		1	2			6/10
Jacob Morris	300	1	3	2		49/10
Elisha Morris						
Bazil Morris						
Michael Miller - Single						
John Moore		2	1			14
William McFarland	225	2	2	5		57/10
Nathaniel McGiffen	200	3	2	3		60
John Miller	100	3	3	4		43/10
John Miller - Duchman	200	2	4	14		63/15
John McVaw Sr	50	1	2	2		18
Joseph Minton	60		1			8
James McVaw	50	1	1			10/10
Isaac McVaw		1	1	1		6/5
Edward McVaw	70	1	1	1		17/10
Benjamin McVaw	80	1	1	1		12

NAME	ACRES	HORSES	COWS	SHEEP	SLAVES	VALUE
William McConkey	150	1	1			22
John Newell	50	1				13/10
John O'daniel - Single						
Samuel Parkhurst	500	5	7	6		123/10
Francis Peck		3	2			15
James Paul	100	2	2	3		19
Isaac Pettit	150	3	3	4		26/10
John Philips	300	3	2	6		87
Phebe Phillips		3	4		1	32/10
Peter Parker	100	3	4	4		53/10
Sarah Philips - Widow		1	1	2		6
Benjamin Ross - Single						
John Rude	200	1	1			15
Jacob Rudde S.	200	1				15
Benjamin Rickey	300	2	3			30
Alexander Reynolds	150	1	2	1		25/10
Morris Rees	100	2	2			32
John Rees	150	3	3	6		61
Nathaniel Ross	100	3	4	5		50
Timothy Ryan	400	3	4	9		70
Benjamin Ryce	600	3	5	6		111
Thomas R(e)ynolds	50	2	1			15/10
Susanna Sheredine	50	1	1			12
Thomas Serjant	300	2	6	8		105/10
Richard Serjeant	400	1	3	2		25/10
Elihu Sanders	20	1	1			15
Stephen Sanders	70	1	2	2		20/10
Joseph Stark	240	2	2			44/10
Abraham Sutton	150	3	2	6		52
Gabriel Swinehart	100	2	3	5		33
Michael Simon	140	3	4	8		66/10
Christopher Seraker /Distill	80	4	5	8		76/10
Daniel Shooster	60	2	2	3		26/10
John Stark		2	2	6		10
Philip Swart	300					20
John Stanley - Single						
William Tegarden		2	3	5		21
David Thomas	100	2	1	1		23/10
James Tucker	370	4	7	14		105/10
William Throop		1	1			6
Michael Thomas	400	4	4	5	3	117/2
Jeremiah Virgin	100	3	2	3		53
John Virgin	200	2				18
Thomas Virgin	100	1				20
Nehemiah Veers	100	2	3	3		40
Stephen Vineyard		2	1			17/1
Thomas Vineyard		1				10
William Vineyard	100	1	2			21
John Vineyard	150	3	8	17		65

NAME	ACRES	HORSES	COWS	SHEEP	SLAVES	VALUE
James Vineyard - Single						
Francis Vineyard - Single						
George Vennom	50	2	3	5		35/10
Isaac Vancamp	210	2	4	3		30/15
Aaron Vancamp /Gristmill	400	2	6	10		82
Laurance Vancamp		2	1	3		6/10
John Weathers - Single						
Colvin Wade		1	1			7
Moses Williams	150	1	1	2		12/10
John Wolverton	200	2	3	7		37/10
Garret Warfull		2				6
Thomas Wiggins		1	2			5
John Whitten	35	1	1	4		18
Philip Wiggins - Single						

1783 BETHLEHEM TOWNSHIP TAX LIST

NAME	ACRES	HORSES	COWS	SHEEP	SLAVES	VALUE £/S
Abraham Arlewine		3	3	3		24/15
John Andrews		1	1			8
Josiah Arnold			1			3
Joseph Arnold		1	2	1		11/5
John Acklen	200	3	3	2		124/10
Isaac Bush	170	3	2	2		98/10
John Buchanna	150	3	2	5		72/5
Isaiah Ball	150	2	3	1		79/5
Zopher Ball	100	2	3	4		53/10
Ulrieck Brekenstaff		3	3	4		22
James Barnet	150	2	3			69/10
James Bradin	150	2	2	6		67/10
Ezekial Braden	100	2	2			49
James C Braden	200	3	3	3		85/15
John Buchias	250	3	3	5		76/10
William Buckinham	350	4	5	9		137/5
John Baker /Distill	300	2	3		1	180
Thomas Baldwine			2			6
David Blair	400	2	3	6		155/10
Robert Branton		1	2			11
David Burcham	50	2	3			16/15
Thomas Biship	300	3	3	2		125/10
Samuel Brown		2	2			16
Jane Beek			1	4		4
Henry Beek	50					4
Thomas Crooks Esqr	340	5	6	12		146
James Currey		2	3	2		20/10
Carry Colvin		2	2			16
Zachariah Castell	65	3	5			50
Francis Casteel	125	5	6	4		85
Philip Chansoler		3	1	5		19/10
Joseph Coal		2	1	2		13/10
Ezra Cary		2	1			13
Daniel Curry		3	3	5		26/5
Robert Callender		1				5
John Cray		3	4			27
Thomas Cornwell		2	2	3		16/15
John Conkle	100	2	2			66
Henry Conkle	200	4	2	8		88
Michael Cocks		2				10
Andrew Cocks			1			3
Archibald Carn		1	2			11
Vallentine Cooper		1	2			11
Michael Clark	100	1	1			64
Christian Crisps	300					100
James Crawford	140					45
Leonard Diven		2	4	5		23/5
Mariam Deval	100	1	1			39

19

NAME	ACRES	HORSES	COWS	SHEEP	SLAVES	VALUE
Thomas Derben	72	1	2	4		33
Isaac Death		2	2	4		17/10
John Dowlen		2	1	2		13/10
George Dorman		1	1	1		8/10
Martin Dagger	575	3	4	12		230
Samuel Davis		1	2	3		11/15
John Davis	250	2	3	7		91/10
Kinsor Davis	100	2	3	5		54/5
James Dixson	200	2	4	6		93/10
Michael Dunfield			1			3
Daniel Drisdel	125	3	5	2		60/10
Jacob Dixes	200	2	3	7		93/15
Thomas Davis Junr	100	2	2	4		50
Thomas Davis Senr		1	1			8
Solomon Denbow		1				5
Joseph Dowdle		2	2	1		16/5
Samuel Evans	70	1	4	4		41
Jonathan Ernet		2	3	4		21
David Enoch	400	4	5	12		138
Paul Everhet		2	2			16
Henry Enoch		3	4			27
Josiah Evans	100	2	2	5		50/5
Henry Frank	250	3	1			98
James Fitspatrick	200	4	4	6		103/10
Tobias Friend		1	1			8
Absolam Fox	50	4	5			45
Philip Friend	375	4	4	7		134
George Friend		2	2			16
George Fruit	50	3	5	4		48
Samuel Folton	120	4	5	20		90
Isaac Falty	75	2	1			33
Jacob Fruzzel		3	2			21
William Gamble		1				5
Bartholomew Griffeth	50	2	2			31
Charles Griffeth	40	1	1			37
Rees Gaddis	100	2	3	3		53/15
James Grimes	40	2	2	2		26/10
Nathan Glass		2	2			16
Eliza Genkins	350	3	4	2		127/10
William Grahams		2				10
William Hardgrass	100	4	4	4		67
Absolom Hoge		3				15
Anthony Hartman	150	3	4	5		78/5
Abraham Hartman	150	3	3	3		75/15
Thomas Hatfield	200	2	4	9		84
Thomas Hatfield		1	1			8
Daniel Hollis		2	2			16
Christopher Horn	300	3	5	7		122
Joseph Hill	300	3	3	3		125/15
Zacharia Huntington		1	3			15

NAME	ACRES	HORSES	COWS	SHEEP	SLAVES	VALUE
John Howel		3	3			25
Zacharia Hurley			3			10
Thomas Hawkins		3	2			21
Thomas Hill	100	2	2			21
John Hardesty	40	1	1			18
Michael Hansel		3	3			25
Robert Hill	160	2	4	2		62/10
Simon Harsh	50	3	3			28/10
Henry Hersh		3	1			18
Henry Hydle	40	2	2			23
David Hartman	200	2	2	2		86/10
Nicholas Hook		2	2	2		16/10
Adam Hartman	100	2	4	3		72/15
Jacob Hook		1	2	2		11/10
William Hill	300	3	3	12		78
William Hill Senr		1	2		1	31
Everhot Hupp	300	2	5	5		126/5
Adam Hanthorn	300	3	3	6		106
Elkeney Holloway		2	2			16
James Hanthorn		1	1	1		8/5
Richard Hart			1			3
John Hartly		1	1	4		9
Benjamin Haywood		1	1			8
Hugh Hails		2	2	2		16/10
John Hails			1			3
John Hatfield	100	2	2			46
John Harvecost	100	4	6	10		70/10
Thomas Hughes	150	1	1			38
Matthias Hook	150	2	6	8		60
John Horable	300	8	7	7	2	264
Thomas Hardy		1	2	3		11/15
Henry Horable	240	4	5	9		117/5
John Henry	200	1	1	1		98/5
William Hawkins	100	2	3	4		50/15
George Helps		2	2			16
Richard Hawkins	130	2	2	7	1	98
Robert Jackson		2	2			16
Edward Joy		2	2	2		16/10
Isaac Julien		1	2		1	41
Christian Just	50	3	3	3		35/15
George Kinder		1				8
Vallentine Kinder	75	2	4	11		45
Peter Kinder	90	1	1			28
Jacob Kinder	50	1	2			21
Henry Kauffman	100	2	2			36
James Kerr		2	2	2		16/10
Peter Lashly	136	3	5	6		71/10
Solomon Lashly	150	3	6	8		65
Isaac Leet	150	2	1			53
Philip Laughlin	100	2	2	6		40/10

NAME	ACRES	HORSES	COWS	SHEEP	SLAVES	VALUE
Peter Lazer		2	2			16
Samuel Lyon		2	4	8		24
Peter Leatherman	250	1	2			91
Christian Leatherman	400	4	4	5		133/5
Daniel Leatherman	250	1	4	4		98
Samuel Latten	100					40
James Largant	300	1				75
Isaac Meek		1	1			8
Paul McCartney	100	2	3	3		50/15
James Mitchel	58	2	2			36
Mitchel Morris		2	2			13
Jacob Meeks		1	1			8
Jacob Meeks		1				5
John Meeks	180	3	7	8		78
Samuel Meek	100	4	5	8		67
Isaac Miller	150	3	6	10		85/10
James McCibben	100	2	3	2		50/10
Daniel McFarlane	100	5	5	8	1	112
Timothy Mayhall		1	1			8
John Miller	50	2	2	5		32/5
Nicholas Miers		2	2			16
Richard Marry		1	2			11
John McCowen	150	2	2	3		66/15
John McGinnis		2	2			16
John McHattan		3	3			25
Michael Moore	40	2	2	3		26/15
Christian Miller		4				20
William Matcalf		3	4			27
John Manning /Gristmill /Sawmill	130	1	3			115
John McRedenour		2	2			16
John Nessonger		2	2	2		16/10
William Picket	200	2	2	6		93
George Prickher	200	2	6	5		99/5
Esable Perry	30	1				15
Jonahs Pots		1	1			8
James Powel	150	1	2	3		61/15
George Peck	100	3	1			48
Henry Palser		2	2			16
Solomon Reese	96	2	2	3		46/15
Ezekiel Rooss	150	3	4	8		79
George Rigdon	80	2	1	2		33/10
Jonathan Ross	240	2	1	2		83/10
Isaac Ruble	150	2	3			70
John Reess	150					30
Leonard Robert	350	3	4	7		129
Thomas Richard	300	3	7	7		118
David Ruble	320	3	8	8		141
Daniel Redford	50	2	3	7		37
Jacob Rigel	100	2	2			46

22

NAME	ACRES	HORSES	COWS	SHEEP	SLAVES	VALUE
George Reed		1	2			11
Thomas Reess	200	3	8	8		111
John Rush	100	2	3			40
Benjamin Roeboch	300	2	3	4		121
Clement Rigg		2	2			15
John Rigg	40	1	1			14
Thomas Reese		2	1			13
Gasper Rigget	50	2	2	3		24/15
John Reynold	300	2	3	2		120/10
Frederick Sellers	100	2	4			42
Martin Spoon	100	2	3	4		41
Christopher Sinetaker	80	3	4	4		48
Peter Shidler	80	2	3			35
Dennis Smith	100	4	3	11		65
George Shidler		1	2	3		11/15
Derby Shawhen	80	3	5	3		60/15
Philip Smith	300	1	2	4		102
Jacob Shidler		1	2	3		12
George Adam Shidler	200	3	3	9		97/10
Williams Sims	100	2	2	8		48
George Swinehart		1	3			15
Adam Simon	200	2	3	5		91/5
Jacob Swineheart	40	2	2	6		27/10
Henry Shidler	100	3	4	4		58
John Shidler	200	2	4	7		93/15
Rachel Shargant		2	2			16
Edward Soams		2	3	9		22/5
Jacob Snuff	150	1	3	7		66/15
Reuben Smith		2	2	4		17
Christian Shank	300	2	2			116
Robert Swaney	50	3	2	4		32
William Seatton	70	1	1			28
William Stanly		1	1	1		8/9
Frederick Tage	400	3	8	15		143
Matthias Tage		1				5
George Tansor	200	3	4	10		109/10
Jacob Tosman		1				6
Elisabeth Tagerden		2	1	5		14/5
Elisabeth Taylor	50					15
John Tucker	100	4	3	5		63
John Varval Junr	40	2	2	1		23/5
John Varval	60	2	1			23
Andrew Wise /Sawmill	80	1	4	2		57/10
Jacob Wolf		2	3	4		21
Thomas Williams	100	2	2	2		46/10
Amos Wilton	50					14
George Weech	400	2	1	2		113/10
Thomas Wright		1	1			8
Isaac West	50	2	1	6		24/10
Samuel Weer	600	2	2	6		207/10

NAME	ACRES	HORSES	COWS	SHEEP	SLAVES	VALUE
Adam Weer		2	2	2		16/10
John Welch	350	2	4			122
James Welch		2	4			22
Adam Wise	75					20
Andrew Young	150	2	3	4		71
Andrew Yates/Tates			1			3
John Larson	200	2	6			98
Daniel McFarlane	400					40
John Moor	300	2	2			46
Samuel Davis	300					30
Henry Bigdol		2	3	7		21/15
Matthias Ault		1	1	2		8/10
Paul Armstrong		1	2	3		11/15
Ann Hupp		2	4	3		22/15
Philip Hupp		1	1	1		8/5
Hugh Hails	600					50
Thomas Davis Junr	200					25
Thomas Davis Senr	300					20
Lewis Right		1	1			8
Isaac Julian	600					60
Henry Aspocke	600					60
Matthias Hook	300					30
William Samuel	300					30
John Connel	30	2	1			19
Thomas Crooks		1				5
Jacob Crow	500					30
Isaac Death	30					5
George Swineheart	40					7
Samuel Miller	350	3	3			55
William Miller	500	2	2			36

"A LIST OF THOSE THAT REFUSED IN THIS TOWNSHIP WITH THE ESTAMATION OF THERE ESTATES"

Kent Mitchel	24
William Miller	40
Nathan Hails	100
Joseph Woodfield	90
Samuel Smith	30
Bartholomew Mc neme	60
Thomas Cook	25
John Ginkens	60
Abraham Smith	50
John Cuzzens	70
William Wilson	30
Adam Weaver	150
Henry Hartzock	30
Conrod Hartzock	40

NAME	ACRES	HORSES	COWS	SHEEP	SLAVES	VALUE
SINGLE FREEMEN						
Robert Stephen						
Henry Wise	80					30
Peter Wise	200	3	4	9		129
Adam Harter						
John Youg/Young		1				5
Jesse Reese						
John Callnder						
Robert Callender						
Robert Stump		1				5
Daniel Frederick	330	1	2			111
John Hill		1				8
James Weer	40	2	3			30
Marmaduke Leet	100					15
John Been	30					15
Doctor Lualen		1				
David Brakenstaff	30	1				20
Philip Frend						
John Beard						
Jacob Leatherman						
Egnatious Bernel/Bernet						
Jacob Brandan	100	1				35
Thomas Hill		2	2			16
Jesse Jackman		1				8
Thomas Bishop		1				5
John Kennedy						
John Brown						
Michael Robe						
Richard Welch						
Isaac McNeme						
Jacob Horable	250	2	4			102
Charles Harlon		1				

1783 CECIL TOWNSHIP TAX LIST

NAME	ACRES	HORSES	COWS	SHEEP	SLAVES	VALUE £/S
John Armstrong /Gristmill	200	4	3	4		227
Mary Andrew /Still	650	3	6	7		315
Thomas Alexander	300					112/10
Samuel Allison		3	2	2		23
Stephen Ashby		4	2			40
John Allison	400	5	6	12		214
Catharine Atcheson					1	40
James Allison	560	5	6	6		257
John Baily /Gristmill	150	4	4	6		195
Rowly Boyd /Distill	200	2	3			135
Thomas Braking	680	3	3	9		335
John Brown	100	2	3			66
John Buchannan		2	1			24
Joseph Brown	600	6	6	8		303
John Bowman		2	1			21
Hugh Bell		2	3	4		31
Thomas Biggart	75	2	2	2		57/10
Robert Boatman	200	3	2			81
Henry Boatman		1	1	1		12/10
James Baggs		1	4			22
Elizabeth Barns	300					112
William Boatman		1				3
Henry Boatman Junr	50	1	1			22
Ephraim Burnwall	56	2	2	2		31
William Brice	100	3	2			66
William Black	150	2	3	1		87/10
Richard Boys	300	2	7	12		156
Thomas Baily		1	1			13
John Boys	250	3	2	4		102
James Brown		2	1	2		24
Sims Bolam	300	3	3	8		152
John Berry	500	3	3	7		239
John Boyd /Taylor		2	1			21
William Bowlin	130					50
Charles Bilderback	200					75
John Brownlee		2	2	4		29
William Bell	100	2	2	2	1	112
Edward Cheese	300	1	4	3		121
Thomas Cotral		2	1			23
Dinnes Coinner	50	2	3	4		140
Peden Cook	150					57
William Coinner		3	1	3		35
Thomas Creal	50	2	3			41
John Creal	300					112/12
John Campbell	1000					300
William Coughran	200	3	4	2		113
Henry Carsey	300	3	3	7		171

NAME	ACRES	HORSES	COWS	SHEEP	SLAVES	VALUE
William Carsey	300	3	3	3		133
Samuel Caughey		2	2			26
Arthur Campbell			1			3
John Cunning		2	1	1		19/10
John Cannon Esqr	800	4	7	13		666
/Gristmill /Sawmill						
Samuel Cross		2	4	3		31
Joshua Cannon		1				10
Cornelious Crealy		1				10
John Campbell			1			3
James Campbell	130	1	2	8		92
Jesse Crawen	250					100
Mary Connyer	100	2	2			36
Daniel Curry		2	3	2		31
Alexr Cowing		1	1	2		14
John Cowing		1	1			12
Alexr Duncan		4	4	4		44
Joseph Downard	100	2	2			66
James Donahee	100	2	3	1		130
Robert Davison		5	3	1		46/5
John Donnahoo	249	2	3			140
Samuel Dunn	250	3	4	6		142
Asariah Dunn		2	3	7		32
James Dinsmore	250	3	3	9		144
William Donnahoe	250	2	2	3		125
William Dunland	10	1	2			46
William Dunlap	110	1	2			67/10
Robert Downard	250	2	5	6		134
John Duncan	100	2	4	6		79
Joseph Davis		2	1			23
Levi Dungan		4	6	5	2	213
Michael Dougherty	50	2	2	3		62
Roger Dougherty	261					98
John Dickson	300					112/10
William Ewing		2				30
Samuel Ewing		2	2			28
Samuel Ewing Junr		1	2	2		17
James Ewing		1				10
Samuel Elliot		2	4			32
Thomas Everight		1				10
John Foset	300	4	5	2		255/10
Thomas Fossett	300	3	2	2		137
George Frazer	600	5	4	14		325
James Foreman	300	4	9	9	3	360
Thomas Frazer	100	3				70
Nicholas Gawn/Gavin	200	3	5	11		129
John Glenn	300	2	4	4		153
Hugh Graham		2	1	2		16
William Gallaher	140					40
Robert Graham		2	2			26

28

NAME	ACRES	HORSES	COWS	SHEEP	SLAVES	VALUE
Josiah Gamble /Gristmill	250	3	3			212
James Gasten		2	3	2		31
Hugh Gardner		1				10
James Gault	200	2	3	6		104
Andrew Gibson		1	2			15
Robert Guttery	260	2	3	7		135
John Grant		2	2			23
Jonathan Gillam		1	1			11
Elizabeth Griffey	400					150
Samuel Graham		2	4	3		33
Edward Gatter		2	4	7	1	44/10
Joseph Hugil		3	2	4		27
John Herrin	100	2	2	2		56/10
George Herrin		1	1	1		11/10
William Herrin	100	1	2	4		46
Obediah Holmes	200					75
James Howlet		1	2	2		24/10
Adam Hickman	100	2	1			48
Robert Hill	200	2	2			106
William Hutton	100	2	3	2	2	200/10
Rvd Matthew Henderson	142	2	2	10	1	140
John Hays	300	3	6	6		183
William Hillis	260	2	2	2		112
John Hall	400	2	2	3		168
Eliasabeth Hews	400	3	3	6		194
William Hamer	50	2	2	5		49
William Holmes	400	2	3	2		173
Matthew Johnston	350	2	3	6		153
John Johnston	300	3	4	7		112
Joseph Johnston	150	2	2			81
Samuel Jeffery	200					50
Robert Ignew		1	2	3		15
William Johnston Senr	250	2	4	5		132
William Johnston Junr	130	3	2	4		118
William Johnston Con		2	1	2		22
James Kirkpatrick	300	3	3	8		115
James Kerns		2	4	6		35
William Keps		1	1	2		14
Peter Kerns	50	1	3	4		38
David Kent		1	2	2		17
Martha Kirk		2	3	4		30
Thomas Lapsly	280					105
James Little	200	2	3	6		107
George Long		2	2	1		26/10
William Lucky	300					120
Christian Lesneth	400	6	4	5		144
William Long /2 Distills	560	3	4	7		355
James Leadly /Distill		1	1			32
John Laughlen	100	3	4	5		93/10

NAME	ACRES	HORSES	COWS	SHEEP	SLAVES	VALUE
James Martin	200	1	2			92
James McLaughlen	280	3	4	7		145
James McCormick	400					100
Jonathan Martin	100	2	3			52
Tobias Mattocks	300	2	4	3		133
John Morgan	200	2	2	3		127
Samuel McCowen	300	3	3	10		125
Kenith McKinsey	200	1	2			66
Benjamin McCormick		3	3	6		42
Christopher Miller	250	3	3	5		170/10
Henry Middleswart	150	1	2			70
Archabeld McIntire		1	1			24
James McBride	50	3	3	5		57/10
Samuel McBride	150	3	4	7		109/10
Matthew McConnal	150	3	6	6		112/10
John McClean		2	2			26
John Martin		1				10
Mary Moore - widow	50	2	2			36
William McLaughlin /Distill	200	3	3	5		42
David McCrory	300	3	4	6		131
William McConnal		1	1			13
Mary Miller		3	1			23
Robert Miller	500	3	5	11		124
Andrew Munroe		1	1			13
William Munroe		2	3			24
William Mitchel	100					37
John McComb	75	2	3	2		50/10
William McKegg	11	3	2	4		31
John Makemson		1	2	5		18/10
James McCready		1	2	4		18
James Money		1	2			16
Alexander McCalaster	350	2	3			160
Daniel McCloud		2	2	4		28
George McComb	100	2	2			66
Sarah Mulholland		1	1	1		11/10
James McClelland	300	3	3	7		163
James McNeary	200	3	3	6		117
Thomas Marchant	60	2	3	6		54/10
Robert McDonald		2				20
Hugh McNight		2	2			26
Samuel McBride Senr	100	3	3	6		102
James Miller	200	2	3	6		107
Samuel Marchant		3	2	2		37
James Marchant		2	2	2		27
Gawn Morrison	400	3	1	7		186
George McColloch	50	3	2	6		49
Alexr McCoy		1	2			16
Daniel McCoy		2	2	2		27
William McCoy		2	2			26

NAME	ACRES	HORSES	COWS	SHEEP	SLAVES	VALUE
Daniel L McCoy		1	1			14
William McDonald		2	2	3		25
Robert Meeks /Distill	200	4	4	6		147
Col. John Navel	900	9	10	26	11	1021
John Nelson		3	4	7		37
William Orram		1	2	2		17
William Orr		1	1			13
John Odonald	400	4	4	10		156
Henry ODonald	250	1	3	4		99
Joseph ODonald		2	2	3		27
John Orr	140	3	3			80
Mary Pickarel		1	1			13
Samuel Parks	500	2	4	5		218
Henry Potter		2	2			26
John Phillps	250	1	4	4		103
Joseph Portor	200	3	3	2		130/10
Charles Phillips	100	2	2			61
James Parker	200	2	2			76
William Price		2	7			41
Hugh Patton	150	2	2			86
Caleb Pumphrey	200					75
Charles Queen		1	2	1		16/10
John Queen	230	4	2	6		129
John Reed Esqr	600	2	4	8		244
George Runo	150	1	2	3		137
Thomas Redman		2	3	3		31
James Reed	363	3	5	14		165
John Reed /Cooper		3				36
Robert Rutherford	1100					550
Stevens Richard	200	1	1	3		89
Murdical Richard	200	1	2			91
Robert Ralston	400	3	5	10		203
James Roberts		1	2	1		16/10
David Rankin Junr	230	3	2	3		117
Marry Rawling	400	5	8	20		287
Nathan Rawlings		2	2	2		27
Andrew Richie	130	2	3			80
Thomas Roberts	250	4	4	8	1	216
Andrew Russel	141	3	4	10		126
Capt David Reed	500	2	4	3		217
Capt Thomas Rankin	550	2	4	4		238
John Robinson	100	1	2	1		41/5
William Russel		2	2	1		26/10
James Ramsey	100	2	2			56
David Rankin Senr	800	6	11	15	2	501
Mary Robertson		2	3	2		30/10
Charles Reed		3	3			39
Thomas Reed	100	3	3			60
Andrew Robertson	300					112/10
David Stephenson	250	3	5	8		148

NAME	ACRES	HORSES	COWS	SHEEP	SLAVES	VALUE
Philip Salkman	200	2	1	1		63/10
Zacheriah Sliddam	300	2	2	7		129
James Scott Senr		1	3			20
John Stillings	300	2	2	4		98
Hugh Stirling	300					112
Thomas Suttles	140	6	4	10		176
Charles Stewart	200					75
Elias Stillwell		1				5
Shadrech Stillwell		1	1			10
James Snodgrass		1	3	1		22/10
William Snodgrass		2	2	2		25
John Springer	300	1	3	5		124
Isaac Springer		2	2	3		27
"Isaac or Enoch" Springer		1	1			13
Hugh Shearer		2	3			29
Elisabeth Shearer		1	2			16
John Struthers	300	2	3	8		134
Archabald Scott	40	2	2			50
Robert Stephenson	900					338
William Sinclear		1				8
William Sinclear Junr	200	1	1			73
David Shearer	300	3	2			130
William Shearer		2				40
Andrew Swearingham	800	2	2	10	1	457
James Scott	300	4	6	10		165
Benjamin Thompson		2	1	4		22
George Therp		2	1	2		22
William Turner		2	2			46
Benjamin Wright		1	3			7
Johnlee Webster	300					112/10
William Williams	100	2	2			140
John Wheeler		1	1			13
Daniel Welch	300	3	3	4		142
John Wilson		1				8
Miles Wilson	200	3	6	14		174
William Wilson Senr	100	2	4			72
John Walker		2	2			26
Thomas Wilson		1	1	2		12
Joseph Walker		3	4	8		39
Robert Wilson		1	2	1		16/10
John Wilson /Still		2				40
Sarah Weights	250	4	5	4		134
James Woodburn	100	1	2			46
Thomas White	150	3	3	9		113
Isaac Wiseman		2	3			29
Robert Welch	100					75
Benjamin Wheally	300					175
Robert Walker	100	2	2	6		65/10
William Wilson		2	3			25
Adam Wiley	150	2	2			66

NAME	ACRES	HORSES	COWS	SHEEP	SLAVES	VALUE

SINGLE FREEMEN

NAME	ACRES	HORSES	COWS	SHEEP	SLAVES	VALUE
John Armstrong						
William Armstrong						
Gawn/Gavin Allison			1			10
Archabald Allison						
Robert Black						
Samuel Brown						
Thomas Brown						
Robert Beer		1				10
William Baggs						
William Boyd						
Robert Bolling						
Thomas Coynner	100	2	4	4		66
William Cornegy		2	3			27
Charles Campbell	40	1				25
Daniel Camoran	40					15
James Chamber		1				10
Hugh Cowing	100	2				52
William Cowing		1	1			13
Robert Dunbar						
Olipher Dornan						
James Ewing		1				10
Alexander Feggen		1				10
Robert Forgison		1				10
William Glenn		1				10
David Gault /Tanyd		1				50
James Gutthery		1				10
Joseph Holmes		1				10
Samuel Henry		1				10
William Hays	500	4	2			236
Robert Hays	200	1				85
David Hutchison		1				10
Doctr David Holmes						10
William Leadly		1				10
David Logan		1				10
Enoch Low	100	2				52
Frederick Leasneth						
Frank Lesneth						
Alexr McConnal	150	3	4	2		73
Patrick McDonald	130	1				50
Alexander McMunn		1				10
Robert McKnight	80	1				30
John May		1	1			13
John Marchant	100	1	2	4		43
James Morrison	400	3	1	7		175
Abraham Neel		1				10
Parks Roberts		1				10
John Reed		1				10
John Robinson		1	1			13

NAME	ACRES	HORSES	COWS	SHEEP	SLAVES	VALUE
Samuel Reed		1				10
James Reed		1				10
Matthew Reed		1				10
John Ralstone		1				10
Alexr Ralstone		1				10
Matthew Richie Esqr /2 Distill	1000	4	6	13		463
Capt Craig Richie		1				10
Andrew Reed		1				10
John Roberts		2				20
James Stephenson		4				30
Daivd Stevenson		3				25
Samuel Scott		1				10
Hugh Sproul	300	1	1			41
James Sproul	150	2	3			57
William Stewart /Distill	300	1				132/10
John Struthers	130	1	1			73
James Sibbet	100	2				57
James Stephenson		1			2	11
Samuel Thompson		1				10
Nathan Tanihill	100	3	2			66
Thomas Walkfield /2 Stills		1				30

"13 more young men that has no property"

1783 CUMBERLAND TOWNSHIP TAX LIST

NAME	ACRES	HORSES	COWS	SHEEP	SLAVES	VALUE £/S
John Armstrong	200	2	3	5		237/10
Abraham Armstrong	250	1	2			150
Charles Anderson /Gristmill /2 Stills	600	3	8	12		825
Thomas Adams Junr	300	2	4	12		280
John Adams		1				10
Daniel Anderson	100					32
Thomas Bowen		2	2	1		18/7
Andrew Burns		1	1			12
Samuel Barnhill		1	1			20
Jacob Blaney		1	1	1		11/7
James Blair	80	2	2	2		104
John Burns		1	1			12
Clifton Bowen		1	1			9
Joseph Ball		2	2			21
Thomas Brown		2	2			18
Alexr Coughran		1	1			9
William Crawford	400	4	6	8	1	506
Robert Cree		2	2	2		22
Patrick Cree		1	1			15
James Carmichael/Sawmill	700	2	3	5	1	618/10
John Crawford	300	3	4	4		334
William Cree	200	2	4	3		177
Robert Crossley	260	3	4			140
Jacob Clone	400	4	7	15		435
Richard Cannon		1				6
Oliver Crawford	100	1	2	4		118
Daniel Clark	70	1	2	4		58
Moses Congee		1	2			14
David Casto	25	2	3			50
John Casto		1				10
Michael Coon		1	1			10
Dennis Dunham		2	2			28
John Davis		1	2			23
Samuel Dutton		1	2	2		15
John Dougherty		2	2	4		22/10
David Duncan	600					679
Joseph Eastwood		1	2			18
Daniel Estell	100	1	2			70
Thomas Eaton	100	1	1			74
James Flennekin	200	2	3	6		228
John Flennekin	300					225
John Green		1	1			12
Richard Gregg	318	2	3	6		355
George Gregg /Gristmill	318	6	5	15		546
John Gates	50	2	4			35
William Gray	98	2	3	7		133
John Hotton/Holton	150	2	3	6		167

35

NAME	ACRES	HORSES	COWS	SHEEP	SLAVES	VALUE
John Hill		2	2			29
John Holt	100	1	2			64
Benjamin Hughes	100	4	8	12		118
Henry Huffman	100	1	2			66
John Huston	50	2	1			64
James Jones		1	1			14
John Jones	100	1	2	3		81
Hugh Johnston		1	1			14
Priscilla Israel			2			8
Isaac Israel Exr	200	2	2			228
Robert Jones	100	2	2			126
Robert Jones Senr	100	2	2			128
George Killgees		2	2			28
Robt Kelsoe		1	3	4		24
Aaron Lusadack		2	2			25
Andrew Lewis		2	2			26
George Lemley	200	2	5	9		89
Andrew McClelland		4	4			66
Charles McDowell	200	2	2	2		129
Anthony Maughone		2	3			34
Peter Miers	300	1	2	8		140
John McElroy		2	3			34
Henry McQuead		2	2	4		30
William McCleerey	318	5	6	6		376
John McClelland	100	2	2			128
John McKee		2	1			24
Joseph Morris		2	2	6		30/10
James Morrarty		2	2			28
James Mordock	400	4	4	12		469
James Porter	300	1	4	3		143
John Province	100	1	1	3		114
Thomas Province		2	4			32
Ruth Rineheart		1	3			24
Joseph Rinehart	70	2	3	6		114/10
Thomas Rinehart	180		3	5		156
Thomas Rinehart Senr	150	2	2			184
Robert Reed		2	3	4		33/10
Joseph Rankin	100	1	3			42
John Rondalds		1				10
Aaron Rollens		1	1			11
Samuel Shannon		2	2	4		30
John Simonton	150	1	2	4		91/10
Frances Seaton		1	1	1		14/10
Daniel Stewart	100	1	2			66
Stephen Stiles	100	1	3	6		72
Jacob Smittle		1				10
Kenner Seaton	100	2	3			172
William Shepheard	200	2	2			228
George Santee		2	2			28
Abraham Scott	300	2	2			328

36

NAME	ACRES	HORSES	COWS	SHEEP	SLAVES	VALUE
Rachel Swan - widow	200	2	3			232
Betty Seaton - widow	250	3	4	5	5	598
Hugh Stephenson		2	3			33
James Seaton		2	1			24
Thomas Shullock	100	2	2			98
Isaac Wood	318	2	2			178
James Winn		1	1			14
Joseph Wilson		1	1			14

SINGLE FREEMEN

NAME	ACRES	HORSES	COWS	SHEEP	SLAVES	VALUE
Alexander Crawford	40	1	2			50
Robert Lewis	100	1	1			110
Richard Seaton		2	1	2		24/10

"20 More young men in this Township That has no property &c."

1783 DONEGAL TOWNSHIP TAX LIST

NAME	ACRES	HORSES	COWS	SHEEP	SLAVES	VALUE £/S
Joseph Alexander	300	3	3	4		196
James Allison	300	2	1	3		175/10
Robert Aglr	400	2	4	3		237/10
James Brownlee	900					450
Thomas Brownlee	300					150
David Barr	150					75
Archibald Brownlee	300					150
Samuel Byers	200					100
Thomas Byers	200					100
James Byers	200					100
Barney Boner	150					75
William Boner	150					75
Charles Boner	150					75
Bryan Bruin	400					200
Ezekiel Boggs	260	2	2	6		161
Robt Carrel	600					300
Hezeklah Clark	200	3	3	2		143
Isaac Coxx	200		3	3		113/10
Jacob Coxx	200					100
Joseph Casey		2	3	4		34
James Caldwell Sr	193	1	5	8	2	154
John Caldwell	193	1	3	6		121
James Clemons	400	4	6	2		265
James Carson	400	1	2	4		220
Robert Corathers		1	1	1		14/10
Thomas Chapman	400	2	2			221
Moses Chaplin	100	3	2	5		89/10
Caleb Clark		2	2	1		28/10
Edward Carles	300					150
John Dunnaven	100	2	1	2		75
Michael Dinnes	200	1	1	2		115
Henry Deets		1				10
Jeremiah Dunn	300					150
George Dement		2	3	1		32/10
Zephaniah Dunn		1	2	3		19/10
Abraham Enlow	400	3	2			238
Michael Ely	100	1	3	6		75
David English	200		1	2		105
Luke Enlow	200					100
Peter Flemming		3	2	1		38/10
Sarah Fillabum		4		1		40/10
Robert French		1	2			18
Henry Fullamwider Senr	300	2	2	6		181
Henry Fullamwider	200	2	1	1		124/10
John Gill	140	2	3	1		102/10
Robert Graham	300	2				170
Hugh Gilliland /Distill	300		2	3		169/10
Samuel Glass	200	4	8	18	3	331

39

NAME	ACRES	HORSES	COWS	SHEEP	SLAVES	VALUE
Neal Gillaspy	400					200
Daniel Gillaspy	400					200
Hugh Glover	100	1	2	1		68/10
Robert Gutry	100	1	1			64
John Grimes	300	2	3	1		182/10
Thomas Gilliland	400	2	3	6		235
Robert Gorley	150					75
Edward Gather	300					150
Thomas Hill	100					50
Everhart & Ann Hupp	200	2				120
George Humphry	400	2	3	6	2	335
Robert Humphrey	400	1	2	8		214
Henry Holmes	300					150
Elizabeth Huston		1	3	2		23
John Howel	200	2	6	11		140/10
John Huff		2	2			28
Samuel Johnson	400	2	3	4		234
Peter Kenteloe		1	1			14
John Kaln	100	1	1			64
Thomas Knoxx	200					100
George Leflar	100		1	3		55/10
Jacob Leflar	600	4	6	2		365
Andrew Link	400					200
John Lane	400	2	1	1		224/10
Margaret Leeper	300					150
John McFeely		1	1			14
John McBride		1	2			18
Christopher Millar	400	3	4			246
Henry Moore	150	2	1	4		101
Nathaniel McDowell		1	1			14
Keeneth McClelland	300	1	3	9		176/10
James Manly		1		2		11
John Moore	300					150
William McDonnough	400					200
Andrew Moore	100		2	1		58/10
John McWilliams	170	2	2	2		114
Samuel Millar	350					175
George McClane	300	2	4	3		187/10
Ann Knight		2	1	3		25/10
James McDonald		1	3	4		24
John McGee	100	1	2			68
Archibald McNeal	150					75
Hugh M. Brekenrige	650					325
Samuel Mason Esqr	550	4	10	16	4	563
Charles McRoberts /Gristmill	500	3	5	10		405
Jno McFarrans	400					200
David McClure	1300					650
Nathaniel McDowell	30	2				25
John Patterson		1				10

40

NAME	ACRES	HORSES	COWS	SHEEP	SLAVES	VALUE
Isaac Philips	200					100
Sarah Philips	200					100
Joshua Russell	200	2	3	4		134
Jacob Rassor		2	2			28
Jacob Rice	1100	5	5	8		624
Abraham Rice	400	3	3			242
James Roney	300					150
Harculus Roney	300					150
James Stephenson	400					200
Walter Summers	240	3	5	4		172
Laurance Streaker	150	2	2	4		105
John Smith	400					200
Samuel Snodgrass	100					50
Jacob "Taylor or Saylor"	200					100
Hugh Sidwell	150	2	2			103
Christian Snidigar		2	2			28
Van Swearingham	400					200
John Smith	400					200
James Snodgrass	50		1			29
Robert Taylor	400	3	4	4		248
Henry Taylor	200	1	1	1		114/10
Samuel Taylor	200	2	2			128
John Templeton	400	1	2	3		219/10
Isabella Templeton		2	1	3		25/10
Robert Walker	300					150
John Williamson Junr	400	3	3	2		243
Jacob Wolf	150	2	3	7		110/10
Christian Wolf	140	1	2	4		90
William Wolf	150	2	2	3		104/10
Thomas Wilson	50		1			29
Samuel Wilson		1	1			14
Christopher Winters	300	3	3	6		195
Benjamin Wells	300					150
Moses Williamson		3	2			38
Jeremiah Williamson		1	1			14
Thomas Williamson		1	1			14
Samuel Williamson	300	3	4	4		198
Zedikiah Williams		2	3	2		33
Basil Williams		2	3	9	1	86/10
Thomas Wallar	700					350
Basel Williams Junr	300					150
Christian Went	300					150
Joseph Wilson	300					150
Richard Yeats Esqr	400					200
Peter Youghoo		1	3			22
Mr. Vance	400					200

NAME	ACRES	HORSES	COWS	SHEEP	SLAVES	VALUE
SINGLE FREEMEN						
Samuel Ankrom		2	1			24
Jonathan Cox	63					32/10
William Bogs		1				10
Samuel Caldwell	400					200
Thomas Lane	400					200
John Summers		1				10
David Williamson	1000					500
Eleazr Williamson	400	1				210
Laurance Williams		1				10
Levin Williams		1	1	1		14/10
Martin Shurry		1				10
Michael Stults		1				10
Philip Hupp	300					150
Jonathan Howell		1	2	5		20/10
Jacob Miller	400	2	3	2		233
James Caldwell Junr /2 Distills	400	3				290

1783 FALLOWFIELD TOWNSHIP TAX LIST

NAME	ACRES	HORSES	COWS	SHEEP	SLAVES	VALUE £/S
Samuel Acklin	45	1	1			21
John Atkinson	111	2	3	5		48
Joseph Allen	853	2	4	9		410
John Allen		1	1			5
John Allen	25		1	1		11
Alexander Andrews		1	1			5
Richard Arsbill		1	1			5
William Almon	300	1	1			97/2
John Adams	450	2	4	7		176
Dugal Boyd	300	2	3	2		105
John Burk		2	2			5
Widow Bandfield		1	1			2
Jesse Buzan		3	1			14
Daniel Brooks	300	3	2	6		132
Nicholas Barts	250	4	4	10		43
John Blandy	230	4	4	10		176
James Babis		1				1
Andrew Black	89	2		1		15
John Baldwine /Sawmill	318					181
John Brooks		1	1			5
Joseph Brenton	290	3	3	8		133
Thomas Baily		1	2	1		9
Joseph Buffington	218	2	2	2		120
John Buffington	60					3
John Buckenliew	100	1	1	4		36
Joseph Brown	166	3	4	6		77
Zephaniah Beal	700	5	8	7		326
Richard Cunningham	80	2	1	3		27
Johnston Campbell	250	3				69
Jacob Coughran	150	2	4	6		30
Henry Conrod	60	2	1			19
Peter Castner	256	2	4	3		132
Nicholas Criss	200	4	6	13		176
Peter Chesroney	240	3	4	13		130
Widow Colvin		2	3	8		14
Vincent Colvin	1639	6	13	20	2	564
Luther Colvin	300	2	2	6		106
William Coburn	60	2	1			26
John Carle	318	3	4	8		127
John Crow	150	3	1	6		58
John Carpenter		2	2	2		10/10
William Coll		1				1
Martha Criss		1	1	8		6
Isaac Chalfin	160	1				48
Bazelor Clark	30	1				5
William Chalfin		1	3	3		11
James Campbell		1	1	1		7
Henry Crabb	200	2	3	2		66

NAME	ACRES	HORSES	COWS	SHEEP	SLAVES	VALUE
Thomas Carson	200	3	4	7		81
Laurance Crow	318	3	5	12		112
Frederick Cooper	300	4	8	10	2	290
Thomas Coxx		2	2	2		8
Daniel Depur	780	3	4	13		290
Jeremiah Davis		2	1	3		4
Abraham Decker	400	3	5	15		171
Tobias Decker	170	3		6		93
John Dunn	50	1	1			22
George Davis		2				10
Moses Davis		1	2			9
John Davis		2	1			7
Abraham Dixson	180	2	2	2		66
Samuel Dixson	318	4	5	10		213
Joshua Dixson	400	3	3	3		224
Henry Dixson	200	3	4	4		167
James Davis		2	2			12
Thomas Dowler		2				12
John Duncan	180	3	4	3		75
Jesse Drake /Gristmill	50	2	2	8		35
Adam Deems		1	2			9
Peter Drake	180	2	4	8		76
Cabeus Dodd /8 oz plate		3	3			50
Moses Doolittle		1	2			10
Archa'd Drumin		1				3
Alexander Duvall		1				3
Mark Deems	90	2	2	7		41
John Deems	150		2	2		36
John Davis		1	1	1		5
Samuel Dunn		1				3
Leonard Everly		2	1			10
Nathan Ellis	50	3	3	7		45
Abner Eastwood						
Ann Ellis	50	1	1			9
William Edward	50	1	2			13
William Evans	200	2	2	6		47
John Everitt	200	2	2	2		47/5
Jesse Ellis		1				5
David England	200	3	1			132
James Ellis	200	3	7	7	1	167
Jeremiah Ellis	125	2	2			33
Samuel Ellis		1	2			10
Benjamin Frye	500	3	4	6	2	373
Philip Fryman	50	2	1			18
James Frye /Gristmill	200	2	5		1	126
William Forwood /Gristmill	481	1	2	2		188
John Flemon	400	4	2	8		132
Robert Fosset		2	2			34
Samuel Frye	318	5	6	19	3	260

44

NAME	ACRES	HORSES	COWS	SHEEP	SLAVES	VALUE
Abraham Frye	318	4	7	15	2	236
Isaac Gibson		1	2	3		8
John Guthry		1	1			6
Christpher Grybill /Distill	111	3	3	1		47
Ann Gillespy		1	2			8
Solomon Gregg	256	1	2			93
Neal Gillaspy		2	7	5	3	120
James Grimes		1	1			4
John Gragg	300	3	6	8		138
Henry Gregg	300	3	6	8		138
John Gribill	300	2	2	3		104
John Hull	215	4	6	2		83
James Hull	100	2	3	1		42
Abraham Hickman	300	2	2	4		82
Charles Hoy		2	2			10
Joshua Harbin		3	7	3	2	90
Richard Hogland	110	2	3	6		57
James Hopkins /Distill	300	4	4	7	1	109
John Hopkins /7 oz plate	450	7	6	12	4	285
William Harris		1	1			6
Moses Henry	120	2	3	5		41
Thomas Hamilton		1	1			5
John Herron		2	2	3		11
Benjamin Harriss		4	4	7		22
Thomas Howard		1	2	5		14
Elizabeth Hook			2			4
John J Hopkins	260	2	2	6	1	130
Thomas Hutson		1				5
Thomas Hollowell		1	2			7
Thomas Hutton	318	4	3	10		135
James Harrow		1	1			5
John House	100	2	3	5		30
Andrew House	100	2	3	6		38
William Howe	318	3	5	5		134
William Hughes	300	2				64
John Husk		1	1	1		4
George Huskins						
William Hawtheway /Distill	150	3	4	4		72
Isaac Harrow		1	1	3		6
Adam House			1			1
James Innis	640	4	7	3	1	274
Jacob Jones	240	5	6	16	2	156
Samuel James		2	1	4		9
Evan Jones		1	2			5
Abel Johnston		1	2	4		10
William Jackman	400	4	7	7		173
David Jamison		2	2	1		10
James Johnston			1			2

NAME	ACRES	HORSES	COWS	SHEEP	SLAVES	VALUE
Jacob Jones	190	3	2	9		74
Nicholas Johnston	200	2	3	5		79
Mary Johnston		3	2	10	2	66
David Johnston		2	2	2		10
Robert Jackman	600	3	6	18	2	548
/Gristmill /2 Distills						
Edward Jackman	318	3	2	3		70
John Jackman	300	2	3	3		110
John Karr		3	2	10	1	44
Nathan Kasbeer		1	1			25
Francis Kellar	125	3	3	3		97
William Knox	300	2	2			115
Hannah Knox	300					100
Robert Louden	300	5	2			79
John Larimore		2	2	2		11
Abraham Leforgee	150	1	3	1		52/5
Henry Lane		2	3	5		14
Jacob Lash		2	2	7		12
Jacob Lady	90	2	1			26
Frederick Leatherman	120	2	2	2		40
James Lowry		1	2			7
John McCourtney	318	2	3	8		18
James Matthews		2	3	3		13
William McCommus	282	3	4	6	2	138
John McCommus	111	2	2	8		49
John Martin		2	2			17
William McCargge	80	2	1			37
Samuel Moore		2	1			8
Alexander Moody	100	1	2	5		32
James McCormick		2	2			11
Joseph McClain						
William McMachan			4	10	2	48
John McCall	200	3	1	2		62
Phillip Miller	120	1	3	2		36
Philip McGarey		2	2			20
George Milford Senr		1	2	8		7
John McGinniss	105	2	3	5		31
Patrick McKinley		2	6	3		21
Kidd Marquis		2	1			3
James Mitchel	250	2	2			93
Jacob Maydon			1			2
Alexander Mcintire	101	2	2	3		48
/2 Distills						
Thomas Mcginniss		1	1			6
Samuel Nigh	50	2	2	3		25
Thomas Nicholas	100	2	2			31
John Nickson	260	2	3			118
John Nichols	75	2	2	4		30
Thomas Nichols	220	4	3	9		69
James Nichols		1				3

NAME	ACRES	HORSES	COWS	SHEEP	SLAVES	VALUE
Constantine O neal		1	1			10
Patrick Offlin						
Ignaslous Ogden		1	2			6
Nathan Offut		2				6
Charles Orsler		2	2	2		11
Stephen Parr		2	2	6		12
Richard Pindary		1	1			11
Thomas Pinnack		1	1			2
Gideon Parrimor	40	2	2			23
John Parkison		2	2			10
Ezekiel Painter	132	4	1			74
Elisabeth Perry		1				1
Isaac Powel	100	1	2	5		37
Isaac Pennington		1	1	1		5
James Prichet		2				6
Joseph Platter	124	3	2	4		58
Nicholas Platter	474	2	4	11		161
Michael Power	150	1	2			50
John Peters				2		0
Evans Phillips		2	2	3		9
Mary Peters / 1/2 Ferry	318	1	2	6		168
Davis Ruth	150	2	2			57
Jacob Rape	50	2	2	3		20
George Riddle	45	2	2	2		23
Robert Robertson		1	1			3
William Riggs	100	1	1	3		34
Jeremiah Riggs	200	3	2	4		75
Henry Rowlin		1				3
Robert Raily	100	4	7	15		90
John Raily	30	2	2	2		21
Edmond Riggs	60	2	3	3	1	36
William Robins		1	1			6
Michael Richard	100	2	1			24
David Richie /Distill	300	3	6	12		142
George Rigle /2 Distill	200					94
Samuel Riddle		4	3	3		19
James Rusk		1	1			6
George Rowler	38	1	2	2		20
John Reed /Distill	45	2	4			50
Eleazr Rigg		1	1			27
Elijah Reese		1	1			20
James Reed		1	1			11
William Risinger	300	2	3	10		116
Alexander Ross		2	2	3		10
Edward Richardson		1	1			5
Samuel Russell						
John Riddle		1	1	2		6
William Rowin		2	2			6
Anthony Shears						
Jacob Springer	120	2	3	8		52

NAME	ACRES	HORSES	COWS	SHEEP	SLAVES	VALUE
Alexr Scott	140	2	2	3		33
William Sparks		1	1	8		8
Jacob Stilwarggon		2	2	7		13
James Shaddock		2	2			11
Daniel Starke		2	2	3		10
James Starke	140	2	3	4		61
Christopher Starke		3	3			20
Jonathan Starke		1	2			8
James Shane	300	2	4	4		108
Stophel Sticker	200	3	3	3		78
Daniel Stephens	100	2	2			44
Daniel Sosburry	40	1	1			17
Henry Spiers /Distill	318	4	7	11	1	198
James Scott		2	3	3		13
George Snap		2	2			7
Obediah Stout	50	2	3	6		24
Peter Snap	200	3	2	4		86
John Snap	45	1				9
Jacob Stroop		2	3	9		14
Joseph Stibbs	300	2	3	6		113/10
John Shoptaw	87	2	2	4		50
William Tubb /Distill	130	3	1	4		54
Jacob Thomas		2	2	1		8/5
Isaac Thomas		1	1			4
Robert Taylor						
James Thomas	70	2	1	4		29
Michael Taylor		3	3			44
William Tribbey		2	1			4
Permelia Thompson						
John Tannihill		3	3	6	1	49
John Venus		1				3
Amos White /Tanyard	175	2	3	5		80
John Ussleton		1	1			3
Charles Wheeler /Doctor	158	4	4	6	3	203
Andrew Waits		2	1	3		3
Charles Willach		2	2	3		11
Jonathan West		2	1			7
Isaac Williams	300	3	2	9		119
Richard Ward		1				1
Augustine Wells	50	1	1			12
Harbourd Wallis	900	7	6	24	9	545
Benjamin White	150	1	1		1	80
Edward West	266	3	7	20		110
Jacob White	120	2	2	1		45
Thomas Wells	200	2	2			65
John Williams		1				4
John Williams.		2	2	3		7
Daniel Whiticar	100	3	2			37
Ephraim Wilson	400	2	3			38
Daniel Watson	100	2	1	2		21

NAME	ACRES	HORSES	COWS	SHEEP	SLAVES	VALUE
John Wilks	120	2	2			40
Edward White	50	2	2	2		34
Enoch Williams	40	2	2			21
John Worth	300	3	3	11		102
William Woods		3	3	4		17
John Wallis	80	3	3	4		32
Edward White Junr		3	3	4		24
William Wood		3	6	8		25
Jacob Young /Distill	140	2	4	4		78
James Young	300	2	2	2		102/5
Hercules Young	318	2	3	6		114

SINGLE FREEMEN

NAME	ACRES	HORSES	COWS	SHEEP	SLAVES	VALUE
Amos Aails						
Eli Allen		1				10
John Almon	100					20
Thomas Almon	150					30
Thomas Broddock		1				2
James Brooks						
Laurance Craft						
Henry Dixson						
Ebinazer Foot		1				5
Jonathan Glaze						
Nathaniel Glaze			2			6
Alexander Hopkins	150					30
Richard Hopkins						5
Silas Hopkins	60					11
Jacob Johnston						
Richard Jackman	50	1				10
Peter Johnston						
James Karr						
George Knox		3				22
Daniel McComus						
Samuel McComus						
Patrick McMachan						
Archibald McKindly						
John Martin		1				6
Nathan Powell		1				26
Peter Platter						
Thomas Parkison /2 Gristmills /Sawmill	300	2	3			502
Daniel Riggle		1				6
John Riggle		1				4
Robert Raley						
William Wallis		1				3

NAME	ACRES	HORSES	COWS	SHEEP	SLAVES	VALUE
James Wallis		2				10
Joseph W. West		1				3
William Williams		1				3

"Also there is 12 single men more than has no property in this
Township"

1783 GREENE TOWNSHIP TAX LIST

NAME	ACRES	HORSES	COWS	SHEEP	SLAVES	VALUE £/S
John Alley		2	3	4		53
William Burk		3	3	5		73/10
William Brown		2	2	4		49/10
John Brown /Hatter	318	2	2	5		149/5
James Belshe	318	2	4			177
Frances Baldwine	318	1	1			73
Joshua Barns		2	2			21
Isaac Bozzer		1				10
Ross Crossley		3	2			60
Thomas Coughran	300					60
John Chaffin		2	2			26
John Cunningham		2	1	3		25
Alexander Clegg			2			6
John Corbey	300	2	2			58
Mary Clawson - widow		2	2			30
Timothy Dougherty		1	1			14
Augustin Dillenger	318	2	4	5		114
Richard Dodson		2	2			26
Andrew Dye	318	5	4	6		108
Thomas Douglass	133	2				100
John Evans	250	3	3	9		153
John Evans Junr		2	2	4		27
David Evans	750	4	7	4		202
John Edwards	318	1	1			54
Widdow Ferry		2	2			23
David Flowers	318	2	2			100
Joseph Freze /Gristmill	318	2	2			156
Jacob Freze		2	4			40
James Flinn	318	3	3	2		82/10
John Guttery	318	2	3	3		73
Frederick Garrison	318	2	3	5		73/10
Leonard Garison	318	1	2			46
Zachariah Gapping	318	4	5	6		155
John Gerrard	318	4	5			152
Hinson Hobbs	500	4	3			122
Samuel Hyde	660	1	5		1	280
William Hudson /Distill	318	5	3	4		254
John Hopewell		1	1			20
Richard Hall		2				20
Matthew Hannan		2	2			50
Robert Jones /Distill	1000	5	5	5		386/10
Aaron Jinkins /Distill	600	5	5	3		215/10
Richard Ivis	318	5	7	13		191
Baily Johnson		1	1			13
John Ivis - Single		1				10
Solomon Knots		1	1	2		14
Benjamin Knots	200	2	1	3		100
James Knots	300	2	2			96

51

NAME	ACRES	HORSES	COWS	SHEEP	SLAVES	VALUE
William Knots		1	1			13
Samuel Kenner	200	2	6	1		138
Mary Lambert		1				3
William Lamestus			2			6
John Long	300	1	1	6		120
David Long	300	1	1	6		100
James Long		1	3	4		28
Eliah Long		2	2			26
John Long Junr		2	2			26
Gidion Long		1	2			16
Jeremiah Long		1	1			13
John Launce	318	3	3			105
Andrew Launce - Single		2	2			26
John Minor Esqr /Gristmill /Sawmill	100	3	3	3		193
William Minor	400	8	8	12	1	358
William McCoy	270	3	5	4		206
Peter Miller		2	4			32
James Mandle	318	2	5	9		118
Abner Mandle	318	1	1			23
Robert Moses - Single						
James Nelson	200	1	1			53
Richard Pain		1				30
Josiah Pricket		2	1			23
John Pricket - Single						
William Robertson	318	2	2	4		147/10
David Rinehart		2	2			50
John Roberts		2	2	2		27
Joseph Ross		1	1			13
Peter Reily		1				20
John Shrier		1	2			21
John Sriver	300	1				30
Lewis Sulser	100	3	2			100
Michael Soap	300	2	5			120
Benjamin Sutton		2	2			30
Stephen Shipman		2	1			23
Martha Stone			1			3
Eliah Stone	200	4	5			190
Henry Six	100	1				90
Moses Taylor		1	2			21
James Winsor		1				10
Lewis Williamson	200					100
Jeremiah Williams		2	1			26
Isaac Wood		1				10
Stephen Gapping		1				10
Leonard Garrison		1				10
Jesse Hill		1				10
Samuel Howard	300					100
John McMachan	600					130
Hussey Hamilton	300					50

NAME	ACRES	HORSES	COWS	SHEEP	SLAVES	VALUE
John Polk	300					60
David Shelby	300					70
Peter Pickenpaugh	300					50
William Boils	300					50
Thomas Clary	300					60
Nathaniel Kidd	300					40
Nicholas Fasts	600					150
John Ross	300					70
Widow Crouse	300					80
Widow Seals	300					70
Everly Leonard	300					60
George Wilson	600					140
John Glascow	600					140
Evans Watkins	300					40
Henry Fricks	300					100
David Bailstone	300					50
George Bailstone	300					60
Daniel McFarlane	300					20
John Ruther	318					50
Nicholas Baker	300					50
James Carmichael	600					200
Robert Shannon	60					10
Brice Wordly	300					100
George Shins	200					50
Jacob Hoover	300					80
John Moore	60					20
Robert Gray	100					30
George Lemley	300					100
William James	300					20
Ebenezer Sutton	300					60
Francis McGinnis	300					80
Isaac Grerard	300					100
Widow Lambert	600					150
William Thomas	300					50
John Corbly	300					70
Joseph Morris	318					100
Jonathan Morris	200					70
Arthur Ginneth	200					50
Joseph Rankin	300					40
Joseph Gerard	200					50
John Green	300					30
Thomas Wolverton	300					60
Henry Jackson	200					40
Charles McDowel	200					30
Amos Mills	340					70
Robert Crossly	300					40
Zepheniah Johnson						30
Isaac Newton	100					40
Michael Burns	300					50

NAME	ACRES	HORSES	COWS	SHEEP	SLAVES	VALUE
Thomas Flowers	400					130
William Hudson	300					50
John Lance	300					40

1783 HOPEWELL TOWNSHIP TAX LIST

NAME	ACRES	HORSES	COWS	SHEEP	SLAVES	VALUE £/S
George Achison		2	2	3		20
Adam Allen		1				3
James Allen		2	2			12
James Anderson	150	1				30
Alexr Anderson	200	1	2			41
Edward Anderson	400	3	4	6	1	172
Peter Anderson		1				8
Allectious Baily		2				10
Jacob Buckston	200	1	2	3		65
Thomas Bay	600	4	4	8		189
Simon Brown	100	1	2			44
John Baker	30	1	1			18
Samuel Buchannan	400					100
Walter Buchannan		1				8
Samuel Bruce	200	3	2	8		74
John Best	300	4	7	10	1	178
Andrew Barber	200	4	5	10		94
John Batsell		3	4	2		30
Edward Brown	50	4	3			50
Thomas Batty	400	4	6	8		138
Francis Boggs		2	2			14
John Comly		2	2	3		22
John Carpenter		3	5	16		45
Thomas Cantwell	100	2	2			42
Thomas Crawford	300	1	2	2		89
William Campbell	200	5	6	12	2	204
James Clark	300	4	4	10		124
John Cowen	100	2	3	5		57
William Caldwell	300	2	2	1		116
George Carothers	50	1	1	2		20
Isaac Cowen		1				8
Ambros Cunningham	150	1				38
Hugh Cunningham		2	2			10
Raph Cotton		3	4	4		39
Peter Coe		2	2			25
John Chapman	300	2	3	8		109
Robert Covens		2	3			25
Thomas Clark		2	3	6		30
William Clark		1				8
John Criss	300					75
David Caldwell	200	2	2	3		67
Robert Cummings	600					150
John Donahee	300	2	4	16		111
Thomas Dowdden	100	2	3	6		63
Edward Dewlen	150					37
John Downing	380	2	4	15		136
John Davis	50	1	2	4		48
James Downing	400	2	2	2		124

NAME	ACRES	HORSES	COWS	SHEEP	SLAVES	VALUE
Timothy Downing	200	3	4	7	1	123
Ezekiel Dewett	400	3	7	11		154
Aaron Delong	300	3	3	6		99
Aaron Delong Jur		1	1	1		10/10
Solomon Delong		1	1			11
Philip Dodridge	150	3	4	4		79
John Dodridge	500	4	4	3		173
Samuel Dunlap		1	1			11
Isaac Ellis		1	2	5		11
William Ellis	250	2	2	8		81
James Finley		1				8
Richard Fowler	150	2	2			55
Thomas Filson		2	2	5		20
Mathew Fowler	200	3	3			81
John Forguson	318	3	4	17		131
John Godard		3	3	3		38
Thomas Garner	100	2	3	7		60
William Gill	700	2	3	9		299
Samuel Gill		1	2	4		25
James Gallespey	300	2	5			132
William Gallespey	100					25
Henry Grimes	300	3	3			120
John Greathouse	400	3	4			132
James Holmes	100	2	3	2		51
William Henry	300	2	2	3		89
James How	300	1				80
Ephraim Hart	200	3	4			86
William Hews	100	2	2	4		49
Samuel Hindman		4	3	3		39
John Hutton		2	3			45
Thomas Halvert	130	2	3	7		63
Thomas Hide	300					48
James Henwood		2	3			30
Michael Huff	150	1	3	5		59
William Huff		1	1			14
James Jackson	318	2	2			95
James Jolliff	100	2	3	2		59
Samuel Johnston	300	3	9	15		146
John Johnston	150	2	2	4		77
Ephraim Johnston	300					75
John Kelly	200	2	2	8		82
John Kelly	200	2	2			75
Elizabeth Kinster	200	2	2			75
Henry Livens	300	4	2			79
Abraham Leighmasters		2	2			17
John Leighmasters		1				8
Frederick Lamb	100	2	3			70
William Lamb	350	2	3			142
Richard Lavens	300	2	2			86
James Lawless	100					25

NAME	ACRES	HORSES	COWS	SHEEP	SLAVES	VALUE
Samuel Leeper	300	3	2	6		133
Samuel Marshall	600	3	3			236
John McCormick	150	3	2			68
John Miricle		2	2			14
Robert McBride		2	1			12
James McDonald		2	2			12
Samuel McBride		2	2			20
Patrick McGohon	100	3	1	7		56
Torrance McCann	182	3	2	12		83
Francis McGuire	318	4	12	7		170
Andrew Moore	100	1	2			31
George Marquise	100	3	3	8		79
Robert Marshall		1				8
Col. James Marshall	400	4	5	12		150
Samuel McKebben		2				16
Thomas Marshall	300	1	1			80
Isaac Milles	100	3	2	10		59
Frances McCalley	200	3	2	8		46
James Marshall	300	2	3	7		93
John Marshall Esgr	200	3	3	4		91
Thomas McKibbin	200	2	3	8		103
Cornelius McEntire	60	2	2			35
John McKibben	200	4	7	12		120
Richard McKibben		2				16
William McClimons		1	1			12
Jesse Martin	900	3	6	17		232
James McMullin		1	3	1		22/10
James Martin	200	3	2	1		86/5
William McCowan		2	2	10		31
Peter McKee	100	3	2			55
Thomas McKee		1				3
Charles McBride	100	2	1	1		54
George McColloch		2	2			18
John Morrison	150	2	3	2		70/10
Thomas Marguis	400	4	4	4		137
George McConnal		1				8
Daniel McGugan	300	3	3	10		120
Arthur McConnal	200	2	3	5		76
Thomas McGuire		1				8
James Newel	400	5	3			150
John Nickles	130	2	2	14		81
James Nailor		1	1	5		12
Thomas Nickles	130	2	2	10		82
Hugh Newell	300	4	4	4		134
Joshua Owings	200	2				80
Brine O neal		2	2			30
William Paterson	400	2	6	22		148
Joseph Patrige		2	2			18
John Poalk	140	2	2			57
Thomas Polk	140	2	1			53

NAME	ACRES	HORSES	COWS	SHEEP	SLAVES	VALUE
Samuel Plummer	50	3	3	6		48
Samuel Plummer		1	1	1		11/5
Andrew Paul		3	3	4		34
Joseph Piles	100					25
Samuel Paterson	200	2	2	3		73
Joseph Paterson		2				6
Baldwine Perkins	600	1				220
William Perren	300	3	3			109
Benjamin Pusley			1			3
Cornelius Quick		2	3			34
Daniel Quimbey		2	2			22
James Robinson	150	2	3			76
David Rundales	400	4	8	6		157
Frances Rayley	200	2	2	4		73
William Randales	400	4	5			147
James Roberts						3
Joseph Reed	200					50
Thomas Rouse	400	1				108
Joseph Reiley	400	3	4	10		140
James Scott		2	3	8		30
Charles Stewart	400	3	3	12	1	198
Thomas Selvey	100	1	1	4		37
William Scott	300	3	5	14		119
Jeremiah Stansburry		3	3	3		35
Joseph Scott	200	5	4	8		105
John Smith Senr	400	3	5	9		142
Samuel Smith		2	1			19
John Smith	60	1	2	3		27
John Scott	100	3	4	8		64
Arthur Scott	300	2	3	8		104
John Steel		1	2	7		17
William Smiley	400	3	3	6		136
William Sheerer	200	2	2			72
John Stephenson	400					100
John Sheerer		2	1			19
Robert Snodgrass	100	1	2			39
Andrew Scott	700	3	5	7		216
Thomas Shain	200					50
Alexander Stevens	200	2	2			72
Joseph Smith	370	4	3		1	175
William Sparks	300	1	3	4		95
George Sparks	400	3	4	6	1	178
Absolom Sparks		1	2			15
Solomon Shepherd	300					75
Arthur Scott		2				16
Luke Summerhorn	450	2	3			71
Susannah Summerhorn	300	1	2			42
Samuel Tetter	300	2	4			103
Isaac Taylor	100	3	7	8		75
John Tennel	300	2	4	5		105

NAME	ACRES	HORSES	COWS	SHEEP	SLAVES	VALUE
John Tweed	300	2	3	2		102
James Taylor	100	2	2			47
Charles Tenel		2	2	6		25
Matthew Templeton	200	4	3			92
Thomas Ury	200	2	2	6		74
Thomas Ury						
John Ury		2	2	5		24
Samuel Ury		2	1			19
David Vance	200	3	3	5		111
Solomon Veel	50	1	3			31
James Vinson	50	3	3	4		49
Brace Werley		4	5	6		49
Morris West		2	2	4		24
Robert Wiggins	350					87
Charles Wells Senr	400	6	8	10	2	270
Charles Wells Junr	1000	5	10	21	3	486
Joseph Wells	500	4	7	16		186
George Wells	300	2				116
Alexander Wells	1150	7	7	16	2	780
Henry Wells	400	4	4	11		148
Joseph Williamson		2	2			22
Alexander Wilson	300	4	2			113
Thomas Wells	200	4	8	4		108
Richard Wells	460	3	4		1	211
Alexr Wells Junr		3	2			30
James Woods	100	4	3			67
Nathan Wells		3	3			34
Jeremiah Wilson		2	3			26
William White		3	3			34
William Williamson	200	2				66
Robert Wells		2	3	7		30
Nathan Wells		2	2	2		23
James White	200	2	2			42
Thomas Williams		2	2			18
Samuel Workman	100	3	2			36
John Waggoner	200					50
Richard [n?] Wells	300	2	2			97
Richard [of James] Wells	400	2	4	10	1	177
David Wilson	300					75
Absolom Wells	400	3	3		1	174
Thomas Ward	200					50
Joseph Wardley		2	2			22
David Wordly		3	3			34
Jonahs Armspoker	100	2	2			47
Ann Lavens	300	2	2			91
James Leeper	200	2	2			52
Amy Bonam	200	4	3	6		97
Alexr Bowlin	200	2	3			86
Henry Bowlin	200					90
Thomas Large	200	2	2			66

NAME	ACRES	HORSES	COWS	SHEEP	SLAVES	VALUE
Archiblad Elson	200	2	2			75
Thomas Barton	200	3	3			70
Josiah Con/Cow		2	3			26
Walter Hill	100	4	2			41

1783 MORGAN TOWNSHIP TAX LIST

NAME	ACRES	HORSES	COWS	SHEEP	SLAVES	VALUE £/S
Frederick Arnold	100	3	3	4		77
Daniel Arnold	200	4	7	7		144
Daniel Arnold Junr	150	2		1		85/10
John Blackburn		1	1			8
Joseph Beedle	100	3	4	6		80
Joseph Beedle Junr		2				6
Francis Beedle		1	1			6
James Bristo	130	2	2	3		23
Francis Baldwine	118					20
Jacob Burge		4	3			22
Groombride Bally		2	3	4		14
Peter Benham	100	2	1	1		18/10
Abel Bell	160	2	6	10		108
Nathaniel Bell	300	2	5	6		122
Nathaniel Bell Junr	300	2	3			120
Abner Brown	150	2	2			80
Paul Brown	40	1	3	4		21
James Bell	240	3	9	10		154
Widow Brown	150	1	4	4		72
Robert Benham	150	3	6	8		86
Daniel Crane	100	2	2	3		33
Silas Crane	100	2	2	5		38
Elizabeth Callender		1	1			5
Michael Coxx	300		1			60
Eleanor Casteel		2	1			8
Holdrige Chidester		2	2	2		11
Samuel Call		1	1	1		6/5
Benjamin Daniel	200	1	4			56
Nathaniel Dunham	140	2	4	6		70
Widow Dunn	100	1				44
Thomas Eastman		4	3			24
Henry Enoch	400	5	17	15		298
Andrew Farly		2	2	3		17
Philip Fox		3	3			25
Henry Fix	60	2	3	3		31
Samuel French		2	2	3		9
Andrew Flude		1				1
William Grooms	260	4	6	8		94
Christian Galmen	300	2	4	3		121
John Goodwine	300	2	3	14		124
Rachel Griffin	300	1	2	3		27
Solomon Grooms	60	3	2	2		31
Philip Grayson	50	2	2	3		25
Archibald Gray	100	4	5			70
John Gray	40	1	1			14/10
Matthew Gray		2	2	1		15
David Gray	100		2			24
Thomas Gilles			1			2

NAME	ACRES	HORSES	COWS	SHEEP	SLAVES	VALUE
Samuel George			2			4
John Gatral	150	3	3			76
Levi Harrod	400	3	4	9		154
Miles Haydan	200	3	4	9		95
Thomas Hardistay			2			2
Richard Hardistay	100	1	2			28
Francis Hardistay		2	3	6		23
Hazekiah Hardistay	50	1	1			12
John Heagle	300	1	2			52
Cornelius Hurley		1				2
George Hoge	300	2	3			90
Samuel House	100	2	2	5		48
William Hartly	100	1	2	1		30
James Hook	800	4	4	5	1	174
Samuel Hateway	60	1	1	3		39
William Hays	600	2	2	2		75
Thomas Hill	636	3	7	15		209
John Justice	400					45
Benjamin Jennings	500	2	4	15		174
Alexr Jackson		2	3	1		26/10
Zepheniah Johnston	200	1	2			54
Richard Jackson	200	2	7	2		141
David Jennings	100	2	3	6		53
Thomas Kelsey	280	2	5	9		133
Nathan Kelley	200	2	3	6		28
John Kee		5	3	9		30
Elias Kelley		1				2
Joseph Linthecum		2	2	2		13
Paulsor Lowry		4	3			25
John Lowry	150	2	2	2		45
Samuel Line	100	1	1	2		21
Jesse Leonard	180	1	4	5		67
Lydia Leonard		1				2
William Leonard	35	3	4	14		95
William Lee	150	2	6	10		84
John Mills	200	3	3	2		61
James Mattheney	100	1	1			30
John Messemore	40	1	1			34
Tobias Moore		1	1			10
Samuel McCray	150	4	3	8		62
Elijah Mills	250	2	3	4		82
Jacob Mills	250	2	3	4		52
Joseph Mills	150	3	3	1		77/10
Joseph Millikan	50	2	2			19
John Moore		2	3	3		17
John Martain	200	1	2			44
John McKinney		1	2			3
Josiah Minor		2	2	2		16
Edmond Manning	30	1	4	9		29
Nathan Meek	200	3	3			70

NAME	ACRES	HORSES	COWS	SHEEP	SLAVES	VALUE
Jeremiah Meek		4	4			30
James Morris	100	2	2	5		35
James Marrandy	300	2	4	4		122
Samuel Marrandy	200	2	3			33
Richard Morris	100	2	3	3		41
Jacob Need	140	3	3	6		58
Widow Owing	200	1	2	3		41
James Parker		3	4	5		29
Reuben Perkins	100	2	2			64
Elisha Perkins	100	2	4	6		62
Jacob Rush	200	3	9	8		110
Tychicus Rose	50	2	5			50
William Rush		2	2			12
John Ross	50	2	3	6	1	82
John Ross Junr	550	4	6	7	1	166
Henry Ross	250	2	5	9		106
Henry Stull	100	2	5	6		87
Benjamin Stilts	600	4	5	6		142
Phillip Swart	150	4	5	8		104
Henry Stull	40	2	2			26
Joseph Stewart	100	2	4			30
Thomas Sletter	200	4	4	6		112
James Seals	300	2	3	4		111
Samuel Seals		1	1			17
Boston Strove	300	1	3			42
Lazarus Timmons	100	2	3	5		37
John Taylor		1	1			6
Widow Viech		2	1	2		9
James Wright		1	2	2		7
Joseph Wilie	200	2	3	5		51
Thomas Wolverton	300	2	3	2		71
Job Walton	50	1	2			18
John Wilie	100	1	3			30
Thomas Wilson		2	1			8
Robt Stump	300					10
William Samuel	300					10
Seth Goodwine	300					10
Capt Brison	300					10
William Hawtheway	600					30
Widow English	300					10
Colvin Carry	300					10

SINGLE FREEMEN

NAME	ACRES	HORSES	COWS	SHEEP	SLAVES	VALUE
Cobus Linthecum		1				2
Ebenezar Brown	400	2				60
Francis Tatter						3
Joseph Blackburn		1				8

NAME	ACRES	HORSES	COWS	SHEEP	SLAVES	VALUE
James Blackburn		1				8
Vallentine Stull		3				12
Reuben Ross						2
John Pettet		1				8
Abraham Arnold	100			1		22
Henry Cline		1				5
David Leonard		1				6
Isaiah Hoge		1				7
William Ross	70	1				34
Robert Ross	70	1				26
John O brian		1				4
John Kenney		1				6

"There is also 5 young men that has no property in this Morgan Township"

1783 NOTTINGHAM TOWNSHIP TAX LIST

NAME	ACRES	HORSES	COWS	SHEEP	SLAVES	VALUE £/S
William Anderson	100	3	3	7		115/10
William Adams		2	1			19
Susannah Aclin	50		1			14
William Byers		3	1			24
Thomas Bounds	300	3	4	6		258
John Bevington /Distill		2	4	6		59
Thomas Bevington		2	1			14
David Brian		2	1			14
James Bruce Junr		1	2	3		25/10
George Bruce		1	1			14
Benjamin Bently M.W.	150	2	2			290
James Bruce Junr		1	3	4		27
William Bruce	223	3	5	6		453
Andrew Bell		1	1			14
Nathaniel Blackemore	300	4	8	10		377
William Blackmore		3	2		2	198
Jehu Bennet		2	2	3		29
William Boys	40	2	2	5		49/10
John Barr /Distill	350	5	5	8		477
John Brown	125	1	2	3		99
Josiah Cathel		1				15
Josiah Crawford	400	3	4	8		389
Andrew Crawford	400	3	4	2		386
Assa Cook		3	7	5		60/10
Joseph Cowenhoven	110	1	2	1		108/10
Gabriel Coxx	620	5	5	9	3	954/10
Benjamin Custard	370	3	4	12		386
Joshua Carman	100	3	2	5		100
Thomas Collins		3	2	5		39/10
Henry Crooks		3	1	8		39
Thomas Crooks		2		3		9/10
Thomas Cummings		1	2	1		14/10
David Crawford		1				5
Robert Crouch	100	3	6	1		120/10
John Crist	300		3			42
William Corns		2	1			24
James Chambers	100	1	2			68
Jonathan Casebears /Distill	90		1	4		56
Agness Casebare		1	1	1		9/10
Thomas Chenith	50	1	1			38
John Clark		1				10
Henry Craig		2	3	3		33/10
Ann Cook	400	2	2	6		324
Lewis Camron	200	1	1	1		134/10
John Devour	300	2	3	5		274/10
Andrew Devoir	800	4	3	7		655/10
Peter Devoir	40	2	2	1		30/10

NAME	ACRES	HORSES	COWS	SHEEP	SLAVES	VALUE
Abraham Deal		1	1	2		15
Thomas Dotherd		1	1	2		15
Nathan Deley	300	4	5	3		531/10
Eleanor Delley	200	3	4	3		247/10
John Delley		1				20
Charles Delley	90	2	2			74
Philip Delly Senr	150	4	7	15		275/10
Philip Delley Junr	100	2	2	2		129
James Demos	100	2	2	2		129
Nicholas Devoir	80	3	3	6		125
Edward Davis		1				20
Isaac Dillan		2	2			23
Henry Devoir	600	1	4	9		479
Thomas Dixson		2	1	2		25
Amey Decker		2	2	2		15
Jesse Edgenton		2	2			18
George Edgenton Junr		4	3			37
John Edgenton	300	4	5	5		262/10
Isaac Edgenton	800	3	4	5		102/10
George Edgenton Senr		1	3	2		20/10
Norrid Edgenton	100	3	1	1		74/10
Archibald Frame		3	3	2		29
James Fowler		2	2			28
Patrick Farlane	300	2	2	7		226/10
James Finch		3	2	4		38
Henry Forgison	144	3	4	2		143
Jacob Figley	200	3	4	15		353/10
Simon Figley	200	1	4	2		327
Vincent Forgison		2	1			15
James Forgison	181	5	3	4		225
Isaac Forgison	100	2	1	2		60
Alexander Gray	200	2	2	3		169/10
James Gibson		2	3	3		20
Patrick Grogran			1			3
George Gillespy	350	4	5	8		414
James Gaham	100	1	4	6		99
James Gardner		2				12
Archibald Hull	100	1	2			114
Sufiah Hughes	150					75
Moses Holladay	300	5	4	3	2	817/10
/2 Distills						
Ezekiel Hopkins	520	3	7	2		439
William Hamilton		3	2			30
John Hardan	50	1	2	3		69/10
William Holmes		1	1	4		13/10
Capt. Henry Heth	300	5	7	12	2	604
Andrew Heth		2	3	3		28/10
John Hamel		2	2			18
Daniel Harris		1	2			15
Thomas Harris		1	1			10

NAME	ACRES	HORSES	COWS	SHEEP	SLAVES	VALUE
Daniel Haggins				2		1
William Hamilton	282	3	3	6		245
Alexander Hill /Distill	100	2	2			108
Samuel Hill	100	2	1			74
David Jolly		2	2	4		21
George Jeckson	300	2	2			51
Samuel Irvin /Attorney	755	6	6		3	794
James Jolley	100	3	2			108
William Jinkins	100		1	3		55
Daniel Jacobs	206	1	3			220
Benjamin Kuckindall /Gristmill /Sawmill /Distill	700	8	10		3	1290
Mary Kennedy		1				7/10
Joseph Kennedy /Distill	100	2	3			118
Ameriah Leck	222	1	1			122
Robert Lytle	400	4	5	7		403
James Logan	50	3	3	7		95
David Levingstone	150	1	2	3		94/10
John Ledim	100	2	2	8		80
John Lain	200	2	1			119
John Morrison	300	3	5	2		201
James Munn	260	2	2		1	158
Abram Morgan		2	2			26
George Millar	300	2	5	8		243
John Munn	800	6	10	8		524
Paul Matthews			1			4
Samuel Meeks	400	2	2	4		230
John Martin	60	3	4	3		70
John Miller Senr		5	4	9		70
John Millar Junr	143	1	1	2		60
John Mitchel	100	3	1			224
Abner Machan		1	1	4		16
Robert McGee	280	3	3	4		324
James McConnel		3		1		15/10
Enos McDonald	100	2	2			74
James McMullen	300	2	2	3		179/10
David McClain	80	2	2	6		71
John McElheney	300	3	5	6		353
James McMahan		2	1	3		25/10
Richard McMachan		2	3			32
Andrew McFarlane	200	5	2	5	1	340/10
James McClane		1				7
Joseph McCune		1	1			12
William McConnel		1	2	3		19
John McGraw	20	1	2			24
Joseph McCollum	150	3	3	4		104
David McCoy		2				20
Henry Newkirk	150	3	3	4		109
James Odonald	200	1	2	3		67/10
Benjamin Parkison Esqr	263	2	2	4		230

NAME	ACRES	HORSES	COWS	SHEEP	SLAVES	VALUE
William Parkison Senr	300	2	2			148
James Payton		1	2			18
William Payton	300	2	2	2		59
Jesse Parimore	89	3	4			96
Thomas Parimore	150	2	3	8		118
John Parimore	150	2	3	4		104/10
Nathaniel Parimore		1	1			16
John Postlewright	150	1	1	4		86
Dorsey Pentecost	2000	7	6	14	1	:711
/Counceler /2 Distills /8 Lots of Ground						
Joseph Parkison Junr	60	1	1	2		146
John Parimore Junr	130	2	1	2		106
William Parkison Junr	400	1	1			424
Benjamin Pegg	200	2	1	3		159/10
William Quigley		2	1	3		26
Charles Ricords	20	1	1			20
John Robins	226	1	1			194
Daniel Robins		1	2	2		19
Thomas Robinson	100	2	1			24
Laurance Robinson	261	2	3	2		156
John Robinson	300	4	3		2	572
John Romine	100	2	1			54
Archibald Ricords		2	1			26
Thomas Rankins	350	3	4	7		299
Hugh Scott	365	4	3	7		356
Joseph Sawins		2	1	2		25
Henry Sawins	500	2	4	4		334
Sarah Sotton	200	1	2	1		78/10
David Scott		1				10
James Spiers		2	3	1		32/10
Edward Staker		1	1			14
John Spivey		2	4	3		37
John Sampson	300	2	1			44
Samuel Swearingham	300	2	5		2	325
John Shannon	200	2	5	7		193
Robert Temple		1				15
William Taylor		1	1			14
Adamson Tanehill		2	2	4		30
George Taylor		1				5
Samuel Trotman	150	3	2	2		135
Ann Thomas		1	1			5
Leverton Thomas	200	2	4	4		188
John Tannihill		2	1	2		25
John Underhill		2	3	3		33/10
Philip Undedam		2	2	8		32
John Vennator	80	1	3	4		82
James Vennator	80	2	2	3		99
Obediah Wilson			1			4
Capt Zedec Wright	400	7	7	12	1	553
Jeremiah Washburn	120	2	3	1		70/10

NAME	ACRES	HORSES	COWS	SHEEP	SLAVES	VALUE
John Wilson /Cooper		2	3	5		34
James Wilson		3	4			46
Samuel Wright		1	2			18
William Wright	300	2	2			228
Andrew Walker	60	3	3			70
George Welch	300	3	3			110
Adam Wickerham	50	1	3	4		204
/Gristmill /Sawmill /Distill						
Jacob Wickerham /Distill	180	2	2	3		221/10
Samuel Watt	100	2	1	2		65
Abner Winds		2	2	5		25/10
William Wilson	140	3	2			146
Aaron Williams	40	1	3	1		35/10
William Williamson	130	2	2	4		70
James Young		1				10
John Yant	100	2	2			68

SINGLE FREEMEN

NAME	ACRES	HORSES	COWS	SHEEP	SLAVES	VALUE
Charles Bevington		2				15
Samuel Barber						
John Bell						
George Barker						
William Barr						
Zeba Cook		1				10
Robert Crooks		2	2			18
William Chinnet						
Philips Deloy						
Samuel Deley						
John Douglass		1				10
William Frame						
John Finch		1	2			18
Zechariah Figley		1				10
John Finley		1				10
John Gardner		1				10
Thomas Gibson		2				20
James Glass						
David Hopkins						
David Jolly		1				10
Henry Morrison	200	4	3	13	1	288
Josiah Munn						
John Mitchel						
David Millar						
James Miller						
Hugh Miller						
Richard Parkison						
Benjamin Parimore						
Elias Peeg		1	1	3		15/10
David Parkison /2 Stills	260					450
Thomas Peyton		1				10

69

NAME	ACRES	HORSES	COWS	SHEEP	SLAVES	VALUE
Henry Ranolds		1				10
James Rankins						
John Rankins						
William Rankins						
James Scott		1				10
Abraham Scott		1				10
Alexr Sewart						
Robert Sheer						
Jeremiah Wright						
John Welkey						
Adam Wickerham		1				10
William Heth	100	1				40

1783 PETERS TOWNSHIP TAX LIST

NAME	ACRES	HORSES	COWS	SHEEP	SLAVES	VALUE £/S
Charles Allison		2	2	5		25/5
William Anderson		1				8
John Atkins		1	1			11
John Anderson	100	2	2	3		73/10
Emaus Agusta		2	2	2		22/10
John Armstrong		2	2	2		22/12
James Anderson		1	1			11
Thomas Armore	100	2	2	2		72/12
Samuel Blackmore	400	4	9	17	3	414/2
Sampson Beaver/2 Stills	700	4	2	1		418/6
Joseph Bealer	300	5	4	8		194/8
John Blackburn	300	2	3	7		177/2
Anthoney Boly	150	4	3	7		118/2
Aaron Barker		2	2			22
John Bowyer		2	2	2		22/12
John Brakenridge	200	1	1			111
James Brakenridge		1	1			11
Abraham Beam	300	3	2	3		180/18
Jacob Beam	100	2	2	5		73/10
Ebenazer Buchannan		1	1			11
Alexander Barr	300	3	6			192
Thomas Bell		1				8
Jacob Bousman/ 1/2 Ferry	300	3	2		1	340
Samuel Brice	100	2	3	7		77/2
James Bryce		2	2	7		24/2
John Barr		1	1			11
William Bennet	100	2	2	3		73
William Black		1	1			11
James Beaty	175	2	3	4		113/14
John Bell	300	4	4	6	2	315/16
Joseph Bell		1	2	2		15
William Benndon		2	2	8		24
Richard Byrn	100	2	2			72
Peter Body	300	2	2	7		174/2
Robert Body	300					150
David Clark		2	1			19
Revd John Clark	100	3	4	8	1	148/8
Benjamin Collins	350	3	3	6		209/16
John Coxx	300	3	4	2		186/12
John Campbell	100	2				66
Edward Campbell		1				18
John Collins	53	3	6	8		69
Josiah Collins						
Benjamin Coe	400	3	6	13		246
Moses Coe /Sawmill	200	3	5	6		171
David Corn	270	3	5	4		175/4
Nathaniel Coulter		1				8
James Coulter		2				16

71

NAME	ACRES	HORSES	COWS	SHEEP	SLAVES	VALUE
Cornelius Conner Senr	150	2	1	2		94/12
Daniel Carrol	300	1	2			164
William Conner		1	2	2		14/12
Alexander Clemmon		1	2			14
John Craells /Gristmill		2	1	5		80/10
Robert Clark	80	1	1	3		51/18
John Conner	100	1	2			64
Richard Crooks	300	8	3	10		127
Samuel Cunningham	100	3	4	6		88
John Cunningham		2	4	7	3	215
Thomas Cunningham		2				6
John Caldwell		3	2			40
John Chambors		1	2			17
Adam Curry	.	2	1			20
Robert Cumming			1			3
Charles Clark		3	4			36
Anthony Dunlavey	225	4	4	6		158/10
Joseph Davison		1	1	1		11/6
Patrick Dugan		1	1			11
John Douglass Esqr	350	3	3	10		220
Robert Dougan	300	3	1			177
Patrick Dorning	300	1	1			161
France Dunlavy		1				8
Joseph Dermek	150	1				83
Duncan Evans		1	1	2		11/12
John Elliot	150	1	2	3		89/18
Robert Estubb	300	2	3	5		177/10
Arthur Eccles	50	2				31
Daniel Elliot	100	2	2		1	140
John Evans		1				8
Richard Evans	200	2	2	5		123/10
Joseph Ervin	200	4	3	5		162/10
James Irwin	300	1	1			161
Mayberry Evans	240	1	2	5		125/10
Henry Eval	250	2	2	3		148
David Elliot		1				8
Henry Eulary		2	4			28
James Ellis		2	2			22
James Ferrel		4	2	10		41
Samuel Forster	80	2	1	3		60
John Forgay	50	2	3	1		51/6
Thomas Finney	300	1	1	3		162
James Forsyth	300	4	4			194
David Forgison		2	1			19
Boston Frederick	100	2	2			122
Capt William Fife		2	2	6		24
John Flemming	40	2	2			46
William Fry /Gristmill	900	3	8	10	3	866
Lewis Frederick	250	2	2			151
Boston Frederick		2	2			22

NAME	ACRES	HORSES	COWS	SHEEP	SLAVES	VALUE
John Fife Senr	400	2	4	5		229/10
William Fife Junr	150	2	4	2		132/12
John Fife	100	2	3			76
William Fife Senr	150	3	3	6		111
Robert Frazer	300	2	3	6		178
Jacob Fights		1				8
Gilbert Fights		2	2			23
Samuel Forgison		2	3			26
Robert Furlow		2	3			26
William Gaudy		2	3			26
Lewis Gallaher						
Thomas Godsel		1	1			11
William Gobban	100	1	2	1		64/6
John Glass		1	2			14
Andrew Glass		1	1			11
Alexander Gilfillan	300	2	2	7		174/5
Alexander Gray	300	2	2	7		174/5
John Green	100	1	1	1		61/3
James Gray		1				8
Thomas Hamilton		1	1			11
Edward Hand	1000					500
James Henry		1	1	5		12/10
John Hopkins	300	4	5	13	3	391
Daniel Harris		2	2	10		25
Robert Henderson	150	1	3	1		93/10
John Haith	100	1	2			64
Joseph Haith	100	1	2			65
Charles Harry	150	1	3			93
James Holiday	300	1	3	4		169/4
Robert Hays		1	1	1		11/6
Christian Hough		2				16
Abraham Hays	80	3	4	3		77
James Henderson		2	1			19
James Hamilton	300	4	4	3		195
James Henderson		2	1			19
Edward Huey	100	2	4	4		79/4
Jacob Henson		2	1	2		19/12
James Hogelin		3	2	6		32
Gilbert Hoblien	100		2	1		56/6
Henry Hulch	200	4	10	8		164/10
Revd Robert Huey	200	4	4	7		146/2
Joseph Hulch	200	2	2	5		123
John Henry	300	3	4	8		201
Marcus Huling		2	2			22
Jacob Haymaker		2	1			19
Frances Hulland		1	1	2		11/12
Major Andrew Hood	75	4	4	7		83/12
Andrew Hood		1	2			14
Thomas James	200	4	3	5		143/10
John Jones	250	3	2	7		157/10

NAME	ACRES	HORSES	COWS	SHEEP	SLAVES	VALUE
Robert Johnston	100	2	2	2		73
Robert Juel	88	2	2	5		67/10
Jacob Jones	150	2	2	4		98/4
John Jones	300	3	3	10		195
Jacob Judy /Gunsmith [Gunsk?]		3	3	3		49/10
Jennet Hoge	100	2	2	1		72/6
Isaac Justice	200	2	2			122
Lewis Kuykendall		1	1			11
Abraham Kuykendall		1	1	3		12
John Kaster		1	1			11
Benjamin Keykendall	300	3	2	8		182/10
George Kester		1	1			11
George Killdue	50	2	2	2		53
James Kuykendall	400	3	2	10		233
James Kindsly		2	2	2		23
Thomas Killdue	50	2	4	1		53/6
David Kennedy /Distill	200	1	1			181
John Kellar	100	2	2	6		78
John Kincaid	300	1	2	2		165
Morris Keyho	150	2	2	2		98
John Kerr		2	3			26
Mardical Kelley		2	3			26
John Lovejoy		1	1	2		11/12
John Lewis	47	2	1	2		44/12
James Lowrie		2	2			22
Moses Louther	50	1	1	2		37
Elias Lane		1				8
Martha Lapsly	25		1			128
Thomas Lapsly	272	2	2	6		150
Conrod Loudibough	300	2	3			176
Peter Loudibough		1	2			14
John Loudibough		1	1			11
John Logan	300	2	3	4		177/2
Robert Laughlin	100	2	9	10		99
Jacob Long	300					150
Adam Logan	400	2	3	4		47
Josep Logan	200	2	3			126
Jacob Long Senr /Still	300	3	5	8	1	262
William Long /Distill	300	1	3	1		180/6
Alexr Long /2 Stills	400	2	4	4		263
James Long	518	2	2	1		316/6
David Long	100	2	2			77
William Lee	300	3	4	4		187
Alexander Ligate	25	2	2	2		47/10
Ennaus McCallister	300	2	1	3		171
William McKee	100	1	1			62
Edward Magner	300	5	6	14	1	174
John Magner		1				8
Henry Magner		2	2	4		23
Patrick McMullen	150	3	2	7		162/5

NAME	ACRES	HORSES	COWS	SHEEP	SLAVES	VALUE
James Matthews	350	2	4	6		205
Frances Morrisson	200	2	2	3		124
Sarah Miller		2	1			20
William Morrison	100	2	2			66
James McGlaughlin		1	1			11
Benjamin Mills		2	2	3	1	85
John Mallady		1				8
William Murduck		2	4	2		28/12
Charles Morgan	130	2	4	4	1	154
Christoper McDonald		1				8
William Masters	45	2	2	1		52/6
William Marshall		2	3	4		27
Robert Marshall		1				8
John McNully		1	1	1		12/6
Robert McKee	300	3	4	5		187/10
William Millar	150	2	2	3		98
John McKinsey		1	1			11
Timothy Mayhall		1	2			14
William Mayhall	190	1	2	4		115
Nathan Matthany		2	3	6		28
Richard Masters	150	2	4	6		105
Edward Mayhall		2	2			22
John Malloney	341	3	3	8		207/10
John Masters	120	2	2			82
John Morrison	400	2	2			222
Thomas McMullan	100	3	1			77
John Miller	300	2	3	4		179/10
Thomas Miller	150	2	2	3		98/10
Thomas Matthew	50	3	6	6		72
Adam McFarson	50	1	1			42
Thomas McGill	160	2	2	4		104
William McGill		1				6
John McEwing	100	1	1			62
John McMean		1	1	3		13/10
William Matthews		2	2	3		23/10
David McKee	250	2	2			147
James McKee	100	1	2			64
John McCulley		1	1			12
Nathaniel McGummery	275	2	4			165/10
John McDowel	300	2	2	2	1	233
Archibald McDowell		1	2	1		14/10
Robert McFarlane		8	4			76
Eneas McClain			2			6
William McDonald		1	1			11
William McGlaughlen	300	2	3			176
John McGlaughlen	270	3	2			180
Zachland McGlaughlen /Still	100	2	2			93
Alexander McCoy		2	2			23
James McGlaughlen	300	3	2	5		181

NAME	ACRES	HORSES	COWS	SHEEP	SLAVES	VALUE
George Murray	100	2	2	2		72/12
John Murray	30	2	2	1		46/6
Alexander McCullay	36	2	2	5		43/10
Widow Millar /Distill	50	2	2	4		59
Joseph McDowell /Gristmill	100					300
Martain McKean	100	3	2	6		82
Hugh McCoy Junr	100	2	2			80
John McCallister		1	1			11
Alexander Miller	300	3	3	8		186/10
Gawin McKee		1	1			12
John Matts	150	3	4	5		112/10
Joseph McNight	100	2	1			69
___ McNight	100					50
William McCandless	65	1	2	7		48/2
Alexr McCandless	65	1	2	5		47/10
William Moore	39	2	2	3		53
Daniel Moor	39	2	2	2		53
Robert McMinn	200	2	2			122
Archibald McDermet	100	2	2	4		73/4
James Miller		2	1			19
Charles McHauffey		2	2	3		25
Robert McDuffey		2	2	4		23/6
Hugh McCoy		2	3			26
William Nickleson	500	2	2	5		273/10
William Nashon		1				10
Edward Nashon		1	1			13
Thomas Neely		2				20
William Nailor		1	1			12
Andrew Nye	400	2	4	2		228
Joseph Neel		2	2	2		23
Henry Nayman	300	2	2	4		173/4
John Neel /Gristmill	15	2	2	4		97/4
John Nickles		2	4	3		29
Christoper Owen		2				20
Samuel Oldham		3	2	3	3	231
Henry O neal						
Mr. Matthews		1	1	1		13/6
John Ornsby	1200					600
John Pack	15		1	1		13/6
Jacob Phyatt Senr	100	1	2			64
David Philips Junr	300	3	3	3		185
John Pursall						
David Philips	300	3	8	14		202
William Philips	300	4	3	8		194/10
Jonathan Philips	100	1	3	3		69
Jonathan Plummer		1	2			14
William Plummer	38	1	1			21
John Paterson		2	3	5		30
John Philips	300	2	3	3		177

NAME	ACRES	HORSES	COWS	SHEEP	SLAVES	VALUE
Samuel Philips	400	2	2	2		222/12
John Purdy		1	3	2		21
Adam Paterson	150	1				85
Joseph Philips	100	2	2	2		73
Joseph Paterson	100	1				58
Robert Potter		1	2	3		15
James Paterson	140	1	2	2		85
William Petten Junr		2	1			19
John Power		1	1			13
Jobb Philips		1	1	4		12/4
James Riggs		1				8
William Ralston		2	2	3		23
Abraham Ralston		1				10
John Reed	92	2	3	5		77/10
John Ross		1	2			16
Robert Richie	100	3	4			86
John Robb	100	2	3	5		81/10
Daniel Rasher	500	2	5			285
John Reed /2 Distills	200	4	7			173
David Radick	300	2	2			172
Joseph Ryan		1	1			13
Thomas Redman	160	4	6	10	2	333
Thomas Ramsey	50	2	2			52
Josiah Richards		3	5			44
James Rutherford	300	2	2			173
William Ryan	100	1	3	4		69
John Ryan	40	1	2	4		69/10
John Redman	100	3	2	9		102/10
George Redman	200	3	3	5		136
Daniel Redman		2	2			28
William Richman	400	2	2	4		229/4
Jacob Rebolt		1	2			14
Jacob Rebolt Senr		2	3			26
Andrew Roads		1	2			14
John Redick		1	1			11
Widow Runno	150	3	3	9		112
Benjamin Reed	300					150
Thomas Strain	200	2	1	8		122/10
James Sharp	200	2	2	3		125
John Sprew		2	2	4		26
Walter Skinner		3	2	4		31/10
Daniel Swearingham	130	3	2	3		96
John Swearingham	500	4	6	12	1	356
George Sickman	204	2	3	6		130
John Stephenson		1	2	1		14/10
John Sea		2				16
John Shannon	60	2	3			106
John Shields	700	2	1			374
Richard Swaswick	300	2	3	6		182
Barbary Smirna - widow	200	1	2			114

NAME	ACRES	HORSES	COWS	SHEEP	SLAVES	VALUE
Nancy Stilley	300	1	2	2		165
Henry Small	100	2	2			72
Paul Spears		1	2	8		16/8
Thomas Sprouls		1	2	4		15/10
John Small	100	4	3			94
William Stewart	150	2				95
James Still		2	3			26
Henry Shaver	50	1	2			68
James Snodgrass	300					150
Benjamin Sweet	400	3	9	8		257
Bazel Swan		2	1	3		21
Anguish Sutherland		1	2			14
Isaac Sellers	300	3	6	8	1	255
David Strabrige	150	1	2			89
Nathaniel Stocks	300	2	4	4		179/10
Edward Sharp	600	4	6	8		385
John Sharp		2	3	5		27/10
Adam Sharp		4	4	5		49/10
George Swaswick	130	2	2	5		98/10
Joseph Scott	300	2	5			185
Daniel Shachan	300	3	7	11		201/10
Robt Snodgrass	150	2	2			96
John Stevenson						
James Stoops		2	5	9		34
Daniel Swiney		1	2	4		15/10
William Shaw		2	2	4		23/10
John Sinnet		1	1			11
Hugh Sterling						
Nehemiah Sharp	200	6	6	8		175
Charles Smith	100	2	4	5		79/10
David Smith		1				8
Thomas Sands		2	1			19
David Steel	200	1	2	4		115/10
Samuel Thompson	250	2	3	2		151/10
James Thompson	235	5	4	2		157/10
William Thompson		1	2			14
Abraham Tout		2	2	2		22/10
John Trumbo	300	6	2	10		231
Michael Thom/Thorn		3	4	11		58/10
Anthony Thompson	200	1	2			114
Robert Thompson /Tanyard	50	2	2	4		106/10
William Thompson	40	1	1	2		52/10
Archibald Thompson		1	1			12
William Tidball	150	3	4	7		113/10
Thomas Titball	150	2	2			99
John Torrance		2	2			22
William Turpine		2	2			22
Daniel Townsend	150	2	3	15		109
John Wall	300	4	9	10		324
James Wallace		1				8

NAME	ACRES	HORSES	COWS	SHEEP	SLAVES	VALUE
Tobias Wood		2	2	1		22/6
John Wallace	600	2	3	3		427
Abraham Wilson	50	2	2			52
William Wilson						
Samuel Wilson	200	2	3	4		131/6
James Wilson	150	2	2			101
James Whittikar	600	2	3	6	3	508
Abraham Whittekar		2	3	3		27
George Weddle	290	3	3	4		190/10
James Warden		1	1	1		11/6
John Wilson		1	1	4		12/6
James Wilson	100	3	1	4		78/4
John White		2	1	2		20/12
Robert Weatherhead		1	1			14
Samuel Watt		1	1	2		11/12
Adam Wolff						
James White Junr		1	2			14
James White Senr		1	2			14
Robert Wilson	150	3	2	12		109
Thomas Wilson	130	2	1			95
William Weightman	300	2	1			169
Thomas Wilson		1	2	5		15/10
James Wilson		2	1			19
Thomas Williams		1	1			12
John Wilkinson		1	1			11
Elijah Veary		1	1	3		12
Andrew Vint	150	1				83
Jacob Miller	50	1				58
Henry Keykendall	100	1	1			61
Thomas Park	50	2	2			46
Martain Owen	100	1	1			61
Thomas Harris		1				8
John Clark						
James Wall		2	1	4		20/4
John McDonald	150	3	3			109
James Parks	150	2	3			101
Isaac Friend	150	1	4			95
John Erwin	200	2	3	4		127/10
Thomas Boyd	200	2	3	3		127
Capt Philip Ross	300	4	9	12	2	335/12
Widow Fowler	200	1	1	4		112/10
John McDermut	300	2	3			176
Thomas Rigdon	300	2	3	5		177/10
Capt John Small		2	1			20
William Stevenson		2	2			22
Ephraim Heuy	100	2	2			72
Thomas Bell		1				8
William Rigdon		1				8
Col. John Campbell	900					

RO 1

1783 ROBINSON TOWNSHIP TAX LIST

NAME	ACRES	HORSES	COWS	SHEEP	SLAVES	VALUE £/S
Samuel Bealer	400	4	7	11	4	363
William Blink	300	3	6	3		84
William Bell	300	3	3	5		97
James Bell	300	2	3	4		86
John Barnes		1	1			10
John Bail	400	2	2	4		92
Richard Chamberland	300	1	3			69
James Baggs	300					100
Charles Bruce	200					38
Robert Bell	1000					200
Hugh Brakinrige	900					250
James Brady						
Alexander Burns	600	3	2	2		187
Jacob Bousman	300					80
Thomas Begger	300					75
William Bagge	300					75
William Carpenter		2				10
Joseph Carlin	100					37
John Campble	300					206
Widow Carmon	200					61
Charles Clark	300					50
Aaron Cherrey	200					40
Adam Coopper	1000					178
John Dunlop	300	2	2			96
Alexander Dunlop	300					52
William Druman	300	2	2			96
Thomas Denton	200					50
Bartholemew Denneston	150					35
James Ewing	600	2	6	6	2	310
Emas Ewing	318					56
Andrew Fink		2				20
Laurance Fezzel	300	3	4			97
William Flennagen		3	3	3		35
Benjamin Fullom		1	1			8
William Furbiss	300					75
William Guy	300	3	2			101
Robert Greenlee	300					50
John Hull	600	3	3	6	1	292
Joseph Henry			2			4
William Hervy	200					32
James Hanna	300					18/15
Matthew Henderson	300					37/10
Jesse Hollensworth	1000					400
Thomas Hanna	108					18/10
William Hall	300					50
David Kennedy	1000					340
Alexr Kidd	318	2	3			106
Abraham Kidd - Single						

81

NAME	ACRES	HORSES	COWS	SHEEP	SLAVES	VALUE
Frances Kilpatrick	200					80
William Kidd		1	1			9
James Little	600	2	2	2		100
Andrew Link	600	2	2		1	166
Thomas Lowdan	318					54
Robert Lowdan	318					54
Jacob Leapheart	400					155
Widow McCoy	100					32
Alexr McCurdy	280					35
Charles Morgan	400					200
Samuel McBride	318					40
Patrick Moore	200					40
Alexander McDowel	300					45
Patrick Murphy	318					40
James McBready	318					43
Widow McCandless	300					87/10
William McGreger	318					66
Isaac Mitchal	100					18
Captain McMackey	318					53
John Morrison	318					54
Robert Moor	318					55
Joseph Mitchal	200					37/10
Henry McBride	318					177
Joshua Meeks	600	6	2	12	3	420
William Marks	300					37/10
William McCandless	350					87/10
Alexr McCandless	350					87/10
Widow McManeme	200					37/10
William McMurray	100					12/10
Benjamin McCormick	300					77
James McAdoo	300					30
Matthew McGreger	318					56
John Meek	318					50
Thomas McMillan	200					33
John McDonald /Distill	1200	5	8	22	3	538
Henry Noble	600	7	6	10	8	395
Samuel Newell	300					75
John Nicles	300					37/10
William Nicles	318					37/10
William Newel	300					38
Hugh Neely	317					80
Alexander Pinkerton	207					50
Robert Pottor	200					50
Henry Pottor	200					50
Jonathan Phlips	300					35
James Paterson	200					60
Charles Queen	318					80
Thomas Rardon	318					80
John Rardon	318					80
William Robb - Single						

NAME	ACRES	HORSES	COWS	SHEEP	SLAVES	VALUE
John Robb	300	2	2			96
John Reed Esqr	300					70
John Reed	300					52
John Scott	200	2	2			81
Patrick Scott	200					53
John Singers	300	2	3	11		75
Abraham Stover	300					53
Joseph Sisney	318	3	2	15		100
Joseph Scott	300					55
John Stephenson	300					75
Josiah Scott	400					100
Hugh Shearer	400					70
Thomas Sproul	200					32
Elizabeth Shearer	300					40
Rev. Joseph Smith	300					75
John Stevenson	300					75
John Spivey	300					53
Bartholemew Tawl		1				6
Timothy Shean		1	2			14
William Turner	300	4	4	6		114
Thomas Thornburge	300					48
Benjamin Thompson	100					25
John Totton	200	3	2			58
George Vallandingham	300	2	9	5	1	162
John Wilson		2	2			18
Alexr Wright Esqr	318	2	5	6		117
Isaac Walker	900	4	3	2		227
Joseph Wilson		2				20
William Woods	300					58
Gabriel Walker	900	5	6	7		220
John Walker	300					52/10
Zadock Wright	300					75
Major Ward	307					76
Joseph Walker	500					125
William Wardan	300					56
James Wardan	100					20
+ Thomas White	318					63
James White	300					40
Robert Witherington	1000					300
Abel Westfall	300					37/10
Joseph Young	300					38
Richard Young	318					40
George Long	318					115
Adam Logan	300					40
William McClelland	300					114
Richard Noble	300					54
Joseph Bealer	318					60
William Tucker	317					111
Samuel Jeffery	318					100
+ Josiah Records	318					100

NAME	ACRES	HORSES	COWS	SHEEP	SLAVES	VALUE
Alexander Dunlap	318					50
Pedden Cook	340					100
John Hervey - Single		1				10
Thomas Scott - Single		1				10
William Milligan - Single		1				10
Patrick McCormick - Single		1				10
William Obany - Single		1				10
William Peoples - Single		1				10
Henry Link		1				10
Andrew Blunk - Single		1				10
Free Chamberland		1				10

+ Names listed between the + marks are from microfilm page 273 (the last page in the Robinson list) but placed here for alphabetical order.

1783 SMITH TOWNSHIP TAX LIST

NAME	ACRES	HORSES	COWS	SHEEP	SLAVES	VALUE £/S
Robert Andrew		2	2			26
John Allen	300	3	5			150
Boston Burcket	300	3	4	7		153
George Blazer	50	1	2	6		49
John Blazer	300	4	4	13		163
Philip Bell	300	2	3	4		172
Thomas Bay	300	3	3	3		146
Arthur Campbell	400	3	7	8		205
Alexr Caul			1			3
John Cooper	400	2	3			234
Thomas Cherry	300	2	3			190
Thomas Cherry Senr	700	6	5	23	1	403
William Casselman	300	2	2			175
David Decker	100	3	4	2		71
James Dumbarr	105	3	3	4		142
John Dodd	100	2	2	1		46/10
Robt Dumbarr	125	3	3	1		90/10
Humphrey Etchison	200	2	3			100
James Edgar	200	3	4	3	1	121
John Eakin	200	2	2	2		97
Thomas Edward	150	2	1			73
Reuben Freshwater	300	3	5	8		202
Christopher Gardner	400		4	4		164
Patrick Gallant		1				10
Garshum Hull	150	3	2	10		90
John Hays	300	2	2	9		90
James Hamilton	300	2	1			138
Matthew Hillis	300	3	4	12		150
Benjamin Jackson	150	1	2			74
Joseph Jackson	300	2	5	7		144
Jacob Johnston	50	2	4	7		65
Philip Jackson	300	2	3	10		145
Samuel Johnson /Gristmill	300	3	4	10		167
Thomas Jackson	250	2	6			158
James Kennedy	100	1	1			123
John Kincaid	200	2	2	6		118
James Leach	100	2	2			126
Brice McGehon	280	2	3	7		135
George McCormick	1000	5	6	12	2	555
George McCasline	100	2	2	3		122
Hugh McDonough	100	1	1			57
James Mathews	200	2	2			146
John McCartney	200	3	2	3		107
Peter Murphey	150	2	1			78
Thomas Moore	300	4	3	6		153
William Martin	200	2	4	4		114
Adam Poe	250	2	3	6		113

NAME	ACRES	HORSES	COWS	SHEEP	SLAVES	VALUE
Andrew Poe	150	2	2	3		77
David Patton	200	2	3			130
Jonahs Potts	300	3	2			136
Joseph Phillis	200	2	3	2		101
Henry Rankin	200	3	2			126
David Rankin		1	2			16
James Revencraft	400	6	4	18		209
John Rankin		2	2			26
Mary Ross	300	1	3	3		131
Thomas Rogers	600	5	2	6	1	349
Thomas Rankin		1	1	2	1	79
William Rankin /Still	1200	11	23	30	4	900
John Stone Senr	200	2	4	12		158
John Stone Junr	100	1.	2			54
John Spiller		2	2			26
John Smith	300	1	2			128
John Strain	200	1	2	5		78
David Thompson	276	2	3			130
William Thompson	100	2	2			46
John Tucker	300	3	5	7		148
Joseph Vance	377	5	5	4		187
Richard Vaghon	300	4	4	4	1	212
Amos Wood	150	2	2	10		84
Abner Wilson		2	1	4		24
David Wilson	200	3	3	6		103
Joseph Wilson	150	2	3	9		90/10
Moses Wallace	100	2	3	3		67
Robert Wallace	300	1		4		112
Uriah Wilson	150	2	3	9		90/10
Isaac Wells	300	2	4	15		180

"EVACUATED Lands in Smiths Township"

NAME	ACRES	VALUE
Thomas Armor	300	108
William Anderson	318	118/7
John Alton	318	120
John Bevington	600	228
Daniel Byers	200	75
Hugh Bell	318	115
John Comly	100	37
Nicholas Cris	300	112
Joseph Clemmons	118	120
Thomas Campbell	200	75
John Clark	200	75
George Clark	200	75
James Carpenter	300	112
Thomas Chain	318	112/10
John Cowin	600	225
John Caruthers	300	112
John Caruther Junr	300	112

NAME	ACRES	HORSES	COWS	SHEEP	SLAVES	VALUE
John Common	318					119
Widow Coughran	300					115
Jacob Coughran	300					150
James Dornal	100					30
John Dungan	300					114
Robert Dungan	318					120
Thomas Dungan	320					120
Michael Dillow	300					114
Duncan Davis	200					80
John Dillow	300					112/10
Levi Dungan	600					337
Nicholas Davison	200					75
James Fulton	200					74
James Furgison	300					112
Joseph Holmes	300					80
Edward Hatfield						
D. Hollensworth	300					112/10
James Holmes	300					112/10
Francis Kilpatrick	318					100
Robert Kenneday	300					78
Andrew Lin	300					112
Andrew Link	318					130
William Lankford	600					225
William Laughlin	300					112
John Laughlin	300					115
Robert Laughlin	300					112
John McDonald	318					80
Christopher McDonald	300					80
Joseph McKinnon	318					120
John Martin	200					75
___ McEntire	200					75
Andrew McClure	300					112
George McColough	100					50
James Miller	300					112/10
Thomas Mullen	100					50
Joseph McCready	300					112
Joseph or Hugh McCready	318					112
William Matthews	317					100
J. Merchant	318					112
Matthew McCaskey	313					112
Henry Nolin	300					115
Abraham Osburn	318					112
Isaac Pearce	300					100
Isaac Peary	150					50
Thomas Park	300					112
William Patterson	200					75
Robert Park	300					100
Matthew Richie	600					225
Joseph Ralston	200					75
Thomas Rogers	300					112

NAME	ACRES	HORSES	COWS	SHEEP	SLAVES	VALUE
Joseph Rogers	318					112
John Rogers	300					100
Levi Stevenson	318					112
William Swan	200					75
Michael Steel	200					75
Thomas Timmon	300					112
John Towlin	318					120
Joseph Tarrance	200					75
D. Valler	300					112
William Vaughon	318					120
James Walker	100					25
W. Woodbreak	200					60
Moses White	200					75
Patrick White	300					112
John White	318					120
Thomas White	318					112
Miles Wilson	300					115
James Wilson	300					100
Isaac Wiseman	300					112
William Wilson	300					115
James White	300					112
John Whithero	400					150
Thomas Whittaker	300					112
John Waggoner	100					50
Robert McGee	100					50
John Leewebster	4500					1175
Nicholas Dawson	300					100
Robert Rutherford	1300					325
Van Swaringin	200					50
McKibbins	400					150
John Stevenson	600					225
Alexr Reed	100					25
Moses Coe	300					112
John Scott	300					100

SINGLE FREEMEN

NAME	ACRES	HORSES	COWS	SHEEP	SLAVES	VALUE
Aaron Bleakman						
Samuel Dumbarr		1				10
John Gardner		2		5		32
Thomas Hogg						
Peter Kidd	500	1				200
David Kerr	300	1				124
Alexander McBride	200					88
Francis McKinney						
Thomas Orlon		1				13
Zacheriah Rankin		2				20
Mathew Rankin	200					50
James Ross	200	1				90
John Ross						
William Wallace						

1783 SOMERSET TOWNSHIP TAX LIST

NAME	ACRES	HORSES	COWS	SHEEP	SLAVES	VALUE £/S
Arthur Forbus	300	1	4	4		135
Alexander Forbus		1				6
Alexander White		2	2	1		16/5
Andrew Swearingen	300					120
Anthony Spaith	40	3	2			40
Abraham Lashly	100	2	2	3		56/15
Abner Leonard						0
Andrew Smith	200					80
Amarias Cravan		3	2	3		22/15
Benjamin Wells	250	2	2	2		116/10
Barney Preston	240	3	2	3		118/15
Bazel Williams		2	2	3		16/15
Benjamin Lashly	60	1	1			32
Charles Hurskins		2	2	2		16/10
Caleb Summers		2	3			18
Caleb Leonard	150	2	1	5		75/5
Conrd Weaver	400	3	5	2		218/10
Chrstian Holmes		4	3	1		30/5
Conrad Eary		2	1			14
Christian Leatherman	200	4	4	7	1	133/15
Chistian Spaith	150	2	4			80
Catherine Kintner	150	2	6	8		86
David Wherry	80	2	2	4		49
Daniel Preston	400	2	2	2	1	206
David Hathaway		1	1			8
Daniel Messonger		1				6
Daniel Williams	180	2	3	2		90/10
Daniel Swickard	200	3	3	9		106/5
Elisha Cravan	50	2	1	2		34/10
Edward Wright		1				6
Edward Mortan	300	4	6	10		168
Edward Morgan		1	5	20		21
Edward Seaborn	80	3	3	7		65/15
Frederick Olt	150	3	3	6		91/10
Frederick Wise	150	2	3	1		78/5
Felty Suster	100	2	2	4		47
Francis Slornater		1	2	5		11/5
Francis Wallace		3	2	3	6	202/15
Frederick Coons		1	2			10
Grace Summers	500	4	3	7		231/15
George Kintnor	300	3	6	8		152
George Bently		1	2			10
George Miers	450	4	7	15		221/15
George Sypole	30	1	1			20
George Reynolds		4	3	8		32
Henry Crites		1				6
Henry Huffman	150	2	2	5		77/5
Hugh Brison		2	2			20

NAME	ACRES	HORSES	COWS	SHEEP	SLAVES	VALUE
Henry Newkirk /Distill	500	3	6	3	1	281/5
Henry Conrad	400	4	4	20		197
Hannah Kemble		1	1	2		8/10
Hugh Forbus	150	1				66
Henry Dickenson	200	2	2	3		96/15
Henry Donahee	80	1	1	3		40/15
Isaac Leonard	150	2	2	10		78/10
Isaac Rose	100	2	2	4		67
John Robinson	200	2	2	2		96/10
John Huffman	258	2	3	3		122/15
John Greenlee	90					36
James Armstrong		1	2	1		10/5
John Felty		2	1	6		15/10
John McFarrain	80	2	3	2		60/10
John McClain		1				6
John Carr	100					40
John Bane		2	1			18
John Stevenson	192	2	4	8		102
John Williamson		1	1			8
James Ramsey	100	2	3	4		59
James Murphey	50	1	1			28
John McClain		1	2			10
James Cammeron		2	3			18
John Stephenson Junr	392					160
John Vance	250	2	2	5		117/5
John Vance Junr		2	2	6		17/10
James Turner	31	2	1	2		24/10
John Gutteridge	100	2	2	5		57/5
Joshua Davis /Gristmill	200	3	3	6		141/10
John Darnold		4	2		1	58
John Carrol	150					60
John Baldwine	102					40
Jacob Swaggler	50	2	1			34
Jacob Spaiht	100	3	3	3		64/15
James Fugate		2	1			14
Joseph Burt	40	2	2			32
Joseph Thomas	50	2	2			36
John McVay	60	2	2	3		40/15
John McCullums		4	3	2		30/10
John Lashly	120	2	1			62
John Masterson	80	1	1	3		40/15
John Cravan	230	3	2	6		116/10
James Lyda	200	3	2	4		23
John Masterson Junr	250	1	3	10		114/10
John Masterson 3d		2	3			12/15
Joseph Hark		1	1			8
James Stewart		3	3			24
Jeremiah Cravan		2				12
James Cravan	160	3	5	8		94
John Millican		2	2			16

NAME	ACRES	HORSES	COWS	SHEEP	SLAVES	VALUE
James Flemming		2	2			16
Jacob Sook	200	2	2			96
Jacob Sook		2				12
John Wallace	300	2	3	2		138/10
James Conner		2	3	5		19/5
John Lyda	640	3	4	7		281/15
Isaac Wells		1	1			8
John Mitchel	200					80
James McConnal		4	4	1	1	62/5
James Boham		1	2	3		10/15
John Stewart		5	2			34
Joseph Williams		1	2	1		10/5
John Hill		2	2	2		16/10
James Clindinning		1				6
John Elliot		1	3	5		13/5
John Studdy	200	4	4	7		113/15
Joseph Cox	300					120
John McNew		1	4	2		14/10
Jacob Booch			1			2
James Wherry Assr	300	3	4	10		148/10
Isaac Darnold		1	1			8
Luther Cary	80	2	2	6		49/10
Lewis Pearce	50	3	2	2	1	72
Michael Shuster	60	2	2	4		41
Michael Miers	350	4	3	12		203
Margaret Book /Distill	260	3	4	12		156
Moses Williamson	50	2	2	2		56/10
Mary Carr		1				
Michael Thomas	300	2	3			138
Matthew Laughlin	300	5	3	13	1	189/5
Nicholas Potter	100					40
Nathaniel Red	300	4	5	10		156/10
Nathaniel Wallace	230	2	1	2		114/10
Patrick McColloch	400	4	4	9		194/5
Patrick Scott	100	2	2			56
Philip Whitten		6				36
Philip Reed		1				6
Patrick Stakes		1	1			8
Peter Sticklet		2	2			16
Peter Leatherman /Tanyard		1				12
Philip Hooper	100	2	3	6		59/10
Philip Black	200	3	2	2		102/10
Peter Black	400	2	3	5		179/5
Richard Elgin	60	1	1	5		33/5
Richard Davis	100	3	2	4		63
Richard Ward		2	1			14
Rudolph Huffman	400	4	8	15		103/15
Robert Ramsey	100	2	3	6		59/10
Robert McComb	400	3	3	6		112/10
Richard Sutton		1				6

NAME	ACRES	HORSES	COWS	SHEEP	SLAVES	VALUE
Robert Lemmon	50	1	3			32
Rosannah Campbell	100	1	1			48
Stephen Bartley		1	2	1		10/5
Samuel Lemmon	50	1	2			30
Samuel Fortner	100	2	2	6		57/10
Shazbeser Bently /Gristmill /Sawmill	800	4	4	8		404
Silas Leonard		2	2			16
Samuel Davison		2	2	7		17/15
Samuel Frazee /Tanyard		2	2	7		27/15
Sampson Nickle	80	2	2			46
Thomas Dickenson	100	3	1	3		60/15
William Wallace /Constable	200	4	3	3		100/15
William Henthorn/Distill	100	3	3	4		75
William Clouse		3	3	7		25/15
William Williamson		2	2	2		16/10
William McComb	350	3	3	6		175/10
William Black		1	1			8
William Masterson Jun		1				6
William Masterson Senr	150	2	2	1		76/5
William Sutton		3	2	5		23/5
William Forwood	300					120
William Johnson		4	4			32
William Wilson		1	1	1		8/5
William Parker Esqr	300	4	4	12		155
Zechariah Masterson		2				6
Zephaniah Bell	80					32
Zephaniah Dyson		2	3	6		19/10
Zepha'h Huntington						0
Vashel Hinton		2	1	5		15/5

SINGLE FREEMEN

NAME	ACRES	HORSES	COWS	SHEEP	SLAVES	VALUE
George Tompow	90	1	1			44
Henry Lyda - no property						
Isaac Newkirk	400	1	3		1	202
Isaac Vance	250	3	1			120
Joseph Nelson	60	1	1			32
James Gutteridge	100	3	2	3		62/15
John Orr		1	1			8
Jeremiah Masterson		1				6
John Wilson	70	1				34
James Guffy - no property						
Samuel Middock - no pr						
Moses Morton		1				6
Martin Swrichart		1				6
Peter Sartor		1				6
Peter Wells - no property						
Richard Williams - no ditto						
Robert Limmon - no ditto						

NAME	ACRES	HORSES	COWS	SHEEP	SLAVES	VALUE
Samuel Parmor		1				6
William McLaughlin		1				6
William Nevin		1				6
William Forbus		1				6

1783 STRABANE TOWNSHIP TAX LIST

NAME	ACRES	HORSES	COWS	SHEEP	SLAVES	VALUE £/S
Joshua Anderson	300	2	2	2		174
Hactor Alexander		1				21
Samuel Agnew	200	3	2			150
Nathaniel Brown	400	1	3	8		225
Thomas Bond	100	2				70
James Brown	100					50
Archibald Boggs	300	1				158
Barney Boner		2	4	6		22
Ann Barnet			1	1		3
Samuel Byers		1	1			10
Ephraim Bilderback	300	3	8	5		236
John Backet	100	2	2			53
Samuel Buchannan	300	2	2			20
James Buchanan Junr	160					80
James Brownlee	200	2	4			132
William Brownlee	318	2	3	9		136
John Brownlee	200	4	4	16		179
Francis Bradick		1	3	3		13
John Bradock	100	3	4	11		76
William Boner		2	4	8		31
John Baird /Distill	320	3	4	2		197
William Buchanan	100	2	2	6		48
Stephen Benet		2	3			24
James Bradford Senr	100	2	3	10		79
James Bradford Junr	200	3	3	3		136/10
William Boshears	300	2	1	7		147
Ezekiel Barnet	100	1	4	1		54/5
John Campbell		2	2	6		31
John Cannon	300					150
Robert Commings		2	1	2		17
Francis Cunningham	100	2	4	6		74
Robert Cunningham	100	2	2	4		70
Paden Cook	750	1	2			118
David Clark /Still	400	2	4	6		249
Joseph Clark /2 Lots	250	2	3	10		133
James Craig	60	2	4	7		67
Nicholas Clemmings		1	2			12
Roley Culbert		1	1			10
Henry Crow		2	2			18
Henry Cotton /Still	200	4	4			139
William Craig	60	2	2			34
John Cross		3	1			26
Noah Cox		1	1			8
Thomas Dill	100	2	2			73
William Douglass		1	1			8
Benoney Dement	150	2	7	15		115
James Dement	200	2	3	4		114
John Dement			1			2

NAME	ACRES	HORSES	COWS	SHEEP	SLAVES	VALUE
Charles C. Dodd /1 Lott			1			154
George Davison		2	1			14
James Drake		1	4	8		20
Benajah Dement	300	2	4	7		175
Enoch Dye	200	2	3	5		107
David Dilley	100	2	3			65
Henry Dickason	200					80
Richard Dickason	300	2	3	4		202
John Dodd	300	3	4			180
Robert Dokes	300	2	3	6		142
John Downey		2				14
David Ervin	200	2	3	5		114
Alexander Eddy	220	4	3	5		152
William Forbus		2	2	6		18
William Forgison	300	2	2	5		182
Palser Frank	200	1	2	4		64/10
William Forgison		1	1			10
David Finley	50	2	3	4		34/10
James Gorrel		2	3	5		24
Alexander Gordon	100	2	1			78
James Gaffney	60	1	2	2		49
Robert Gibson		2	2	3		31/10
William Gibson	200					83
James Gault	150					75
John Gates		2				8
Listen Glass	150	2	3	3	2	191
Robert Giffen	30	2	2			35
James Goudy	60	1				44
Robert Goudy	70	2				37
Robert Greenlees		1	2	1		10/10
Thomas Hamilton	700	1	4	7		428/10
Hannah Hawkins		2	1	5	1	24
John Hill	30	2	2			36
Obediah Holms	100	5	5	8		145
Abram Holms	120	1				56
Paul Huff		3	1	8		30
David Hosick	80		1	8		30
Andrew Hipinhamer	20	1	1			28
John Haslip		2	1			19
Robert Hamilton	200					180
James Haslerige		1	3	3		21/10
James Hunter		2	4	3		26
John Huston	300	2	2	2		202
Henry Holms	50	2	2	1		33/10
David Hamilton	300	2	2	5		200
William Huston	400	2	6	12		338
Laurance Huff		1	1	3		10
William Hall		1				8
James Herring		1	1	1		10/10
James Hanna	40	1	2	1		32/10

96

NAME	ACRES	HORSES	COWS	SHEEP	SLAVES	VALUE
William Hays	110	1	3	6		72
Elijah Hyet	300	1	3			15
John Henry		1	2			12
Benjamin Johnston		6	8	13	2	123
William Johnston	300	3	4	12		168
John Jamison		2	2	5		24
John Jackson	350	2	2	2		194/10
Isaac Israel /Distill	300	3	6			194
Peter Jolly	300	3	3	6		150
Henry Jolly	200	2	2	2		101
John Jamison		2	2			21
William Jordon	200	3	5	6		130
William Irvin	100	2	3	5		66
Edward King		2	2			20
Edward Kummins	42	1	1			31
Isaac Leet	330	2	4	16		220
George Latimore	400	1	2			312
George Leming	300	2	2	4		159
Daniel Leet	600	3	2			360
Nicholas Little	300	2	5	10		165
Nicholas Little Executor	600					240
William Laughlin	50	2	3	3		56
James Leeper	30	2	2	4		30
Samuel Leeper	100	2	3	3		59
William Malkemson		2	2			20
Robert Malkemson		1	2			12
Andrew Malkemson		1	1			12
Joseph McCready		1	2	5		13/10
Andrew McClure	300	2	2	4		211
James McDowel	300	3	4	1		212/10
Alexander McCollough		2	1	3		11/10
Daniel Merrick		2	2	3		22/10
John Mordock	100	3	2	5	1	128
Alexander McCoy	110	1	2	1		68/5
Charles Martin	100	1	1	1		54/5
Thomas Manery	250	3	2			222
Widow McDowel	300	2	2			38
John McDowel	350	3	6	8		288
Revd John McMillan	450	4	3	7		238
Henry Martin	300	2	3	7		167/10
Aaron Marshal		2	1	2		21/15
Andrew Moore	400	3	3	8		217
William McComb	300	2	3			165
Jonathan Marklin	300	3	1	16		208
Alexander McFerson	200	2	4	10		109
William Morrisson	100	2	2	3		71/10
Robert Moore	400					160
John McFadden		2	2			20
James McConkey /3 Lotts			1			22
John McMillan	36	2	2	2		31

NAME	ACRES	HORSES	COWS	SHEEP	SLAVES	VALUE
James McElroy		2	2	2		18
Thomas Montgomery	200	2	2	6		100
William Montgomery	350	3	3	15		174
James McBurney	190	2	2	9		105
Jacob Norris	35	1	1			27
William Norris	300	3	5	14		180
William Nelson		2	2	2		21
George Nox		2	1			12
James Navel		2	1	8		19
Elijah Nuttle	300	3	3	12	2	412
Andrew Nickel	100	2	2	6		62
Thomas Nickel	50	2	1	2		52
Susanna Norris	100	2	3	8		72
Frances Nation		1				8
Charles O Donnald	200	2	3	7		110
Samuel Osborn	150	3	4	5		92
James Paterson	400	2	2	3		229/10
Thomas Philips		1	2			12/10
Reason Pumphrey	275	5	7	23	2	386
Zachariah Pumphrey	275	3	4	12	1	363
Daniel Peck		3	4	6		35
Peter Patterson		4	2	9		40
Samuel Pollick	170	2	2	8		104
Nicholas Peas /Distill /Gristmill	300	3	3	12		216
William Ross	110	2	2	3		76
John Ralston	150	2	2			98
Harculas Roney Junr		2	3	4		24
Harculas Roney Senr	160	1	3			70
Elijah Rittenhouse		2	2	2		21
Daniel Rawlings		1	1	3		10/10
Ann Roberts	125	1	1			64
David Riddle	150	3	5	16		120
Nathan Roberts	100	1	2	1		53/5
John Raily	90	1	2			52
Joseph Riddle	50	2	2	3		47
Van Swearingen /Sheriff /2 Lotts /"post of Honer & profits"	700	3	2	11	2	470
George Sharp /"Col. Canon's Land"	400	2	3	4		265
Samuel Shannon	180	4	2	2		140/10
David Snodon Jun	70	1	2			51
David Snodon	70	1	4	3		60/10
John Sparr	150	2	3	4		89/10
Thomas Scott /Prothonotary /1 Lott						15
Lodiwick Smith /Distill	300	3	6	6		212
James Scott	100	2	2	3		55
Robert Slogdon	300	2	4			178
John Smith	100	2	2	4		51/5
David Shepherd	300	1	2	6		240

NAME	ACRES	HORSES	COWS	SHEEP	SLAVES	VALUE
John Smith		1				8
Matthew Steen	300		3			96
Samuel Sellecks	360	2	2			114
Samuel Stewart	300	2	2	6		143
Josias Scott	300	3	5	10		205
Jacob Shiveley	300	4	5	5		212/10
Samuel Leeper	300					63
William Thompson	250	1	2	8		142
John Templeton		1	1			10
Aaron Torance	200	3	4	4		133
Michael Tygart	85	1	2			32
Henry Taylor /4 Lotts	200	4	4	10		270
John Virgin	100					50
Abram Van Middleswart		4	4	4		43
Brice Virgin	400	2	4	7		223
Mary Vannemon	300	3	3	6		225
George Vannemon	300	4	7	10		248
Garret Vannemon	100	3	3	6		133
John White Senr	300	2	3	6		211
John White Junr	300	2	3	3		225
Thomas Wilson	400	1	3	6		136
John Wellman		1	2			20
Hugh Wiley	40	1	1	2		31
James Wilson /1 Lot	400	2	3	2		207
Peter Wolf	250	2	3			149
Thomas Waller		2	1		1	65
James Wilson		2	3	4		24
Robert Walker		1	1			10
Samuel Workman	125	2	3		1	136
James Workman	125	2	2	4		72
Thomas Woodward	100	2	2	9		73
John Wright	150	2	2	2		91
Richard Yates	700	7	9	20	4	532
Robert Young	260	1	4			144
William Zeans	160	1	2			170

SINGLE FREEMEN

NAME	ACRES	HORSES	COWS	SHEEP	SLAVES	VALUE
William Alexander						
James Byers						
Thomas Beers						
Charles Bilderback		1				8
James Brady						8
Edward Bess						
James Bailey		1				10
William Bailey		1				10
David Bradford		1				8
Jacob Bilderback						

NAME	ACRES	HORSES	COWS	SHEEP	SLAVES	VALUE
John Bica						
John Cotton						
Hugh Cotton						
James Cunningham						
John Finley						
Cornelius Gaiter						
Obediah Holms		1				8
Joshua Hasleridge						
John Henry						
William Leet		1				8
James Latimore		1				8
John Little						
William Love						
Thomas Makemson		1				8
William Marklin		1				8
Moses Middleswart						
Jacob Middleswart						
John Hogg	500	1				392
John Riddle	90	1				83
James Roney	90	1				44
John Raily						
John Sharp		1				8
James Steel		1				8
George White		1				8
Nathaniel White		1				8
James White	200	1				120
Samuel White	100	1				68
Andrew Vannemon		1				10

SECTION 2

THE 1790 FEDERAL CENSUS

FOR

WASHINGTON COUNTY, PENNSYLVANIA

by

Raymond Martin Bell

and

Katherine Kendall Zinsser

EVOLUTION OF COUNTIES AND TOWNSHIPS FROM WASHINGTON COUNTY, PENNSYLVANIA

(Boundaries Approximate)

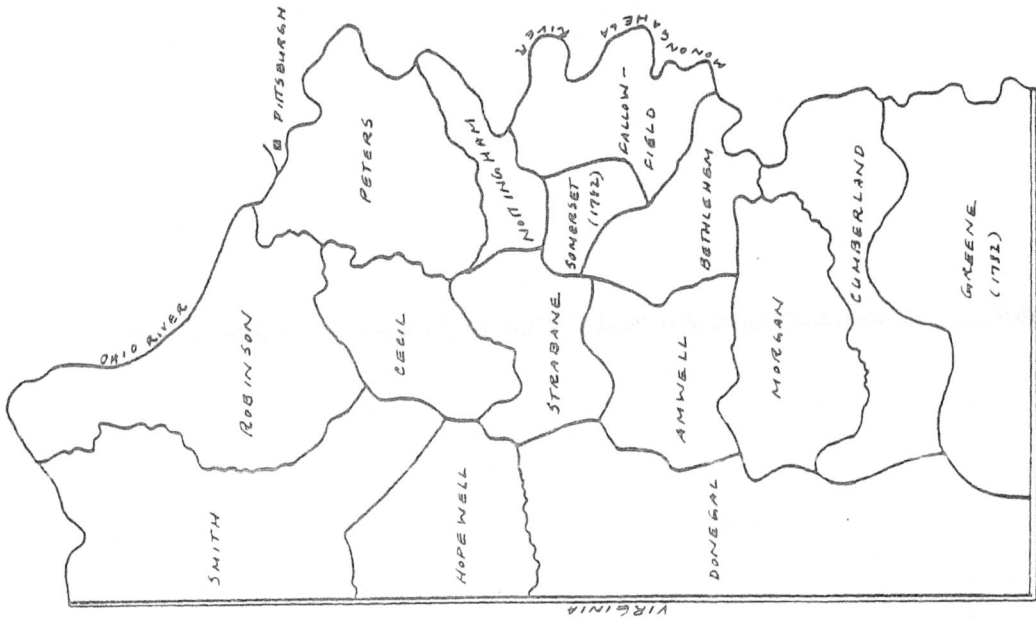

1800

GREENE CO. FORMED 1796
BEAVER CO. FORMED 1800

1790

ALLEGHENY CO. FORMED 1788

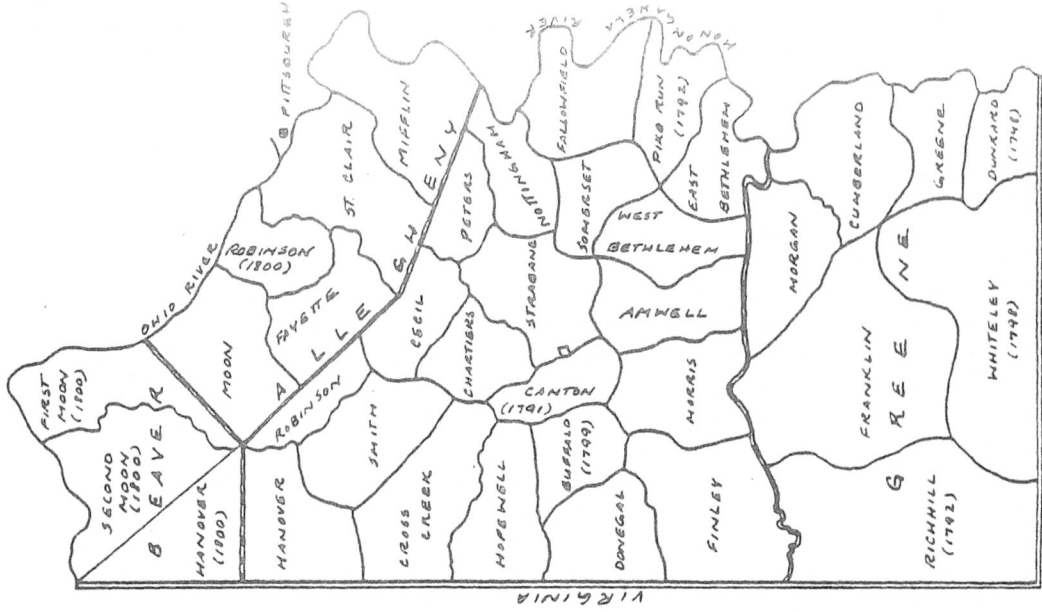

1781/2

WASHINGTON COUNTY, PA

THE 1790 FEDERAL CENSUS FOR WASHINGTON COUNTY, PENNSYLVANIA DIVIDED BY TOWNSHIPS

by Raymond M. Bell and Katherine K. Zinsser

Many researchers find locating the township of their ancestor's property in Washington County PA frustrated by the fact that the 1790 Census for Washington County was not returned by townships. Using tax records and warrantee maps, we have divided the 1790 Census into townships as nearly as possible.

The 1790 Census contains errors. The genealogist attempting to pinpoint an ancestor's residence should use both Census and tax records, especially if the area is near the Washington County boundary with Allegheny County. Some common problems with the Census are misspellings of names, duplicate entries for the same household, and errors made when transcribing copies of the lists from the original.

Tax lists provide the only references complete enough for comparison with the Census, yet some persons did not own taxable property and were therefore not included in the tax lists. Also, the rapid migration through the area meant some people were not residents long enough to be taxed. Thus some names appearing on the Census could not be placed for lack of reference.

We have divided the area that comprised Washington County at its formation in 1781 into three parts: Part I is present Washington County; Part II is present Greene County; Part III is lower Allegheny County. The map on p. 104 shows these divisions more clearly.

Part III deserves special explanation. Lower Allegheny County was separated from Washington County by two legislative acts dated 24 Sept. 1788 and 17 Sept. 1789. Although the final boundary between Washington and Allegheny Counties had been established on paper by the time the 1790 Census was taken, some public officials were not familiar with its exact location. The Census returns for lower Allegheny County were grouped together under the heading "Portion taken from Washington County". There is ample evidence the Washington-Allegheny County border was blurred in the minds of local residents. For instance, the 1789 Washington County Tax Lists include parts of lower Allegheny County under the old Washington County townships of Hanover, Robinson, Cecil and Peters.

For Part III only, we have replaced the last two columns "All other free persons" and "Slaves" with "Allegheny Twp." and "1789 Washington Co. Tax List" respectively. A township code in the Allegheny Twp. column indicates where a person of that name was located on either the 1791 or 1794 Allegheny Tax Lists. The 1789 Washington Co. column gives a township code where a person of that name lived just as the border was being established. A question mark means that name could not be placed using the sources available to us. A key to the code letters used for each township is provided on the first page of Part III. The map on p. 124 gives more detail on Allegheny County boundary changes.

Our lists are cut-and-pasted from Heads of Families at the First Census of the United States Taken in the Year 1790: Pennsylvania, from a reprint of the United States Bureau of Census publication [1908] by the Genealogical Publishing Co. of Baltimore, MD, 1970. Where possible we have preserved the original order of the names, but the reader may find some names juxtaposed on our lists because of our cut-and-paste method that do not appear so on the original lists. Care should be taken to not make assumptions about neighboring families based on our lists. Our lists are not difinitive; the researcher will want to compare data indicated on our reworked Census against other sources.

1790 CENSUS PART I: PRESENT WASHINGTON COUNTY, PA

AMWELL

NAME OF HEAD OF FAMILY.	Free white males of 16 years and upward, including heads of families.	Free white males under 16 years.	Free white females, including heads of families.	All other free persons.	Slaves.
Amelick, Phil.	2	1	3	....	
Anderson, Jacob	2	2	6	....	
Adam, Jacob	1	2	2	....	
Anderson, Richard	1	2	3	....	
Bilby, Richard	1	1	6	....	
Bean, Nathan	1	4	4	....	1
Bean, Isaac	1	3	6	....	
Bean, Joseph	1	1	2	....	
Corey, William	1	3	6	....	
Baldwin, Caleb	1	2	4	....	
Carter, James	2	2	6	....	
Coleman, Nath'l	5	5	4	....	
Carey, Jeremiah	2	3	1	....	
Cook, Noah	2	2	4	....	
Cook, Ziby	1	3	1	....	
Carmichael, Jno.	2	3	4	....	
Campbell, Joseph	2	2	2	....	
Cumberland, Arthur	1	2	1	....	
Colson, Samuel	1	4	3	....	
Carter, Eleanor	....	1	5	....	
Clark, Samuel	1	3	7	....	
Cachler, Christian	1	1	6	....	
Cook, Stephen	1	3	7	....	
Clark, Ezekiel	1	4	3	....	
Covalt, Epeneniah	2	4	4	....	
Cary, Daniel	1	2	1	....	
Cooper, Lemuel	1	2	2	....	
Cooper, Moses	1	2	5	....	
Cooper, Zebulon	2	3	5	....	
Kettelton, Abm	1	1	1	....	
Dickeson, Jno.	1	2	8	....	
Dodd, Daniel	3	3	4	....	
Dodd, Neal	1	2	3	....	
Dodd, Thadius	1	2	4	....	
Day, Jeremiah	2	2	2	....	
Eddy, John	1	1	2	....	
Addison, Caleb	1	2	3	....	
Eddy, Joseph	2	2	2	....	
Evans, Daniel	3	2	3	....	1
Evans, Abm	1	1	4	....	
Frail, Jno.	1	1	4	....	
Gordon, Thos	1	1	2	....	
Greggs, Jno.	2	1	4	....	
Galloway, Enoch	1	2	2	....	

AMWELL

NAME OF HEAD OF FAMILY.	Free white males of 16 years and upward, including heads of families.	Free white males under 16 years.	Free white females, including heads of families.	All other free persons.	Slaves.
Gregg, Solomon	1	5	4	....	
Gregg, Amos	3	5	2	....	
Graham, William	1	1	2	....	
Griffey, Chas	1	2	1	....	
Isaacs, Benjamin	1	4	4	....	
Braseley, Jno.	1	2	1	....	
Beabout, Ebenezar	3	2	2	....	
Bartholemew, William	1	2	2	....	
Barkshore, Jno.	1	2	2	....	
Clark, Jabez	1	1	2	....	
Miller, Hugh	1	2	1	....	
Ryan, Joseph	1	4	1	....	
Heaton, Ebenezar	1	3	3	....	
Hewitt, Phillip	3	2	6	....	
Hook, Jacob	1	1	1	....	
Harris, John	1	3	3	....	
Holloway, Jacob	1	1	2	....	
Hatfield, William	1	1	1	....	
Horn, John	1	4	1	....	
Husong, Jacob	1	2	3	....	
Hays, David	2	2	2	....	
Johnston, Abm	3	2	4	....	
Johnston, John	1	2	4	....	
Jennings, Joseph	1	5	6	....	
Jennings, John	1	3	3	....	
Johnston, Abm, Senr	2	5	3	....	
Ritten, Thos	1	3	4	....	2
Ritten, Theophilus	1	3	3	....	
Luce, Mathias	1	3	5	....	
Laycock, William	2	1	4	....	
Lewelling, Francis	1	2	5	....	
Lackey, Thos	3	1	1	....	
Laycock, Joseph	2	1	1	....	
Laycock, Elisha	1	4	1	....	
Laycock, Abner	1	1	1	....	
Leazar, Joseph	2	2	1	....	
Leazar, Peter	1	2	5	....	
Larrison, John	1	3	2	....	
Jammeson, Jno.	1	1	4	....	
Vinneman, Solomon	4	3	4	....	
Noble, William	1	1	1	....	
Knap, Jno.	1	4	5	....	

AMWELL

NAME OF HEAD OF FAMILY.	Free white males of 16 years and upward, including heads of families.	Free white males under 16 years.	Free white females, including heads of families.	All other free persons.	Slaves.
Mustard, James	1	2	3	....	
McGary, William	1	3	3	....	
McCleland, William	1	2		....	
Moore, Gershom	1	3	2	....	
Hickson, Rebecca	....	2	2	....	
Howell, Daniel	1	1	3	....	
Hewitt, Peter	1	2	4	....	
Hill, John	1	2	6	....	
Helms, Michael	2	2	3	....	
Helmes, Thomas	1	3	3	....	
Helms, Mich'l, Jur	2	1	3	....	
McCarmick, William	1	3	2	....	
Miller, John	1	4	3	....	
Masters, William	3		2	....	
McCollam, John	1	2	4	....	
Miller, Michael	1	1	2	....	
Morris, Robert	2	1	3	....	
Morris, Jacob	2	2	4	....	
Morris, Jacob	1	1	1	....	
McFarland, William	2	3	5	....	
Morris, Elisha	2	1	4	....	
McFarland, Daniel	1	1	4	....	
McCullough, Samuel	1	2	3	....	
Porter, Simon	1	2	5	....	
Petitt, Isaac	4	1	3	....	
Parker, Thos	1	1	2	....	
Peck, Jacob	1	1	6	....	
Junier, Isaac	1	1	2	....	
Phillips, John	1	1	2	....	
Ross, Saml	1	....	2	....	
Ross, Nath'l	1	1	2	....	
Rose, Abner	1	1	2	....	
Reese, John	2	4	9	....	
Reese, Morris	1		2	....	
Sutton, Abm	1	1	3	....	
Sutton, David	1	1	2	....	
Slusher, David	1	1	2	....	
Sergeant, Sampson	2	1	1	....	
Stout, Moses	1	1	2	....	
Smith, John	3	1	3	....	

The following pages reproduce a census table with three districts. Column headers (repeated for each section):

- **Free white males of 16 years and upward, including heads of families.**
- **Free white males under 16 years.**
- **Free white females, including heads of families.**
- **All other free persons.**
- **Slaves.**

AMWELL

Name of Head of Family	16+ M	<16 M	Females	Other free	Slaves
Swinhart, Gabriel	1	5	3		
Simon, Michael	1	7	4		
Sirecan, George	2	2	7		
Shuster, Daniel	2	2	7		
Shuster, Martin	1	1	1		
Scott, Nehemiah	4		3		
Tombough, William	1	2	2		
Tucker, James	1	2	4		
Terry, William	1	1	1		
Thorn, Abm	1	2	3		
Tucker, Moses	1	2	3		
Vancamp, Aron	1	2	3		
Vineyard, John	4	1	2		
Vineyard, Thomas	1	2	3		
Vancork, Jno	4	1	3		
White, Edward	2	5	3		
Wolverton, Jno	1		5		
Weckem, Lemanuel	2	1	3		
Wiggens, Thos	1	2	3		
Young, Geo	1	1	1		

EAST BETHLEHEM

Name of Head of Family	16+ M	<16 M	Females	Other free	Slaves
Parkison, William	1	2	3		
Read, David White	1	2	3		
Doolittle, John	1	2	1		
Wier, Adam	2	3	3		
Miller, Joseph	1		3		
Dickey, Andrew	1	1	3		
Vowles, Abm	3		5		
Vowles, Powell	1		4		
Prinsley, Jno	1	4	4		
Chaffind, Nathan	1		4		
Hunt, Richard	1	4	3		
Sniden, Adam	2	3	1		
Chaffing, William	2		2		
Gripps, Jno	1	2	2		
Poiser, Peter	1	2	2		
Dorsey, Joseph	4	2	7		6
Peters, William	1	3	2		
Powell, Benjamin	1	1	2		
Walker, Geo	1		2		
Weaver, Jacob	1	1	3		
Thomas, Joseph	1	3	3		
Holleway, Geo	1	2	4		
Helps, Geo	1		2		
Smith, Samuel	1	1	3		
Hamilton, Henry	1	3	3		
Davis, John	1	3	7		
Faulker, Allen	1	1	1		
Faulker, Thos	1	2	1		
Powell, James	3	6	2		
Townshend, Joseph	1	2	3		
Carson, Jno	1	3	4		
Wood, Ebenezar	1	2	2		
Heald, Nathan	1	2	2		
Faulker, Robert	1	3	5		
Agline, John	1	1	4		
Riggs, Eleazar	1	4	1		
Riggle, Jacob	1	4	5		
Welch, John	2	2	5		
Holton, Chas	1	2	1		
Lashley, Abm	1	1	3		
Hill, Stephen	1		3		
Hughes, Thos	1		2		
Charles, Daniel	1	1	1		
Charles, Solomon	1	1	3		
Hughes, Thos, Senr	1		2		
Joy, Edward	1	1	5		5
Bell, Zephaniah	1	1	2		
Miller, Jno	1		2		
Heald, Hugh	1	3	2		
Jones, Robert	1	2	2		
Hawkins, Thos	1	2	5		
Darby, Thos	1	2	2		1
Hargrove, William	1	2	3		
Harsock, Henry	1	3	3		
Wise, Andrew	1		7		
Hartman, Anthony	1		3		
Hilton, John	2	2	2		
Frederick, Jacob	1	2	2		
Kender, Valentine	1	6	4		
Seller, Frederick	1	2	1		
Baker, Geo	1	2	2		2
Rose, Jno	1		4		
Nosenger, Jno	2	2	4		
Nosenger, Ruddy			2		
Lashly, Peter	2	1	5		1
Pricker, Geo	1	2	4		
Shawhen, Derby		2	4		
Wear, Robert	1		3		
Montgomery, William	1		3		
Enochs, Henry	1	4	5		
Leed, Jacob	1	4	3		
Buckingham, William	3	1	6		
Bishop, Thos	1	1	3		
Bishop, Thos, Senr	1	1	2		
Stone, William	1	3	2		
Frederick, Daniel	1		1		
Hill, Robert	1		1		
Megrover, Philip	1	3	4		
Snuff, Jacob	3	4	4		
Henderson, William	1		2		
Townshend, Jno	1	3	3		
Townshend, Benjamin	1	4	3		
Magnemea, John	1		2		
Pentor, Ezekiel	1	3	3		
Yost, Christian	1	3	3		
Woodnield, Joseph	1	1	3		
Hutton, Joseph	1	1	3		
Dermon, Geo	1		3		
Callender, Robert	1		4		
Rigdon, Geo	1	2	4		
Brenton, Robert	1		2		
Swainey, Robert	1	3	2		
Hughes, Abm	1	3	3		
Poiser, Henry	1	4	3		
Ross, Alexander	2	4	4		
Mettle, Joseph	1	3	7		2
Harmal, John	1	4			5
Williams, Abel	1		2		
Ellis, Amos	1		3		
Richarison, John	3	1	6		
Green, Joseph	2	5	4		
Wilson, William	3	3	6		
Simms, Nathl	1		2		
Smith, Abm	1	2	5		
Smith, Henry	1	1	5		
Moody, Alexander	1	5	3		
Allshouzh, Henry	1		5		
Atkeson, Richard	1	3	4		
Ackey, John	1		2		
Ruble, David	3		4		
Ruble, David, Jur	1		2		
Porry, James	1	2	1		
Huffman, Henry	1	3	6		
Geess, Jacob	1	4	3		
Brant, Jno	1	1	5		
Clark, Jno	1	1	3		
Hopp, Everhard	1	7	2		
Perkins, Reuban	1		3		
Moore, Michael	1	5	5		
Boryard, Jesse	1	1	2		
Baker, Jno	2	1	6		1
Nosenger, Peter	1	4	6		
Wise, Frederick	1	4	4		
Hester, Adam	1	3	2		
Jenkins, Isaac	1		3		
Ronnalds, James	1	1	3		1
Blair, David	1	2	4		
Alexander, Henry	2	2	4		
Harvecost, Jno	2		2		
Harvecost, Joseph	1	1	4		
West, Jonathan	1	4	2		
Baldwine, Thos	2	2	6		
Alexander, Joseph	1		3		
Alexander, Isaac	1		2		
Crow, Abm		4	4		
Weaver, Jno	1		1		

WEST BETHLEHEM

Name of Head of Family	16+ M	<16 M	Females	Other free	Slaves
Allum, William	1	1	4		
Braden, Jas	2	2	3		
Bell, Andrew	2		1		
Beaty, James	1	1	1		
Rush, Isaac	1		4		
Barringer, Andrew	3	3	3		
Ball, Zopher	3	3	3		
Braden, Ezekiel	1	2	2		
Braden, James	3	2	2		
Barnett, Ignatius	3	1	2		
Buchias, John	1		2		
Braden, Jacob	1	2	2		
Phillips, Chancellor	2	1	2		
Cox, Christopher	3		2		
Conarestill, Henry	1	3	3		
Craft, Samuel	1	3	5		
Crooks, Thos	3	1	7		
Clingan, Richd	1	1	4		
Dustman, Henry	2		2		
Davis, Aron	2		4		
Drake, Peter	1	4	4		
Dickeson, Benjamin	1	1	3		
Doke, Mathias	1	3	4		
Densor, Jno	2		4		
Dager, Martin	2	1	3		
Dixon, James	3		3		
Dake, Frederick	3	2	2		
Dake, Michael	1	2	5		
Durham, Joshua	3		4		
Drisdell, Daniel	1	4	4		
Deroney, James	1	1	3		
Dowdle, Joseph	1	1	3		
Dowdel, Michael	1		3		
David, Enoch, Junr	1		2		
Evans, Samuel	1	4	3		
Miller, Adam	1		2		
Enochs, David	2	2	3		
Evans, James	1	1	3		
Evans, Walter	1	2	2		
Fox, Charles	1	1	2		
Fox, David	1	1	3		
Frazer, William	1		2		
Fox, Absalom	1	4	4		
Fruit, George	1		3		
Fisher, Gasper	4	4	4		
Griffith, Barcley	1	1	2		
Griffith, Francis	1	3	2		
Gaddis, Reese	1	2	5		
Graham, James	1	2	3		
Friend, Philip	1		3		
Friend, Philip, Jur	2	3	3		
Hill, Robert	1	3	3		2
Boggs, Andw	1	2	5		1
Hoflard, Rudolph	2		2		
Harsh, Simon	1		4		
Harsh, Geo	1	1	6		
Harsh, Henry	1	4	4		
Hill, Joseph	3	4	5		
Horn, Christopher	2	1	3		
Hostick, Michael	2	2	5		
Hill, James	2	2	5		
Hill, Thomas	2	2	5		
Hill, William	2	2	5		
Hedge, Absolom	1	2	4		
Hartman, Abm	1	4	5		
Jenkins, Eliazar	2	4	2		
Runkle, Jno	2	2	4		
Runkle, Henry	2	3	4		
Kelly, James	2	2	4		
Liel, Isaac	1		3		
Lewelling, Phillip	2	4	5		
Lacey, Moses	1	1	2		
Lawrence, Joseph	2	2	5		
Lorr, Bolsor	4		5		
Lashley, Jacob	1	5	4		
Leatherman, Daniel	1	3	3		
Leatherman, Michael	1	1	1		
Lickens, William	1		2		
Meeks, Samuel	1	1	3		
Meeks, Richard	1	5	4		
McCartney, Paul	1	3	4		
Hanstil, Michl	2	1	3		
Hull, Thos	2	2	4		
McCartney, Abel	2	2	2		
McFarland, Abel	2	1	4		
Moore, Andw	1		1		
Myers, Jacob	1		1		
Miller, David	1	2	3		
Meek, Jno	2	1	2		
Myers, Stephen	2	2	3		
Miller, William	1		1		
Oliver, William	1	2	4		
Parkeson, Jno	2	1	4		
Rose, Ezekiel	1	3	5		
Reynolds, William	1	3	3		
Ross, Benjamin	1	2	4		
Rush, Jno	1	2	2		
Richards, Casper	2	2	6		
Roberts, Lennard	2	3	6		
Richardson, Thos	3	3	5		
Reese, Thos	1	2	3		
Reese, Thos, Jur	1	4	6		
Redinor, Jno	1		2		
Riley, Peter	1	1	2		
Rigdon, Geo	1	2	1		
Riggle, Jno	1		1		
Shidler, Peter	1	2	4		
Shidler, John	1	6	7		
Spoon, Martin	1	2	2		
Snider, Peter	1		2		
Shidler, Jno (Black Smith)	1	6	7		
Swinehart, Geo	1	1	2		
Sutton, David	4		3		
Swinehart, Adam	1	2	6		
Sundaker, Christopher	1	2	4		
Shidler, Henry	1	5	3		
Swinehart, Peter	1	2	4		
Shidler, Geo	2	4	2		
Swinehart, Jacob	1	4	2		
Simon, Jacob	1	2	2		

NAME OF HEAD OF FAMILY.	Free white males of 16 years and upward, including heads of families.	Free white males under 16 years.	Free white females, including heads of families.	All other free persons.	Slaves.
WEST BETHLEHEM					
Shiddler, Jacob	1	3	2		
Simon, Nicholas	1	1	1		
Teetor, Francis	1	1			
Jacobs, Thos	1	2	5		
Taylor, Peter	1	3	1		
Taylor, William	1	1	3		
Ulrick, John					
Ulrick, Stephen					
Wise, Peter	1	3	2		
Walton, Amos	1	2	3		
Walters, Geo	1	2	2		
Weer, Samuel	2	2	4		
Weaver, Adam	3	4	2		
Young, Andw	3	1	4		
Buckingham, John	1	2	4		
Sutton, David, Junr	1		2		
Chaffin, James	1	4	2		
Grimes, James	1	2	5		
CECIL					
Brakin, Thos	3	4	4		
Lauder, Moses	1	3	3		
Henry, Frank	1	3	3		
Gaslin, James	1	3	3		
McCleave, Geo	1	1	3		
McQuidd, Timothy	1	2	3		
Coutter, Richd	4		2		1
Matthewson, Robert	4		3		
Matthewson, William	1	3	3		
Hutson, William	2		3		
Logan, Samuel	2		6		
Moore, Mory		2			
Dunlap, William		5			
McLaughlin, William					
Parson, Willis	2	1	3		
Ralston, Robert	5		2		
Brown, Samuel	1	2	2		
McRory, David	4	1	3		
Waits, Sarah		3			
Neel, Jno		1	5		
Parks, Robert		2	4		
Blair, Joseph		2	2		
Montgomery, John		1			
Porter, Robert			1		
Feed, James			2		
Miller, John	2	2	2		
Oliver, Andw	1	2	2	2	
Hays, Robert	1	2			
Welsh, Daniel	2				
Smith, Thomas	2		4		
May, Alex	1	2	2		
May, Saml	1	2	1		
May, John	1	1	3		
Reed, John, Esqr	2	1	5		
Hunter, John	4	1	1		
Acheson, Matthew	1	2	2		
Cowen, Henry	2	4	3		
Johnston, Matthew	2	4	4		
Orman, Thomas	2	4	4		
Richie, Andrew, Senr	3	4	4		
Graham, Samuel	2	1	6		
Andrew, John	2	1			
Roberts, William	2	2	3		
Little, James	4	4	3		
McLaughlin, James	1	1	2		
Douglass, Pat	1	3	2		
Campbell, John	3	1	2		
Stephenson, David	2	1	2		
Warneck, Robert	1	2	3		
Short, Thos	1	2	2		
Moorehead, Samuel	1	2	1		
Stephenson, Alexander		2			
Dennahew, Elizabeth			2		
Hunter, Robert	1	2			
Knox, James	1	2	3		
Hannah, William	1	2			
Hannah, William	1	2	3		
Hall, Benjamin	2	3	2		
Gances, Benjamin	1	2	2		
Gances, George	1	2	2		
Gance, Nicholas	1	1	2		
Cheese, Edward	1		2		
Hudgill, John	1	2	1		
Flemming, Thomas	1	2	2		
Tannehill, John	2		3		
McBride, Samuel	1	3	3		
White, John	2		3		
Dinny, Walter		4	5		
Downer, Joseph	1	2	3		
Martin, James	1	1	3		
Dobbins, Lennard	1	1	1		
McGuhon, Brice	1	2	4		
Glenn, John	1	3	4		

NAME OF HEAD OF FAMILY.	Free white males of 16 years and upward, including heads of families.	Free white males under 16 years.	Free white females, including heads of families.	All other free persons.	Slaves.
CECIL					
Armstrong, John	1	2	6		
Futton, Andrew	1	2	4		
Colvin, James	1	3	4		
Russel, Thos	2	5	1		
Herring, Jas	1	6	2		
Cowden, John		2	1		
Brassland, James	1		4		
Graham, Michael	1		3		
Guy, Henry	1	2	2		
Andrews, Nathl	1		3		
Black, Will		3	3		
Craig, James	1	2	3		
Culberson, Elias	1	3	1		
Donnald, Chas	1	5	4		
Faucett, Jno	3	4	4		
Faucett, Thos	2	4	4		
Hill, Robert	1		4		
Johnston, Adam	1	4	3		
Long, William	1	3	6		
Lisnett, Francis	1		3		
McBride, Wm		2	3		
McConnell, Matt	3	5			
McConnell, Alexr	2	7	2		
Oram, Wm	1	1	2		
Parks, Jno	1		5		
Parks, Samuel	1		2		
Reed, David	1	4	4		
Robey, Wm	1		3		
Sheean, Jas	1	2	4		
Steell, David	1	5	3		
Taggart, Jno	2	5	3		
Walker, Jno	1		4		
Wilson, Robert	1	2	3		
Sprowl, James	1		4		
Patterson, Jno	2	2	4		
Crea, Patrick	1		4		
CHARTIERS					
Cowen, Henry	1	2	3		
Hannah, James	1	3	2		
Lee, Thomas	1	2	4		
McMichael, Henry	1	2	3		
McDonald, Martin	1	2	4		
McClean, Robert	1	2	4		
McMullin, Robert	1	2	4		
McClean, James	1	2	4		
McClean, Samuel	1	2	3		
Chapman, Richard	2	2	2		
Thomas, Joseph	1	2	3		
Henderson, Revd Mattw	2	2	5		1
Walker, Andw	2		5		
McClusky, Robert	1	5	3		
Russell, Andw	1	1	5		
Woodburn, James	1	1	1		
Strothers, Jno, Jur	1	1			
Strothers, Jno, Senr	4	5	7		
Scott, Archibald	1	1			
McCall, Thos	2	1			
Hays, William	2	3	1		
McClelland, Hans	2	3	4		
Russell, Jno	2		4		
Holmes, William	1	2	3		
Nelson, John	1	2	4		
Cannon, Joshua	1	2	1		
Donald, Henry	1		2		
Donald, John	2		3		
Henry, Robert	3	3	4		
McRory (Widow)			4		
Baggs, James	3	2	5		
Scott, Isaac	1	3			
Leard, Jno	1		3		
Crisswell, William	1		4		
Singhorse, Abm	1	2	4		
Weaver, Isaac	3	1	4		
Jordan, Jno	1	1	3		
Garett, David	4		4		
Gault, James	2	2	3		
McCall, Jno	5	2	2		
McClean, William	2		1		
Ritchie, Andw	2	4	3		
Campbell, Chas	2		2		
Tannehill, Agnes	2		3		
Sloan, Thomas	2		2		
Hays, Jno	2		1		
Holmes, Joseph	1		2		
Thomson, Jos	2	2	5		
Ewing, Matthew	2	4	5		
Boys, Jno	2	4	4		
Miller, James	2	1	4		
Cahey, Nathl	3	1	2		
Phillips, Thos	2	6	2		
Garrell, James	3		3		

NAME OF HEAD OF FAMILY.	Free white males of 16 years and upward, including heads of families.	Free white males under 16 years.	Free white females, including heads of families.	All other free persons.	Slaves.
CHARTIERS					
Taylor, Geo	3	1	2		
Spears, William	1	1	2		
Adams, William	1	1	3		
McKnight, Patr	2	1	1		
McClelland, James	2	1	1		
McConnell, James	1	1			
Hammond, John	1		4		
Mercer, James	3	4	5		
Paul, John	2	4	1		
Wallace, Gavin	3	1	4		
Porter, Joseph	1	4	2		
Nesbitt, Jonathan	3	1	2		
Robinson, Henry	1	6	2		
Robins, John	1	3	4		
Morrison, John	1	1	3		
Merchant, Thomas	1	1	3		
Galbraeth, Samuel	1		2		
Guttery, Robert	1	1			
Guttery, James		2	2		
Linsley, John	1	6	2		
Hannah, Samuel	1	3	4		
Mull, Henry	1	2	2		
Steveson, George	1	2	5		
Steveson, Jno	2	2	5		
Miller, John	1	2	1		
Teenan, James	1	1	3		
Boll, Hugh	1	1	3		
McDowell, Thomas	2	1	5		
Patton, Hugh	1	3	4		
McKnight, Alexr	1	2	1		
Miller, James	2	5	2		
Merchant, Ann		2			
McGaughan, Jno	1	1	2		
Shearer, James	3		2		
McKnight, Hugh	1	2	4		
Hammond, David	1	1	2		
Hammon, Robert	1	1	2		
Cowden, James	2	2	1		
McComb, Geo	1	2	4		
Castle, Alexr	2	2	1		
Agnew, Samuel	5	1	3		1
Wilson, John	1	1	3		
Russell, Robert	1	1	2		
Hornett, Noah	1	1	4		
Kirkpatrick, Alexr	1	1	4		
Ramsay, James	1	1	2		
Ramsay, Thos	1	1	1		
Sinclair, William	1	1	2		
St Clair, William, Jur	6	1	4		
Allison, Jean	1	1			
Merchant, James	1		4		
Lex, Phil			4		
Lex, James	1	1	5		
Welch, Robert	4	2	5		
McBride, Samuel	2	2	9		
Thompson, Robert	3	1	2		
Macelroey, James	2		2		
McCoy, Angus	2				
Dougherty, Roger	2		2		
Elliott, James	2	2	3		
Maxfield, Henry	1		2		
Maxfield, Thos	1	1	3		
Maxfield, Samuel	1		3		
Johnston, William, Senr	1		3		
Hughes, Elizabeth			3		
Hughes, Robert	1	2	2		
McNary, James	4	2	5		
Johnston, William, Jur	2		3		
Wallace, Geo	1				
Clark, Henry	1	3	6		1
White, Jno	3		5		
Wherry, Joseph	3	1	1		
Foreman, James, Senr	1	2			1
Foreman, James, Jur	1	1	2		
Steel, Robert	1	1	2		
McCullough, Geo	1		7		
Wylie, Adam	1	4	1		
McClean, Jno	1		6		
Leeper, James	1	4	6		
Miller, John	2	3	4		
Coutter, Adam	1	3	5		
McDonald, William	1	1	2		
McDonald, Archibald	1	3	3		
Woods, Samuel	2	3	4		
Morrison, Gavin	3		4		
McAllester, Alexr	4	1	3		
Montgomery, Robert	6	4	5		
Gibson, Andrew	4	5	2		1
Allison, William	4	2	4		
McCall, James, Jur	1		4		
Fry, Jno	2	3	2		
Rice, Edwd	1	1	4		
Sears, James	3	3	4		
Roach, Wm			4		
Ross, Daniel	1	4	5		

CHARTIERS

NAME OF HEAD OF FAMILY.	Free white males of 16 years and upward, including heads of families.	Free white males under 16 years.	Free white females, including heads of families.	All other free persons.	Slaves.
Morrison, James	1	1	2		
Simson, Jeremiah	1	1	3		
White, Thos	2	3	3		
Reed, David	2	5	2		
Kerr, William	3	3	3		
Laughlin, Sarah	3	3	4		
Hutcheson, Thos	2	4	3		
Bowland, Matthew	1	3	3		
Bowland, William	1	3	2		
Leadly, James	1	3	3		
McClean, Jno	1	3	3		
Todd, Jno	4		3		
Monroe, Andrew	4		6		
McCoy, Daniel	2	1	2		
Church, James	1		6		
Marshall, William	2	2	6		
Ritchie, Craig	2	2	2		
Dehaven, Abm	2	2	2		
Cannon, Jno	5	3	6		1
Weaver, Thos D	1	3	4		

CROSS CREEK

NAME OF HEAD OF FAMILY.	Free white males of 16 years and upward, including heads of families.	Free white males under 16 years.	Free white females, including heads of families.	All other free persons.	Slaves.
Nerns, Joseph	1	2	5		
Glenn, David	3	1	4		
Patterson, William	5	3	5		
Tennel, John	2	5	4		1
Bees, Thos	2	5	2		
Buxton, Jacob	1	3	3		
Ray, William	2	1	2		
Marshal, John	3	4	4		
McGibbons, Thos	3	3	4		
Giffens, Samuel	1		1		
McGibbons, John	3		4		
Ferguson, Andrew	3	1	4		
Reynolds, David	2	4	3		
Martin, Isaac	1	1	5		
McComb, David	2	2	1		
Scott, John	1	1	4		
Scott, Matthew	1	2	6		
McCauly, Francis	2	1	4		1
Stewart, Jno	3	1	7		
McComb, Robert	1	1	6		
Sloan, Willm	1	1	2		
Walker, Andw	1	4	2		
Wilkeson, John	1	1	2		
Beacon, Thos	2		2		
Young, William	1		4		
Glass, Robert	1		2		
Johnston, John	1	1	2		
Robinson, Robert	3	2	7		
Smith, Samuel	2	2	3		1
Carson, Samuel	1		1		
Morrison, John	1		2		
Duper, James	1	2	5		
Bush, Robert	2	4	4		
Calwell, Joseph	2	1	5		
Jackson, James	1	3	4		
Hart, Epm	1	3	4		
Stevenson, John	1	2	1		
Leeper, John	1		3		
Ackleson, Robert	2	1	3		
Hughes, William	3		3		
Dennahoe, Ann			7		
Cummins, Samuel	1		3		
Fowler, Jonathan	1	1	1		
Johnston, Samuel	2	2	3		
Johnston, Isaac	1	1	2		
Johnston, Stephen	1	2	2		
Henwood, James	1	1	4		
Henwood, Elisha	1		1		
Marshal, William	2	1	3		
Lisle, Aron	2	2	3		
Sitesfield, James	1	2	1		
Davis, Philemon	3		2		
Robinson, James	1		3		
McClurg, William	1	2	4		
Kirk, James	1	2	4		
Graham, Henry	3		3		
McCaskey, Wm	1	1	2		
McConnel, Thos	1	1	3		
Waggener, John	3	2	5		
Smith, Ebenezar	1	1	3		
Glenn, Joseph	1	1	3		
Glenn, Hugh	2	2	4		
Hays, David	2	1	5		
Smith, William	2	2	4		
McKinsey, Aron	1		4		
Brown, Edwd	3		5		
Hofstaker, Olesy	1	2	4		
Cowen, Isaac	1	3	3		
Rannal, William	1	2	4		
Marcus, Thomas	2	3	5		
McMullin, Samuel	1		2		
Robb, Robert	1				

CROSS CREEK

NAME OF HEAD OF FAMILY.	Free white males of 16 years and upward, including heads of families.	Free white males under 16 years.	Free white females, including heads of families.	All other free persons.	Slaves.
Newell, Hugh	1	4	3		
Marcus, John	1	3	3		
Palmer, Samuel	1	1	2		
Boyd, John	1		4		
Brown, John	1		2		
Nicholas, James	2	1	1		
Brown, Caleb	1	2	2		
Brown, Joshua	2	1	3		
Mackenson, Robert	1	1	7		
Smith, James	1	3	1		
Adams, Jno	1		3		
Criswell, James	1	2	3		
Smith, Jonathan	1	2	3		
Grant, Jno	1	3	4		
Robinson, Samuel	1	2	2		
Stephenson, Jno	2	6	5		
Kelly, Danl	2	2	5		
Marsh, Thos	2	1	3		
Criss, Jno	2	5	3		
March, Wm	2	3	7		
Wells, Richard	1	6	3		
Ward, Thos	3	3	5		
McGary, William	1	1	3		
Wells, William	1	1	3		
Wells, Thomas	2	3	5		
Pollock, John	1	4	1		
Davison, James	1		3		
Levins, Ann	1		1		
Sparks, Selethial	1	2	2		
Allison, Archibald	1	2	1		
McCready, Robert	1	5	3		
Lovejoy, Joseph	1		2		
Davis, David	2	3	3		
Robinson, Elisha	2	2	3		
Wells, Richard	1		2		2
Rennolds, David	1		3		
Acheson, Ralph	1	3	2		
Wells, George	1	4	5		
Thorn, William	1	1	4		
Scott, Joseph	1	4	4		
Hannah, James	2	2	5		
Campbell, William	3	2	2		2
Campbell, John	1	6	2		
Campbell, James	2		3		
Marshall, John	1	3	5		
Marshall, Thomas	3	1	4		
Wily, Thomas	2	3	6		
Beaty, Thomas	2	5	4		
Cowan, John	2	1	2		
Fegan, Alexander	2		2		
Smith, Nicholas	1		3		
Lemuel, Peter	1	5	4		
Walker, Robert	1	3	5		
Henwood, Joseph	1		4		
Boyd, John	1	2	5		
Armstrong, Robert	1		2		
McGechon, Ann		4	3		
McCloud, Jno	1		2		
Moore, Samuel	2	4	2		
Young, Goodman	1		3		
Gardner, Jno	1	1	5		
Clark, James	1	2	2		
Clark, William	1	2	1		
Galleher, John	1	1	1		
Watson, James	4	3	6		
Loeper, Samuel	1	4	4		
Thomson, Samuel	1	2	2		
Robinson, Thos	1		2		
Morrison, Joseph	2		4		
McGarah, Henry	2	1	2		
Johnston, John	1	3	4		
McGarah, John	1	1	5		
Morrison, John	1	2	5		
Wells, Alex	4		4		4
Wells, Henry	3	2	5		1
McGuire, John	1	1	5		

DONEGAL

NAME OF HEAD OF FAMILY.	Free white males of 16 years and upward, including heads of families.	Free white males under 16 years.	Free white females, including heads of families.	All other free persons.	Slaves.
Armstrong, Thos	1	2	3		
Alexander, Jos	1		4		
Archibald, Richd	1	1	2		
Ankaim, Samuel	1		2		
Anderson, Jno	1	2	2		
Allison, James	1	2	1		
Allison, John	1		2		
Byers, Samuel	1	4	4		
Brownlee, James	3	1	3		
Bair, John	1	1	1		
Brady, James	1	4	3		
Bell, Robert	1	3	2		
Bell, James	1		3		
Begs, Andrew	2		3		
Begs, Jno	1				

DONEGAL

NAME OF HEAD OF FAMILY.	Free white males of 16 years and upward, including heads of families.	Free white males under 16 years.	Free white females, including heads of families.	All other free persons.	Slaves.
Brownlee, Thomas	1	1	1		
Bole, James	1	2	1		
Burns, Sarah	1	5	4		
Bickett, James	1	2	1		
Bryson, Jno	2	3	3		
Chambers, James	4	1	7		
Carson, James	1	3	4		
Cheney, Samuel	1	2	1		
Crawford, William	1	1	2		
Clark, Benjamin	1	2	2		
Conley, Jno	1	2	1		
Cox, Isaac	1	2	4		
Callwell, David	1	2	2		
Cole, Barnet	1	2	1		
Craig, Daniel	1	1	1		
Deed, Henry	1	1	3		
Derrenger, Jno	1	3	5		
Dennis, Michael	1	2	2		
Davis, Samuel	1	2	2		
Dradin, James	1		2		
Dilling, Geo	2	2	3		
Dilling, Jno	1		2		
Dowling, John	1	2	2		
Ely, Michael	1	3	6		
Ely, Michael (Smith)	1	2	2		
Irvine, Thos	1	2	1		
Finley, Robert	1	3	5		
Flick, Jno	1	2	1		
Ferguson, William	1	1	2		
Fisher, Jno	1		2		
Fullenwider (The Widow)		2	2		
Gather, Edward	1	1	5		
Graham, Robert	2	2	4		
Graham, Jno	2		2		
Glover, James	2		4		
Gorley, Robert	1	1	6		
Grimes, Jno	1				
Gray, William	1	1	1		
Gordon, Thos	1	2	3		
Gill, Andw	1		1		
Glover, Hugh	1		4		
Hill, Elisha	1	2	5		
Hawkins, Hannah	1		5		
Horn, Hartman	2	4	4		
Hill, Thos	1	2	1		
Hawkins, Jeremiah	1	1	3		
Heaton, Jno	1		2		
Hawkins, William	2	3	2		
Hemphill, John	2		3		
Holliday, James	1	4	3		
Hutcheson, Joseph	2	1	3		
Herring, Andrew	1	2	3		
Holmes, Thos	1	2	2		
Howell, Jonathan	1	2	4		
Huffman, Christian	1	2	2		
Hitt, Jno	1	2	2		
Hupp, Phillip	1	2	6		
Johnston, William	3	2	4		
English, David	1	4			
Jamison, Jno	1		3		
Ishbaugh, Simon	1		3		
Jeffery, Jno	1	1	3		
Johnston, Thos	1	2	4		
Cain, John	1	1	3		
Kelly, John	1	1	3		
Knox, Thos	2	1	4		
Leatherman, Frederick	1	3	3		
Leffer, Geo	1	1	2		
Leffer, Jacob	1	2	2		
Lester, Isaac	2	1	1		
Leak, David	1		1		
Lain, Jno	1		3		
Lain, David	2	1	3		
Laurence, Jno	2	2	3		
Moore, Andrew	1	4	1		
McLaughlen, Edward	1		1		
May, Jno	1	2	4		
Deeds, Andrew	1	1	3		
Miller, Jacob	1	2	2		
Miller, Jno	1	2	2		
Miller, Christian	1	2	5		
Martin, David	1	3	3		
McRoberts (The Widow)	1	3	4		
McRoberts, William	1				
McClure, Francis	1	2	3		
McNeall, Archibald	3	3	6		
McMaugh, Patrick	1	2	2		
Marshall, James	2	3	5		
Miller, Francis	1	1	4		
Marshall, Jno	1		1		
McCleland, Kenith	1		1		
McDowell, Nathl	1	4	3		
McKee, Joseph	1	2	2		
Shane, Timothy	1		3		

DONEGAL

NAME OF HEAD OF FAMILY	Free white males of 16 years and upward, including heads of families	Free white males under 16 years	Free white females, including heads of families	All other free persons	Slaves
McCullough, James	1		1		
McConnel, William	1	3	1		
McConnel, Robert	1				
Mounts, Jno	1	2	2		
McWilliams, Jno	2	2	2		
McConnell, Alexr	1	1	1		
McConnell, Samuel	2	1	2		
McConkey, James	1	1	3		
McClean, Geo	1	3	2		
McKee, Jno	2		2		
Matthews, James	1	2	1		
Matthews, John	2	1	2		
Mathers, James	1	3	2		
McMullin, Jane	2	1	4		
McKinney, David	1		3		
Matthews, John	1	2	4		
McClemments, David	2	3	6		
Morris, Isaac	1	2	3		
Martin, John	1	2	2		
Paxton, Joseph	2	3	4		
Paxton, Samuel	1	1	2		
Perry, Jno	2	1	2		
Porter, Jno	1	2	1		
Porter, James	2	1	2		
Power, William	1	1	4		
Rice, Jacob	1	2	2		
Rice, Abm	1	4	3		
Raser, Jacob	1		1		
Rice, Henry	1				
Reese, Daniel	1				
Russel, Joshua	3	3	6		
Rogers, Samuel	1	2	3		
Renison, Wm	1		3		
Riddle, Wm	1	3	1		
Stephenson, Jas	1	1	3		
Sinclair, John	1	2	2		
Scott, John	2		3		
Simler, Gasper	1	2	4		
Striker, Laurence	2	2	8		
Spriggs, Ebenezar	1		5		
Sharp, Jno	1	2	6		
Sellar, Jacob	1	2	5		
Summers, Walter	2	2	2		
Summers, Jno	1				
Travis, William	1	1			
Tayler, Robert, Senr	1	1	1		
Taylor, Robert, Jur	1		2		
Taylor, William	1		1		
Taylor, Samuel	1		6		
Templeton, Jno	1	1	1		
Waller, Thos	1	1	5		
Waller, Richd	1				
Williamson, David, Esqr	1	1	5		
Williamson, Eliazar	1	1	4		
Williamson, Joseph	1	4	1		
Williamson, James	1				
Williamson, Samuel	1	4	5		
Walker, Robert	1	2	3		
Walker, Alexr	1				
Wilson, Thos	2		3		
Williams, Bazil	1				
Williams, Levin	1	2	1		
Williams, Jerrett	1				
Wolf, Jacob	1	2	5		
Wolf, William	1	2	3		
White, George	1	3	4		
Winters, Stoppel	1	4	3		
Wolf, Peter	1	3	2		
Whitehill, Thomas	1	1	2		

FALLOWFIELD

NAME OF HEAD OF FAMILY	Free white males of 16 years and upward	Free white males under 16 years	Free white females	All other free persons	Slaves
Mitchell, James	2	3	4		
West, Edward	3	1	1		
Allman, William	1	4	2		
Nichols, Thomas	3	1	6		
Prichard, James	1	1	6		
Johnston, Robert	1	1	3		
Reess, Elijah	1	6	3		
Morton, Moses	1	2	2		
Shaplaw, John	1	3	2		
Depew, Daniel	2	3	5		
Hall, Thomas	1	2	6		
Hyatt, Shadrach	1	1	2		
Clark, Geo	1	3	3		
Morris, Benjamin	1	2	3		
Conley, Nicholas	1	4	4		
Hamilton, Jonthn	1	1	5		
Shoush, Christian	1	2	1		
Stacker, Christopher	2	2	3		
Irish, Peter	1	1	2		
Wygand, Cornelius	1	3	4		

FALLOWFIELD

NAME OF HEAD OF FAMILY	Free white males of 16 years and upward	Free white males under 16 years	Free white females	All other free persons	Slaves
Hill, John	1	1	5		
Bough, Peter	1	2	2		
Crossin, Patrick	1		2		
Coulter, Thos	2	1	2		
Mesenger, Abner	1		3		
Johnston, Nicholas	1	3	4		4
Gunce, Samuel	2	1	1		
McRurry, James	1	5	4		
Mathorn, Jacob	2		4		
Carr, William	2	1	2		
Guthery, John	1	5	2		
Morrison, William	2	1	4		
Jamison, David	1	3	4		
Nye, Samuel	1	3	3		
Boyd, Dugal	3	1	3		
Goodburry, Nathan	3	1	2		
Emlin, John	3	2	4		
Seevers, Abm	1	2	4		
Powers, Michl	1	3	2		
Stillwagon, Jacob	2	2	6		
Regner, Conrod	2	1	2		
Young, James	1	6	4		
Grabble, Christian	2	2	3		
Everly, Leannard	1	3	2		
Yesserounds, Peter	2	3	2		1
Colvin, Vincent	2	3	2		1
Burk, John	1	1	2		
Crooksharp, James	1	1	5		
Durbin, Phillip	1	2	1		
Beedle, Abner	1	2	5		
Wirt, Martin	1	1	2		
Johnston, John	1	2	2		
Coulter, Abigail	3	3	4		
Orr, Humphrey			2		
Sullivan, Danial		1	1		
Hoy, Charles	1	3	4		
Wallace, Jno	2	4	3		
Parks, Micajah	1	4	2		
Ferton, Thos	2	4	4		
Hill, Alexr	1	4	4		
Fry, Abner, Jnr	1	4	4		1
Cooper, Frederick	1	4	5		10
Bartly, Stephen	1	5	3		
Speers, Henry	1	2	5		3
Wooley, Samuel	1	1	4		
Mefford, John	1	2	3		
Bonaim, Zachariah	1	3	4		
Ellis, Jesse	1		3		
Ellis, Hezekiah		1	4		
Ellis, James, Senr	1	1	2		1
Ellis, James, Jnr	1	1	1		
Ellis, Nathan	1	3	2		
Downden, Clement	1	3	2		
Crawford, William	1	3	2		
Kerr, Moses	1	1			
Crabbs, Philip	1		3		
Crabbs, Jacob	1	1	2		
Crabbs, Henry	1	2	2		
Hawk, John	1	3	4		
Crosshorry, Robert	1	3	2		
Hull, Geo	1	2			
Charles, George	1	1	1		
Shields, John	1	2	1		
Sickle, John	1	2	2		
Ringland, Jno	2		2		
Chedester, Silas	1	2	3		
Chedester, William	1		3		
Knox, Geo		2	3		1
Knox, Jno	1	2	3		
Brenton, Joseph	2	1	6		1
West, Thomas	1		2		
Adams, John	3	4	5		
Riley, Thos	1	2	4		
McAdams, Jno	1	2	4		
White, Benjamin	1	1	3		
Moore, Daniel	1		2		
Road, John	1	4	5		
Flinn, Geo	1	3	3		1
House, Jno	1	2	3		
Whittacre, Daniel	1	6	4		
Watson, Daniel	1	2	4		
Martin, John	2	1	2		
Scott, Alexr	1	3	4		
Whinnatt, William	1	2	4		
Stivers, Jno	1	3	2		
Neal, Samuel	1	3	2		
Carrell, Thos	1	6	1		
Riggs, Ed	2	1	6		1
Riggs, Samuel	1	1	1		
Hull, Amos	1	1	6		
Baker, Isaac	1	4	4		
Ward, Richard	1	4	3		
McArdell, Patrick	1				
Harkim, Peter	1	1	2		
Sparr, Martin	1	3			

FALLOWFIELD

NAME OF HEAD OF FAMILY	Free white males of 16 years and upward	Free white males under 16 years	Free white females	All other free persons	Slaves
Chester, Joseph	1	3	3		
Hall, Joseph	1	1	5		
Chatfield, Lewis	1	1	6		
Brown, Jno	1	2	1		
Quimby, Samuel	1	1	4		
Sutherland, Alexander	1	1	1		
Rape, Jacob	2	1			
Rape, Thos	1	1	3		
Roe, Samuel	1		3		
Case, Thos	1	1	2		
Bellsitt, Peter	1	1	1		
Baxter, Samuel	3		6		
Boundwell, Josh	5	1	3		
Case, Meshack	1	1	2		
Teeple, Isaac	1		2		
Nicholas, Thos	2	3	3		1
Woods, Jeremiah	2	1	3		
McCombs, William	2	1	4		
White, Edward	1		2		
Pinsock, Thos	1	4	2		
Watson, Jas	1	1	3		
Forken, Thos	1	2	3		
Casner, Peter	3	1	5		
Flemming, Peter	2	1	2		
Prior, Thos	1	3	2		
Spiers, Robert	1		2		
Thompson, Thomas	1	1	3		
Mitterfield, William	1	1	2		
Legg, Thomas	1	5	2		
Hughes, Hannah		1	3		
Imbrey, James	1	4	4		
McHorg, William	1	3	5		
Lane, William	2	2	3		
Morrison, Joseph	1		2		
McCord, William	1	1	4		
Province, Chas	1	1	2		
Parker, William	4	2	2		
Perry, Edwd	1	3	2		
Park, James	1	2	1		1
Innis, James	1	1	1		6
Holden, Richard	1				
Johnston, Robert	1	6	2		
Rogers, Andrew	1	2	2		
Hamilton, Daniel	1	3	2		
Parkison, Thomas	2	3	3		
McNutt, William	3	4	2		
Carr, James	3	1	3		
Vanhorn, Bernard	3	3	5		
Shaver, Thos	2		1		
Teel, Jacob	1	1	2		
Ritchie, David	3	1	3		
Jewell, William	1	2	3		
George, Robert	1	3	2		
Rice, James	2	2	5		
Fry, Abraham	1	1	2		5
Young, Jacob		4	2		
Worth, John	2	1	3		
George, Alexander	1	2	4		

PIKE RUN (formed 1792) from FALLOWFIELD

NAME OF HEAD OF FAMILY	Free white males of 16 years and upward	Free white males under 16 years	Free white females	All other free persons	Slaves
Dixon, Henry	1	2	8		
Woods, Jacob	3	3	2		
Bundle, Aron	3	2	6		
Ingland, David	3	1	5		
Allen, John	1	4	2		
McGauhey, David	1	1	2		
Allen, Joseph	2	1	3		
Case, Henry	1	2	3		
Platter, Christian	1	1	1		
Dunshea, William	1	1	2		
Shane, James	1	6	4		
Fortune, Jacob	1	2	4		
Roller, Geo	1	1	1		
Platter, Joseph	2	1	2		
Platter, Peter	1	1	2		
Gibson, David	3		2		
Phoebs, Nicholas		1	2		
Platter, Nicholas, Jur	1	1	2		
Dixon, Joshua	1	2	5		
Finney, John	1	2	2		
Thornton, Josaph	2		1		
Cull, William	1	7	1		
House, William	2	4	6		
Jackman, Henry	1				
Williams, Robert	1	1	1		
Chaffin, John	1	3	3		
Jackman, Robert	2	4	4		5
Phillips, Henry	1	3	2		
Smith, Elisha	1	2	3		
Patterson, James	1	4	6		
Johnston, Caleb	1				

FALLOWFIELD (PIKE RUN)

NAME OF HEAD OF FAMILY.	Free white males of 16 years and upward, including heads of families.	Free white males under 16 years.	Free white females, including heads of families.	All other free persons.	Slaves.
Gregg, Daniel	1		2		
Nixon, John	1	2	2		
Dixon, Samuel	3		2		
Hays, Joseph	2	1	2		
Hays, Sarah		2	2		
Miller, Thomas	1	2	4		
Kennear, Thomas	1	2	4		
Phillis, Solomon	1	1	3		
Hanly, Jno	1		3		
Chaden, Mary			3		
Large, Samuel	2	3	3		
McCartney, John	2		3		
McCartney, John, Jur	4	2	4		6
Gillespie, Neal	1		3		
Askew, John	1	3	2		
Brown, Joseph	3	3	2		
Taylor, Samuel	1	2	2		
Devall, Alexander	1	5	4		
Whitelatch, Chas	1		3		
Ellis, Amos	1	3	3		
Dowler, Thos	1	2	2		
Earl, Edwd	1		1		
McFaddon, Jno	1	4			
White, Amos	1		3		
Vale, Saml	1		3		
Badger, Sarah			3		
Wheeler, Chas	1	1	6		
Hutton, Thos	5		3		
Mills, Henry	1	1	2		
Henderson, Alexander	1	3	5		
Perry, Sarah	2	2	2		
Wilson, Amos	1		6		
Waits, Andrew	1	5			
Slavin, Bryan	1	2			
Springer, Jacob	1	4	3		
Jamison, David	1	4	3		
Grigg, Henry	4	1	3		
Jackman, William	1	3	3		
Hanen, Moses	2	4	3		
Babbs, James	1		3		
Higgens, John	1	3	2		
Kerr, Robert	2	2	3		
Cavinaugh, Patrick	1		2		
Mosdale, Jonathan	1	1	2		
Vandegrist, Jacob	1	1	3		
Stewart, Jno	1		3		
Ryder, Christopher	1		2		
Patterson, Andrew	1	1	2		
Miller, Harry	1		2		
Chess, John	2	6	2		
Albert, John	1		1		
Gregg, John	2	3	2		
Risinger, William	2	4	1		
Wallman, Nicholas	1	2	2		
McClov, William	1		3		
Thomas, James	2	1	3		
Allman, Jno	2	3	3		
Rigg, Clement	2	2	5		
Rigg, Hosea	1	1	2		
Dwire, Thomas	2	4	4		
Evritt, Jno	2	4	5		
Everitt, William	1	3	4		
Feely, William	1	2	5		
White, James	1	2	2		
Crow, Thomas			2		
Crow, Margaret	1	4	3		
Crow, John	1	3	3		
Higgins, William	1	1	3		
Robinson, Zachariah	1	1	2		
Jackman, William	2	3	6		
Riggs, Jeremiah	1	3	4		
Riggs, William	1	3	3		
Earl, John	1		2		
Dean, Michael	2	2	3		
Jackman, Richard	2	5	3		
Dunkin, Luke	1	3	3		
Young, John	3		3		
Soosby, Sampson	1		3		
Young, Morgan	1		2		
Frederick, George	1		3		
Wallace, David	1		2		
Wilks, Samuel	2		3		
Steel, Jesse	1		3		
Bartly, John	2	1	3		
Allman, Thomas	1		3		
Thompson, Amillas		3	4		
McCall, John	1	3	4		
Carson, Thos	1	3	2		
Carson, Thos, Jnr	1		2		
Carson, James	1		3		
Cloud, Thomas	1	2	2		
Collett, James	2		3		
Miller, Phillp	1	3	1		
Hull, John	1	3	3		
McFarlin, Baptist	1	2	2		
McRory, David	1		3		
Stanley, William	2	4	4		
Riley, John	2	4	4		
Deems, Mark	1	4	2		
Deems, Adam	1	1	2		
Hails, Joseph	2	2	1		
Hubbs, Elijah	1	1	3		
Riley, Robert	1	1	4		
Riley, Robert, Jur	1		2		
Pedon, Isaac	1	2	3		
Vandusan, Michl	1	1	2		
McMullin, James	1	2	3		
Pedon, Joseph	1	2	3		

FALLOWFIELD (PIKE RUN)

NAME OF HEAD OF FAMILY.	Free white males of 16 years and upward, including heads of families.	Free white males under 16 years.	Free white females, including heads of families.	All other free persons.	Slaves.
Carrol, Jno	3	2	4		
Litten, Samuel	3	3	5		
Teal, Asas	2	1	2		
Baker, Joshua	1		2		
Riggle, Michl	1	2	3		
Weaver, Conrod	1	4			
Wallace, Herbert	4				11
Pedin, Samuel	1		2		
Tice, Jno		4	2		
Jones, Josh	1		3		
Riddon, James	2		3		
Pedon, Samuel, Jur	2		3		
McQliton, Andr	1	3			
Conrod, Henry	1	2	1		1
Conrod, Jno		2	2		
Hackett, Andrew	1	1	1		
Clouse, William	1	1	1		
Green, John	1		4		
Bow, Thos	1	1	3		
House, Thos	2		2		
Offard, Nathan	2		2		
Riggle, Geo	2	1	4		
Darnel, Isaac	4	5	5		
Flemming, Jno	1	2	6		
Hopkins, Jno	3	1	1		5
Hopkin, Jno, Jur	1	2	2		2
Headly, Francis	1		1		
Headly, Jno C	1	2	2		
Baker, Jno	1	1	2		
Rail, John	1	1	2		
Powell, Nathan	1	2	3		
Reddy, Lawrence	1		4		
Stibbs, Mary	1	1	3		
Berry, William	2	1	7		
Hines, Benjamin	1		2		
Clark, Bazel	2	2	4		
Bailey, Henry	1		3		
Brooks, Jno		2	3		
Powell, Isaac	1	5	2		
Buffinton, Jno	1		2		
Runnion, Jos	1		2		
McComb, Daniel	2	2	2		4

FINLEY

NAME OF HEAD OF FAMILY.	Free white males of 16 years and upward, including heads of families.	Free white males under 16 years.	Free white females, including heads of families.	All other free persons.	Slaves.
Lurey, Robert	1	1	4		
Campbell, Daniel	1	2	2		
McKinsey, Daniel	1	2	2		
Sebraio, Daniel	1		1		
McCoy, Daniel	1	3	4		
Davis, Samuel	1	1	2		
Adams, John	1	3	4		
Beham, James	2	3	3		
Harper, Thos	1	3	3		
Robinson, John	1	2	4		
Sletten, James	1	2	3		
Sletten, William	1	3	3		
McFarren, John	1	2	4		
Gooden, Alexr	1	1	3		
Steson, Robert	1	1	4		
Boner, William	1	1	8		
Boner, Charles	1	2	3		
Brownlee, John	1	3	3		
McDonald, George	1	2	3		
McArthur, John	2	1	5		
McDonald, Daniel	2	1	3		
Davison, Geo	1	1	6		
Armstrong, James	1	1	3		
Mays, Chas	1	4	3		
Smith, William	1	1	3		
Roney, Hercules	2	3	3		
Kirk, Isaac	1	2	2		
Gunn, Jno, Senr	1	2	3		
Enlow, Luke	1	2	2		
Enlow, Elliott	1	2	2		
Vance, John	1	1			
Byers, Thos	1	2	2		2
Byers, Samuel	1	2	3		
Byers, Ebenezar	1	2	3		
Sutt, Valentine	1		1		
Jackson, Hugh	1	2	2		
Leeper, Margaret	2		3		
Fitzpatrick, Hugh	1	2	3		
Henry, Robert	1	2	3		
Hannah, Thos	1	1	3		
Cunningham, Robert	1	1	2		
McCoy, William	1	3	3		
Gunn, William	1	3	1		
McGuffey, William	2		2		
Little, James	1	1			
Rush, James	1	3	3		
Nicholson, George	1	1	3		
Armstrong, Andrew	1		4		
Enlow, Abm	1	3	4		
Teegard, William	1	6	4		
Ingland, Samuel	1	1	2		
Evans, John	1	3	3		
Carrol, Robert	1	7	4		
Gorly, Thos	2		4		
Weathers, Jno	1	4	4		
McMillen, Jno	1	3	3		
Sergeant, Richard	1	1			

HANOVER

NAME OF HEAD OF FAMILY.	Free white males of 16 years and upward, including heads of families.	Free white males under 16 years.	Free white females, including heads of families.	All other free persons.	Slaves.
Cunning, Robert	1		4		
Duggan, James	1		2		
Moore, Augustine	1		5		
Johnston, Andrew	3	1	3		
Edgar, Robert	1		1		
Douglass, Robert	1	3	1		
Timmons, Thos	1		1		
McCoy, Hugh	1	3			
Bowman, Robert	1		2		
McConnel, Dennis	1		2		
Carothers, Thos	2	3	3		
Anderson, William	1		3		
Moore, Isabella	1		1		
Stephens, Thos	1	3	3		
Glascow, Samuel	1		1		3
Carothers, James	1		1		
McKinney, Isaac	1		1		
Davison, Robert	1	2	5		
Patton, David	1	4	3		
Lewabbery, Isaac	1	1	1		
Brady, William	1	2	1		
Quack, Cornelius	1	1	5		
McCulloch, Alexr	1	1	1		
Miller, Alexr	1	1	2		
Kevkendall, Henry	1		2		
Hannan, Andrew	1		2		
Hall, Adam	1	1	2		
McCullough, Geo	1	1	2		
Harson, Henderson	2	1	1		
Manteeth, David	1	1	2		
Bell, Hugh	1	2	2		
McCready, Joseph	1	3	4		
McCaskey, Matthew	1	1	1		
Leulin, Alexander	1	1	1		
Ewing, James	1		2		
Aikens, John	1	2	2		
Moore, Samuel	2	1	1		
Moore, Jno	1	3	2		
Crose, Martha		1	4		
Brooks, Arch	1	1			
Miller, John	1	3	5		
McDonald, Path	1		1		
Dunnon, David	1	3	3		
McCaslin, Geo	1	2	2		
Dugan, Robert	1	5	2		
Blazer, Geo	1	3	3		
Ralstone, Archibald	2	1	3		
Dungan, Levi	1		2		
Kerr, Jno	1	2	2		
Stephens, Isaac	2	3	3		
Devour, Elijah	1		1		
Pool, John	1	2	2		
Walter, Jacob	1		2		
Wilson, Miles	1	2	4		
Dorman, Path	1		1		
Proudfoot, Jacob		2	3		
Russell, Robert	2	3	5		
Moore, Jno	1	3	2		
Potts, Jonas	1	2	3		
Jackson, Joseph	1	3	4		
Phillips, Thos	1	4	2		
Devilling, Francis	1	2	1		
Fitzpatrick, Jno	1	2			
Poe, Adam	1	6	1		
Comely, Jno	1	2	6		
Flemming, Robert	1		1		
Miller, Isaac	2	1	2		
Buchannon, John	1	3	3		
Nelson, Joseph	1	1	3		
White, Jno	1	2	3		
Clemmons, Alexander	1	2	2		
Gibson, Robert	1	2	2		
McNary, David	1	1	3		
Casteman, Henry	1	4	2		
McClurg, Robert	1	1	2		
Duke, Mark	1	3			
Eaton, William	1	1	3		
Laughlin, William	1	2	1		
Armour, Thos	1		1		
Moore, William	1		1		
Holms, Thos	1	1	4		
Tisten, John	1	3	1		
McDowell, James	1	1	2		
Brooks, Benjamin	2	3	4		
Wright, Benjamin	1	5			
McCready, Hugh	1	1	1		
Hill, Roger	1		2		
McMillan, Hugh	1	1	2		
McMullin, William	1	1	1		
Pecker, Jno	1	1	4		
Gifford, James	1	1	1		
Swearingen, Samuel	3	2	3		2
Lankford, William	1	4	3		
Jenkins, William	1	4	2		
Kerr, David	1				

NAME OF HEAD OF FAMILY.	Free white males of 16 years and upward, including heads of families.	Free white males under 16 years.	Free white females, including heads of families.	All other free persons.	Slaves.
Law, Thos	4	1	2		
Law, John	1	2	2		
Scott, Elizabeth			3		
McClelland, William	1	3	4		
McConnell, Arthur	2	2	1		
Taterfield, Daniel	1	1	3		
Kennett, Valentine	1	5	3		
McConnel, George	1	2	2		
Galbraith, William	2	2	2		
McCann, John	1	3	4		
Wells, Alexr	1	3	3		
Pillars, Jno	1	3	3		
Bolls, Thomas	1	2	4		
Ferguson, Robert	1	2	4		
McCullough, Robert	1	2	2		
Hall, Thomas			1		
Carothers, Robert		3	2		
Smith, Isaac	1	5	2		
Sprie, William	2	3	2		
Critchfield, Jno	1	5	2		
Harriman, David	1	2	4		
McFaddin, Jno	1	3	3		
Jamison, Jno	1	3	5		
McFaddon, Samuel	1	1	2		
Reaves, Nathan	2	1	7		
Thompson, James	1	2	1		
Sprie, Benjamin	1	2	2		
Sprie, Thos	2	2	2		
Alles, William	3	1	2		
Newell, William	1	3	2		
Tolbert, Richard	1	2	4		
Beck, Sarah			3		
Strong, Elizabeth	2		1		
Sharp, George	2	1	2		
Gill, William	1	1	6		
Gill, Samuel	1	5	2		
Henry, William	2	2	3		
Sharp, Geo Jur	1	2	1		
Smilie, William	4	3	3		
Cruthers, Geo	2	3	3		
Slemmons, William, Jur	2	1	3		
Caiwell, Robert	1	1	2		
Gillespie, James	1	7	1		3
Sparks, Geo	1	1	2		
Smith, John	1	2	2		
Slemmons, Samuel	1	2	4		
Harriman, Geo			3		
Martin, James	1	1	1		
Montgomery, David	1	1	3		
Hicks, William	1	1	2		
Ross, Jno	1	1	3		
Ramsay, Geo	1	1	3		
Pharrell, Joseph	1	2	3		
Smith, Alexr	1	2	5		
Todd, James	1	2	3		
Martin, Robert	2	4	3		
Fowler, Patrick	3	5	4		
Gault, Jno	1	5	3		
Buchannon, Jno	3	4	3		
Buchannon, William	2	2	4		
Chesnutt, Samuel	1		3		
Scott, Jno		1	3		
Warden, Samuel	1	1	2		
Bines, Thomas	4	2	2		
Levins, Henry	1	5	5		
Cummings, Robert	1	3	4		
Maholland, James	1	1	2		
Wells, Edward	1	2	3		
Harvey, William	1	5	3		
Teetor, Samuel	1	2	2		
Frazier, James	2	2	2		
Wills, Robert	1	1	1		
Bess, John, Jur	1	1	2		
Wells, Joseph	1	3	2		1
Scott, Arthur	1	3	2		
Tilton, Thos	1	3	2		
Newcome, Jno	1	2	2		
Henderson, Andrew	1	2	6		
Welch, Geo	1	3	3		
Stewart, Benjamin	1	1	4		
Canton, William	1	1	2		
Kent, Joseph	1	2	4		
Hollen, Gabriel	1	2	4		
Vance, Arthur	1	1	4		
Mellen, Thos	1	3	4		
Harrod, Henry	1	3	4		
Harriman, Robert	1	3	3		
Kelly, Jno	1	3	3		
Hide, Thos	2	3	2		
Sharp, Jno, Jur	1	2	2		
Gillespie, William		1	4		
Perrin, Joseph	1		1		
Perrin, Ann	1		4		
Washburn, Nathaniel	3	4	6		

NAME OF HEAD OF FAMILY.	Free white males of 16 years and upward, including heads of families.	Free white males under 16 years.	Free white females, including heads of families.	All other free persons.	Slaves.
Wilken, Robert	1	1	1		
Marriott, Hezekiah	1	2	2		
Moore, James	1	2	3		
Gilchriest, Jno	1	1	3		
Alexander, David	2	3	3		
Hill, Walter	1	2	2		
Bacon, Mishack	1	4	3		
Wells, Chas	1	1	3		
Buchannon, Walter	1		3		
Piles, Joseph	1	2	2		
Irvine, Christopher	1	1	2		
Fulton, James	1	3	3		
Bess, Jno	2	1	5		
Merrick, Daniel	1	1	4		
Chambers, Jno	1	2	1		
Sharp, Jno	1	2	2		
Stewart, Allen	1	2	2		
McRichards, Robert	2	2	3		
Blair, James	1	2	3		
Marrot, Matthew	1	2	6		
Hawkens, William	1	2	1		
Davids, Jno	1	1	4		
Andrew, Edward	1	2	2		
Merrick, Moses	1	2	3		
Harriman, Sankin	1	1	4		
Robinson, James	3	4	2		
Sparks, Geo	2	1	2		
Matthews, Augustine	2	1	2		
Sharp, Jno, Senr	2	1	3		
McKee, Thos	1	1	4		
Little, James	2	2	6		
Wilsou, Chas	1	3	4		
Cunningham, Ambrose		3	4		
Scott, James	1	2	5		
Moore, William	1	1	3		
Hastings, Alexander	1	1	3		
McKee, Samuel	3	2	3		
McKee, Peter	1	1	3		
Templeton, Matthew	1	4	4		
Wilkins, Archibald	1		5		
Wilkins, Archibald, Jur	1		4		
Wilkins, James			4		
Moore, James	1	2	1		
Cook, James	1	1	3		
Kelly, William	1		3		
Fisher, Samuel	1	1	2		
Anderson, Benjamin		3	2		
Patterson, Jas	2	5	3		
Templeton, Jas			3		
Callwell, David	1	1	2		
Anderson, Peter	1		1		
Snodgrass, Robert		4	3		
Doolan, Jno	1		3		
Cummings, Paul	2	4	3		
Congleton, Moses			1		
Smith, Revd Jos	2	1	5		1
Callwell, Samuel	1	1	3		
Slemmons, William	1	1	2		
Steel, William	2	2	1		
Bealy, William	1		1		
Bealy, James	1	1	1		
Lowrie, John	1	3	4		
Anderson, Alexr	3	3	2		
Steel, Samuel	1	3	5		
Snodgrass, Samuel	1	3	3		
Stewart, William	2	3	4		
Smith, Thos	1	1	2		
Doddridge, Phillip	2		5		
West, Moses		3	4		
Hines, James	1	3	4		
Cox, Noah		2	8		
Welch, Mary			4		
Pemberton, Jno	1	2	4		
Tweed, Jno	3	2	3		
Hannah, Hugh	1	3	3		
Dixon, James	1	1	2		
Wilken, John	1	1	3		
Hannah, William	1	3	3		
Vincent, James	1	3	6		
Smiley, Jno	1		3		
Porter, Hugh			4		
McKinney, Samuel	1	2	6		
Caiwell, Margaret			3		
McGregor, Jno	1		3		
Brown, Jno	1	2	2		
Welch, Robert	1	1	1		
Mitchell, Mattw	1	1	6		
McEwings, Will	1	1	3		
Repeth, Will	1	1	5		
Doddridge, Jno	1	2	3		
Ward, Talbert	1	2	4		
Rouse, Benjamin	1	3	4		
Stewart, Chas	1	1	4		
Ford, Wm	1	3	3		
Shannon, Thos	1	5	3		

NAME OF HEAD OF FAMILY.	Free white males of 16 years and upward, including heads of families.	Free white males under 16 years.	Free white females, including heads of families.	All other free persons.	Slaves.
McGuire, Thos	1	5	3		4
Spencer, Jos	1	2	2		
Callwell, Thos	1	4	4		
McGuire, Francis	1		3		
Baker, Job	3	4	3		
Wells, Sarah		1	1		
Baker, Elizabeth	1	3	3		
Armstrong, Ed	2		3		
McConnell, Jno	1	2	2		
Gates, Valentine	1	2	2		
Gates, Geo	1	3	3		
Clements, Adam	1	2	2		
Delong, Aron	1	1	1		
Simmons, Lawrence	1	3	4		
Simmons, Saml	1		1		
Garven, James	1	3	2		
Buchannon, Elizabeth	1	4	4		
Moore, Robt	1	3	1		
Buchannon, James	1	4	3		
Urie, Thos	1	1	1		
Urie, Solomon	1	1	2		
Urie, Samuel	1	1	1		
Money, James	2	1	2		

MORRIS

NAME OF HEAD OF FAMILY.	Free white males of 16 years and upward, including heads of families.	Free white males under 16 years.	Free white females, including heads of families.	All other free persons.	Slaves.
Goble, Ebenezar	1	2	3		
Extell, Thos	2	1	6		
Linken, Hannah			2		
Minton, Savannah			1		
Johnston, Nehemiah	1	1	2		
Tuttle, Daniel	1		2		
Tuttle, Isaac	1	2	3		
McPherson, Malcolm	1	1	1		
Hall, Hugh	1		1		
Rowley, Constant	1	2	4		
Green, William	1		2		
Prowder, Joseph	1	1	2		
Lazey, Moses	1		2		
Axtell, Danl	3	4	3		
Craig, Robert	1	1	2		
Allison, Patrick	1	1	2		2
Lee, Richd	1	2	6		
Craig, Jno	2		2		
Goble, Caleb	1	1	2		
Johnston, David	1	2	2		
Axtell, Luther	1	2	4		
Cundite, David	1				
Randles, Benedict	1		4		
Balchey, Humphrey	1		3		
Acheson, John	1		2		
Martin, Epm	1	5	2		
Lindsley, Joseph	1		4		
Baldwine, Lemuel	1		1		
Paste, Jeremiah	1		2		
Dilley, Isaac	1	4	2		
Pipes, Joseph	1	1	2		
McVay, Edward	1	2	2		
Lindsly, Jesse	1	1	2		
Dilley, Israel	1	3	3		
Hunt, Jonathan	2	2	4		
Post, Joseph	1	2	2		
Draper, Jno	1	1	2		
Post, David	2	2	2		
Richy, Benjamin	2	1	5		
McCraken, David	1	1	5		
Frazey, Benjamin	1	4	3		
Clutter, William	2	2	6		
Shuball, Jno	1	1	5		
Parker, James	1	2	2		
Pettit, Jno	1	2	4		
Sheetz, Zachariah	1	4	2		
Jackson, Alexr	1	3	3		
Coe, Joseph	1	1	3		
Coe, Joshua	1				
Coe, Joseph, Jur	1	1	1		
Clutter, Jno	1	2	6		
Dilley, Samuel	1	2	8		
Hathaway, Abm	1	4	2		
Lindsly, Caleb	1	1	3		
Lindsley, Jno	1	1	2		
Lindsley, Dumas	3	1	4		
Cook, John	3	2	4		
McVay, James	2	4	2		
Lindley, Abm	1		3		
Lindley, Caien, Jur	1	1	4		
Wingatt, Caleb	3		4		
Michelrath, Thos	1	1	3		
Ball, Mathias	1	2	4		
Craft, Chas	3	1	2		
Oliver, David	1	1	2		
Creacraft, Chas	1		6		
Dickeson, Henry	1	2	3		
Dickeson, Assey	1	1	3		3

MORRIS

NAME OF HEAD OF FAMILY.	Free white males of 16 years and upward, including heads of families.	Free white males under 16 years.	Free white females, including heads of families.	All other free persons.	Slaves.
Roberts, Nathan	1	4	2		
Davis, John	1	1	1		
Vaughn, Alexr	1	3	2		
McPherson, Alexr	1		3		
Haslip, Samuel	2	1	6		
Cooper, Nathl	1	1	5		
Goble, Stephen	2	1	2		
Wallace, Jno	1	3	2		
Lewis, Jno	2	1	3		
Dotty, Henry	1		1		
Hatheway, Richard	1	5	2		
Bryant, David	1	4	2		
Brison, Jno	2		2		
Preeden, Benjamin	1	1	1		
Milligan, William	1	1	1		
McVay, John	1		1		
Simson, Simon	1		2		
Saunders, Stephen	1	5	3		
Archer, Jno	1		1		
Goodin, Abm	1		1		
Dibb, Lewis	1	1	2		
Doyle, Aron	1	4	4		
Doyle, Icabad	1		1		
Ross, Edwd	1	1	4		
Ross, Phoeba			1		
Fordyce, Elizabeth	1	1	1		
Doyle, Price	2	3	3		
McVay, Jno	1	2	4		
Wingate, Daniel	1	1	2		
Ralston, Saml	1		4		
Purcell, John	2	3	3		
Lindley, Levi	2	2	1		
Lindley, Levi, Jur	1				
Headly, Joseph	3	3	5		
Headly, Thos	1		1		
Golden, Mathew	1	1	2		
Carns, Jno	1	1	2		
Clark, Isaac	1		1		
Cary, Colvin	1	2	6		
French, Aron	2	2	3		
Miller, Benja	2	2	2		
Williams, Moses	1	5	1		
Hatheway, Nathan	2	2	5		
Reese, Benja	1	5	4		
Bennett, Joseph	1	4	4		
Wingate, Zibe	1	2	2		
McVay, Isaac	1	2	2		
Clark, Hezekiah	1	3	1		
Clark, Jno	1	3	2		
Clark, Joseph	1		1		
Babitt, Job	3	5	3		
Babitt, Aron	1	1	1		
Carmichael, Jno	1		2		
Parkhurst, Samuel	3	4	2		
Reede, Jno	3	2	1		
Reede, Jacob	3	1	1		
Holness, Frederick	1	1	4		
Lindly, Caleb	1	1	3		
Leary, Abijah	1	1	3		
Miles, John	1	2	1		
Craig, William	1		2		
Coleman, Leanard	1	4	2		
Lindly, Napthalin	1	1	1		
Lindley, Zibe	1		3		
Sergeant, Edwd	1		1		
McCohn, David	2	1	6		
Craft, Lawrence	1		5		
Dolly, John	1	1	4		
Craft, Lawrence, Jnr	1	2	1		
Craft, John	3		6		
Craft, Thos	1		1		
Elliott, William	1	4	3		
Ackerson, Thos	1	1	1		
Brownlee, Thomas	1	2	3		
Hull, Solomon	1	2	2		
Bowers, Elias	1	1	1		
Adkerson, Geo	1	3	2		
Day, Samuel	1		5		
Day, Samuel, Junr	1		2		
Day, Daniel	1	3	1		
Day, Ananias	1	2	3		
Day, Moses	1		2		
Day, Darling	1				
Sergeant, Thomas	2	3	1		
Vay, Benja	1	3	3		
Kimble, Jos	1	2	3		
Brison, William	1	2	3		
Wier, William	1		2		
Ferguson, Robert	1	1	2		

NOTTINGHAM

NAME OF HEAD OF FAMILY.	Free white males of 16 years and upward, including heads of families.	Free white males under 16 years.	Free white females, including heads of families.	All other free persons.	Slaves.
Dovour, Henry	1	6	3		
Gibson, Robert	1	1	3		
Madden, Jno	1	2	3		
Devour, John	2	2	5		
Brierly, Jno	1	5	2		
Osburn, William	1	2	1		
Galloway, Jas	1	2	2		
Stephenson, Jno	1	4	2		
Marcus, Jno	2	2	6		
Marcus, Samuel	1	2	1		
McCabe, James	2	1	2		
McDowill, Mattw	1	1	2		
Millener, Jno	1	2	2		
Meloney, Thos	1	2	2		
Caldwell, Joseph	2	2	3		
Caldwell, Robert	1	1	2		
Hopkins, David	1	4	2		
Derrough, Jno	3	2	5		
Goudy, Wm	2	3	4		
Leggett, Robert	1	4	2		
Crawford, David	1	1	1		
Ferguson, Margaret	3		1		
Ferguson, Vincent	1		4		
Munn, Jno, Senr	1		2		
Munn, James	1	4	2		
Munn, Jno, Jur	1	2	2		
Munn, David	1	2	4		
Byers, William	1		3		
Cook, Joseph	1		2		
Gladden, Joseph	1	2	2		
Cook, Ann		1	3		
Collins, Josiah	1		2		
Collins, John	1		2		
Patterson, Thos	1	1	2		
Patterson, Jno	1	4	3		
Seers, Samuel	2		5		
Sawings, Joseph	1		3		
Scott, Hugh, Esqr	3		3		
Quigley, Wm	1		6		
Ruwark, Shedrach	1	3	2		
Thomas, Leverton	2	5	4		
Goudy, William, Senr	2	3	7		
Casebare, Jonathan	1	2	2		
Irvine, Jas	1		2		
McKee, Robert	2	3	3		
Williams, Aron	2	1	6		
Devour, Andrew	1	6	3		
Reed, Jno	1		2		
Gray, Alexr	1	4	2		
Wilson, William	1		3		
Hannah, William	1		2		
Hannah, Hugh	1	1	5		
Robins, Jno	1	2	4		
Gibb, Alexander	2	2	4		
Newkirk, Henry	2	2	4		
Vannatters, Jno	2	3	5		
Armstrong, William	2		1		
Crawford, Benja	1	1		4	
McMullin, James	1		4		
Benson, Isaac	1	2	3		
Bounds, Thos	1	2	3		
Clark, Jno	2	2	4		1
Cryts, Jacob	1	1	1		
Murdith, Thos	1		1		
McHaffen, Chas	1	2	3		
Parkenson, Benjamin	1	3	5		1
Masters, Richard	1		3		
Yant, John	1	3	3		
Marshal, Hugh	1	2	2		
Lash, Isaac	1		5		
Scott, Hugh, Jur	2	1	2		
Parkinson, William	4		5		
Miller, George	2	1	5		
Marshal, William	1		4		
Davis, George	1	3	4		
Stephen, Samuel	2	3	5		
Gibson, William	1		2		
Hamilton, James	1	2	6		
Parkenson, Joseph	2	3	2		2
Parkenson, James	2	3	4		
Montgomery, Robert	1		4		
Parkinson, Martha	1		2		
Devour, Peter	1		3		
Duncan, James	1	2	3		
Phillips, Joseph	2	1	3		
Garvin, Thos	1		1		
McDonald, Enos	1	2	4		
Montgomery, Ezekiel	1		4		
Montgomery, Samuel	1		3		
Leadarn, John	1	1	4		
Johnston, Chas	1		3		
Bryan, David	1	2	4		
McElvay, Patw	1		6		
Young, James	1		2		

NOTTINGHAM

NAME OF HEAD OF FAMILY.	Free white males of 16 years and upward, including heads of families.	Free white males under 16 years.	Free white females, including heads of families.	All other free persons.	Slaves.
Craig, Jno	1	2	3		
Paylor, Michl	1	2	6		
Little, Amos	1	2	4		
Brannon, Oliver	1	2	3		
Tally, John	1	2	3		
Hamilton, John	4	1	2		
Stantown, Richard	1		1		
O'Donald, James	1	1	3		
Baldwin, John	2	2	2		2
Ferguson, James	2	2	4		
McKinny, Jenny	2		6		
Hone, Ruth		1	6		
Hone, Peter	1	1	1		
Mitchell, John	1	1	3		
Scott, Samuel	1	4	3		
Ramage, William	2	1	2		
Hoppar, Jno	1	4	3		
Barr, Jno	3	1	2		
McCune, Joseph	1	4	4		
Cryts, Andw	3	1	1		
Love, John	1	1	1		
Kennedy, John	1	2	3		
Boys, William	1	4	5		
McAully, Saml	1	3	4		
Hays, Jno	1	2	4		
Watt, Samuel	2	3	3		
Welch, John	3	4	4		
Welsh, George	2	3	1		
Jacobs, Daniel	3	3	2		
Wickerham, Peter	1	3	2		
Davis, Francis	2	2	2		
Scott, William	4	1	1		
Mitchell, William	2		3		
Scott, William, Jur	1	2	3		
Coins, William	4		2		
Ault, Andw	1		1		
Crawford, David, Senr	1	1	1		
Wickerham, Adam	2		1		
McKnight, William	2	2	1		
Grey, John	1	2	4		
Donaldson, David	1	1	3		
McCoy, James	1		1		
Jacobs, Sarah		2			
Jacobs, David	1		1		
Taters, Elisha	1	3	5		1
Pegg, Benjamin	1	2	4		
Porter, Robert	1		4		
Waddle, Alex	1	4	3		
Fragly, Jacob	4	1	4		
Myers, Mattw	1	2	2		
Hanley, Michl	1	2	1		
Gibbing, Geo	2	1	7		
Adley, William	1	1	1		
Beaty, Thos	1	4	6		
Meeks, Samuel	4	1	3		
Farland, Patrick	1	4	5		
Little, Saml	1	2	2		
Coulter, Jonathan	1	3	1		
Patterson, Jno	1	2	2		
Farland, James	1	2	3		
Chambers, James	1		1		
Bently, Joseph	2		1		
Kennon, Thos	1	1	1		
Logan, Jas	1		1		
Daily, Chas	2		1		
Daily, Nathan	2	2	2		
Naylor, William	1	1	1		
Keykendall, Cobus	3		1		
Keykendall, Benja	1	1	3		
Hall, Mattw	1	1	1		
Daily, Chas, Senr	1		1		
Daily, Phillip	1	3	2		
Chambers, James	1	2	2		
Chambers, Joseph	1		1		
Daily, Saml	1	3	1		
Nailor, Wm, Senr	1	1	1		
Nailor, Ralp	1				
Nailor (Widow)	2	2	2		
Welsh, Valentine	1	3	4		
Cox, John	1		1		
McDonald, Jno	1		1		
McClean, Saml	1		1		2
James, Robert	1		1		
James, William	1	2	5		
Hopkins, Edward	1	4	5		
Holdcraft, John	1	4	5		
Holdcraft, John, Jur	1	2	1		
Underhill, Jno	3	2	6		
Barber, Samuel	1		1		
Bradford, Elizabeth	1	2	2		2
Estep, Elisha	1	1	4		
McFarlane, Andw	3	4	1		2
Dunshea, William	2	1			
Morrison, Henry	1				

NAME OF HEAD OF FAMILY.	Free white males of 16 years and upward, including heads of families.	Free white males under 16 years.	Free white females, including heads of families.	All other free persons.	Slaves.
NOTTINGHAM					
Evans, Jno.	3	4	2		
Livingstone, Joseph	1	3	3		
Nellson, John	1	2	2		
Todd, John	3	1	3		
Morrison, John	1	6	5		
Mitchell, Robert	1	3	3		
James, Thomas	1	3	6		
PETERS					
Brice, Josiah	3	1	6		
Brice, James	1	1	2		
Welsh, James	1	2	4		
Crawford, Josiah	4	3	4		
Crawford, And°	2		3		
Hamilton, Danl	3		3		
Westty, Burrows, Jr	1	2	3		
Harbuckel, Joseph	2	2	5		
Huston, Daniel	2	1	2		
Hickby, Obadiah	2	3	3		
Mills, Benjamin	2	1	3		2
Harney, Nancy	2	1	3		
McBurney, James	2		2		
Gault, Adam	2	1	2		
Gault, Jno	2	1	5		
McNeal, Neal	2	2	5		
Rush, Caleb	1	2	4		
Clark, Jno	1	2	4		
Keykendall, Abm	1	3	2		
Dickson, Henry	1	1	2		
Henry, Robert	1	2	4		
Lusk, John	2	1	2		
Gailey, John	2	3	3		
Newill, William	1		3		
Begs, John	1		1		
Maloney, John	1	3	6		
Lusk, Robert	2		2		
Tweedle, Alex	1	3	6		
Hazen, Nathl	3	4	5		
Masters, Jno	1				
Masters, Richard	1	4	6		
Townshend, Daniel	2	1	6		
Bailey, Elias	1	3	1		
Leard, John	1	1	1		
Campbell, Edward	1	1	4		
Campbell, John	1	1	5		
Hamilton, Thos	1	3	5		
Magner, Henry	2	1	4		
McMullin, Wm	1		3		
McMullin, Jno	2	1	3		
Powers, Jno	2	5	3		
Polk, Thos	1	2	5		
Wilson, Obediah	1	1	4		
Sharp, Peter	1		2		
Anderson, Jno	2	2	4		
Huey, Revd Robert	2	2	4		
Thompson, William	4		7		
Long, Jacob, Senr	1		2		1
Green, Chas	1	1	3		
Mitchell, James, Esqr	1		4		
Dunlavey, Anthony	3		4		
White, Jno	1	1	2		
Breckenridge, John	1		3		
Newgen, James	1	2	2		
McCartney, James	1	2	3		
Coins, David	1	2	4		
Conger, Ishmael	1	1	2		
Watson, William	1	2	4		
Swearingen, Jno	3	3	5		4
Blackmore, Eberilla	1	4	4		3
Allison, Chas	1	3	3		
Boyer, Jas	1	1	2		
Crooks, Richd	2	1	2		
McLean, David	2	1	2		
Hemphill, James	1	2	3		
Richarson, Jonathan	1	2	3		
Phillips, Revd David	1	1	4		
Phillips, John	1	6	4		
Phillips, Benje	1	1	2		
Phillips, Wm	1		2		
Peate, Elizabeth	2		2		
Mackey, Andrew	1	2	2		
Coe, Moses	2	1	4		
Wynes, Abner	1	3	8		
Anderson, Samuel	2		2		
Beabout, John	2		2		
Beabout, Danl	1	3	4		
Morrison, William	3	4	3		
Sharp, James	3		6		
Reed, James	1		4		
Thomson, Saml	1	2	3		
Thomson, Hugh	1	3	1		
Lisle, Robert	1	3	1		
James, Valta	1				

NAME OF HEAD OF FAMILY.	Free white males of 16 years and upward, including heads of families.	Free white males under 16 years.	Free white females, including heads of families.	All other free persons.	Slaves.
PETERS					
Simson, Robert	1	1	3		
Armstrong, Willm	1	2	2		
Dickey, William	1	2	2		
Morrison, Francis	2	3	4		
Buchannon, James	2	2	7		
Turner, Jno	1	3	2		
Coulter, Nathl	1	1	3		
Anderson, James	1	1	3		
Long, Jacob, Junr	1	1	2		
Hughly, Edwd	1	2	4		
Moss, James	7	1	4		
Donaldson, David	1	1	2		
Allen, Oneas	3	4	2		
Gasten, John	3		3		
Gasten, William	1	1	4		
Wallace, Robert	1		3		
Wallace, Saml	1	2	2		
Estep, Robert	1	5	5		
Bartley, James	1	3	3		
Millenger, David	1	1	4		
Lovejoy, Jno F	1	2	3		
Magner, Edwd	3	2	3		
Bielor, Saml	3		5		
Dillen, Mathias	1	3	4		
Applegate, Obadiah	1	2	6		
Stephenson, Jno	1	2	4		
Gamble, Saml	1	1	3		
Blackburn, Jno	2	3	3		
Shuster, Phelty	1	2	2		
Boly, Anthony	2	1	3		
Bell, Robert	1	1	2		
Brynan, Peter	2	1	2		
Wilson, Thos	1	1	2		
Navson, Richard	1	4	2		
Patterson, Jas	1	1	5		
Macky, Jas	2		2		
Miller, Joseph	1		1		
ROBINSON					
McClurg, Jno	1	4	6		
McCandless, Elizabeth	3		3		
Johnston, William	1		1		
Singars, John	2	2	7		
Flenniken, William	1	3	2		
Wright, John	1	1	3		
Reed, John	2	1	3		
McCoy, James	4	3	2		
White, John	1	1	3		
Moore, Robert	1		4		
Tiddball, Abm	1		3		
Carlisle, Jno	2	3	4		
Scott, Thos	1	1	2		
Scott, Josiah	1	2	1		
Wright, Jno, Senr	1		3		
Scott, Jno	2	1	1		
Scott, Samuel	1	1	2		
Lytle, Epm	1	3	2		
Fullom, Benjamin	4	2	3		
Andrew, Moses	1	2	2		
Baily, Alexander	5		5		
Brown, Thos	1	1	5		
Shearer, Hugh	1	1	2		
Russel, William	1	2	4		
Bailey, Alexander, Jur	1	2	2		
Baily, William	1		2		
Dunlap, John	1	5	2		
Dunlap, Alexr	1	2	2		
Wright, Alexr	5	2	4		
Henry, Joseph	1	5	4		
Stewart, Daniel	2	2	6		
McBride, James	2	6	1		
Queen, Chas	1		6		
Queen, John	1		6		
White, Thos	1		1		1
Patterson, Revd Joseph	3	2	5		
Wilson, John	1	1	3		
Chamberlain, Mary			4		
Ryan, William	1	4	3		
Biggart, Thos	2	4	3		
Brown, William	1	1	4		
Swearingen, Danl	1	3	4		1
Cormichael, Jean			1		
Walker, Robert	1	1	3		
Matson, Isaac	1	1	4		
Kerr, Jas	1		2		
Wilson, Jno	1	2	3		
Whitesid, James	1	3	4		
McDonald, John	4	9	1		2
Clark, John	1	1	3		
Clark, James	1	1	2		
Howard, Samuel	1	1	2		
Wallace, Samuel	1	2	1		
Hunter, Samuel	1	2	2		

NAME OF HEAD OF FAMILY.	Free white males of 16 years and upward, including heads of families.	Free white males under 16 years.	Free white females, including heads of families.	All other free persons.	Slaves.
ROBINSON					
Kedd, Alexr, Senr	2		1		
Allen, John	3	1	1		
Kerty, John	2	1	6		
Holmes, Robert	1	1	1		
Criswell, James	2	3	4		
Dunlap, Jno	2		4		
McClean, Andw	1	1	3		
Marcus, Robert	2	2	4		
Thomson, William	3	1	6		
Thomson, Elizabeth	1		5		
Phillis, Joseph	1	4	3		
Phillis, Joseph, Senr	1		4		
Crooks, Robert	1	1	2		
Crooks, Thos	1	2	3		
Scott, Jno	1	4	1		
Hays, David	1	3	2		
White, Jno	1	1	2		
McAdams, Gilbert	2	3	4		
Smith, Jno	3	3	4		
Long, Jno S	3	5	4		
SMITH					
White, Moses	1	2	2		
Wallace, Robert	1		1		
White, Patrick	1		2		
Merchant, Samuel	1	2	4		
McElroy, James	2	1	2		
Marcus, Robert	1	1	2		
McCoy, Daniel	1	2	4		
McCoy, William	1	3	1		
Miller, James	1	1	2		
McGee, Robert	1	3	2		
McGee, William	1	2	1		
Montgomery, Hugh	1		1		
Merchant, James	1		1		
Oldham, Moses	1	1	2		
Pharo, Andrew	1	1	2		
Rogers, John	1	1	1		
Spiller, John	1	1	3		
Scott, Joseph	1	1	2		
Stone, John	1	2	2		
Strain, Samuel	1	2	3		
Hatfield, Edward	1	2	1		
Holmes, James	1	5	1		
Johnston, William	1	2	3		
Jackson, Benjamin	1	2	2		
Jackson, Phil	1	4	2		
Kennedy, Robert	1	2	2		
Kendesy, Jno	1	2	5		
Kimble, Nathan	1	2	2		
Lisle, Robert	1	2	2		
Lisle, John	1	3	2		
Moody, James					
McKebbans, Richard	1	2	2		
McCready, Alexander	1	2	3		
McDennough, Hugh	1	3	5		
Marks, Samuel	1	2	2		
McMullin, Alexr	1	1			
Coventry, Jno	1		1		
Campbell, James	1	2	2		
Cook, James	1	1	2		
Rogers, Thomas	1	1	2		
Cooper, Henry	1		2		
Cook, Jno	1		2		
Crawford, James	1	2	3		
Cooper, John	1	2	3		
Criswell James, Jur	1	2	4		
Day, Geo	1		2		
Dunbarr, Samuel	1	2	2		
Dunbarr, Robert	1	1	4		
Martin, Robert	1	2	3		
Lamb, John	1	2	2		
Meloney, Samuel	1				
Hillis, Matt	1		6		
Kedd, William	1		2		
Ravenscraft, James	2	2	7		
Ravenscraft, James, Jur	1		2		
Stewart, Joseph	1		3		
Rhea, James	1		4		
Smith, John	1	2	3		
Mahan, David	1	3	2		
Russell, Abm	1	3	2		
Dobbins, James	3	5	3		
Stearn, John	1	2	3		
Kedd, Alexr, Jur	1				
Hull, Rachel		3	4		
Boatman, William	1	2	3		
Duff, James	1	1	2		
Clouky, William	1		1		
Thomson, Samuel	1	3	2		
Marcus, Samuel	2		1		
Piles, Josh	2	3	2		

NAME OF HEAD OF FAMILY.	Free white males of 16 years and upward including heads of families.	Free white males under 16 years.	Free white females, including heads of families.	All other free persons.	Slaves.
SMITH					
McCarty, Jno.	1	2	7		
Guy, Henry	1	4	3		
Acheson, Humphray	2	2	4		
Henderson, John	1	1	1		
McKibbon, Richd.	1		1		
Thompson, Robert	3	1	5		
Acheson, Matthew	4	1	3		
Acheson, David	1	1	2		
Glass, Jno.	1	3	1		
Ross, Jno.	1	1	2		
Clark, Mary	1		2		
Colvin, James	1	2	3		
Patridge, Robert	1	1	3		
Martin, William	3	3	2		
Holland, Jno.	1	1	2		
Ross, James	1		3		
McGeehon, Duncan	1	2	4		
Freeman, Thomas	1		3		
Hays, Thos.	2	3	2		
Hays, Moses	1	2	2		
Hays, Joseph	1	2	2		
Hays, William	1	1	2		
Hays, Andw.	1	3	2		
Rankin, Henry	1	3	1		1
Montgomery, Hugh	1	1	3		
Hutcheson, John	1	3	2		
Welkey, William	2	1	1		
Gasken, James	1	1	2		
Smith, John, Jur.	1	2	3		
Leech, James	1	1	4		
Bowman, Robert	3		2		
Murphy, Cornelius	1		3		
Thompson, Benjamin	3		3		
McCandless, William	2	4	3		
Cherry, Mary	2	1	1		4
Cherry, Thos.	1	2	2		2
Smith, Christian	1		2		
McKibbans, Richd.	1	1	2		
Ranken, Thos.	1	2	2		1
Ranken, William	5		3		2
Link, Andrew	1		5		
Donaldson, John	2		3		
Stewart, David	1	2	1		
Stewart, George	1	4	3		
Cornal, Jno.	1	2	2		
Robb, Jno. Senr.	1	3	2		
Robb, Jno. Junr.	1		2		
Robb, William	1		3		
McVay, Edward	2	1	1		
Edgar, James, Esqr.	3	3	4		2
Wilkins, John	1	1	3		
Bays, Samuel	1	4	3		
Murphy, Peter	1	4	2		
McClurg, John	1	1	2		
Elder, Thos.	1		2		
Cook, James	1	1	2		
Cook, John	1	1	3		
Vance, Joseph	2	3	3		
Vance, Mary	1		2		
Little, J. Cooper	2	1	2		
Cooper, Henry, Senr.	1	2	4		
Burkett, Rosannah		4	4		
Burkett, Geo.	2		1		
Montgomery, James	3		1		
Montgomery, Humphrey		5	2		
Campbell, Arthur	2	2	4		
Newill, Hugh	1	4	3		
Cline, Michael	1	1	1		
Hutton, Alexr.	3		1		
Fullerton, Henry	1		1		
Low, Isaac	1	2	2		
Cooper, John, Senr.	1	2	2		
McKee, William, Senr.	1	2	2		
Dodd, John	1	3	2		
Stephenson, James	3	1	3		1
McBride, Alexr.	1		1		
Fitzpatrick, Jno.	3	2	3		
Moore, David	2	1	3		
Rankin, Mattw.	1	3	2		
Ross, James, Senr.	1		3		
Ross, Mary	1		3		
Farnsworth, Henry	2	3	5		
Leech, James, Senr.	4	1	5		
Dooland, Michael	2	1	4		
Wallace, William	2	2	3		
Coe, Peter	1	2	3		
Thompson, Saml.	1	2	2		
Thompson, Robert	1	1	3		
Vaugher, Richard	1	1	3		
Wilson, Samuel	3		3		
Long, Ellsl.	1	3	2		
Lemly, John	1	2	1		
Miller, James	1		1		

NAME OF HEAD OF FAMILY.	Free white males of 16 years and upward including heads of families.	Free white males under 16 years.	Free white females, including heads of families.	All other free persons.	Slaves.
SMITH					
Mickelroy, James	2		3		
Nangle, Andw. Sr.	1		2		
Wily, James	1	1	2		
Barr, Samuel	2		2		
Barr, Robert	2		1		
Thompson, David	1	1	2		
SOMERSET					
Speck, Jacob	1	2	7		
Carey, Luther	2	6	2		
Jennings, Hugh	1	3	1		
Campbell, Duncan	2		5		
Snider, Geo.	1	1	5		
Leanard, Coleb	2	3	1		
Leanard, William	1	1	4		
Leanard, Silas	1	2	1		
Leanard, Isaac	2	1	5		
Myers, John	1	1	2		
Tombough, George	2	2	4		
Clouse, Christopher	1	4	4		
Fry, Peter	3	2	3		
Winthorn, Geo.	1	2	2		
Burt, Ebenezar	1		2		
Black, Philip	2	2	1		
Carr, Mary	2		3		
Crossly, Thomas	1	2	3		
Dalcly, John	1	2	4		
Dawson, James	1	3	2		
Davis, Richard	1	1	2		
Eaton, James	1	2	3		
Forbes, John	1	2	4		
Glaze, Nathan	2	1	3		
Isaac, Geo.	1	3	4		
Lyda, Henry	1	2	2		
Morrow, John	2		1		
Morrow, David	1	1	2		
Morrow, Chas.	1	1	3		
McCelven, Jno.	1	2	4		
McMinn, William	2	1	3		
McDinnough, Henry	1		1		
McCain, James	1	3	1		
McNealy, Joseph	2	2	2		
Poker, Michael	1	3	4		
Snider, Abm.	1	3	4		
Smith, Andw.	1	1	3		
Speck, Anthy.	2	3	1		
Sparks, William	1	3	4		
Streat, Charles	1	3	2		
Tyce, Jno.	1	3	3		
Vance, Isaac	1	2	3		
Vance, Jno.	1	2	3		
Wood, Joseph	1	1	3		
Summers, Chas.	1	2	3		
Porter, William	2	1	1		
Blain, Wm.	1		1		
Elliott, Christopher	1		3		
Hoesick, Geo.	1	1	3		
Thompson, William	2	6	3		
McManus, James	3	2			
Smith, Martin	2	1	2		
McComb, Robert	2	1	2		
Vinneman, Andw.	2	1	6		
Cameron, James	1	6	1		
Vann, Jacob	1	6	3		
Wherry, James	1	2	5		
Diven, Leanard	1		3		
Bryson, Hugh	1	1	2		
Diven, Jacob	1		1		
Swazier, Jacob	1		1		
Scott, Patrick	1	1	4		
McCulloch, Patrick	4		3		
Huffman, Rudolph			2		
Huffman, David			2		
Wallace, James	1	1	6		
Crosser, Rebecca		8	1		
McComb, William	1		6		
Black, Peter	2	1	2		
Cockran, William	2		4		
Neely, Joseph	1	2	2		
Ramsay, Robert	3	3	2		
Ramsay, James	1		1		
Ramsay, Joseph	1		1		
Ramsay, Jno.	1	1	1		
Kintner, Andw.	1	2	4		
Kintner, Geo. Jur.	1	1	1		
Patterson, Peter	1	2	2		
Forbes, Hugh	1	1	4		
Smith, Andw.	1		4		
Scott, Catharine		2	5		
Forbes, Alexr.	1		1		
Forbes, Arthur	1	1	1		

NAME OF HEAD OF FAMILY.	Free white males of 16 years and upward including heads of families.	Free white males under 16 years.	Free white females, including heads of families.	All other free persons.	Slaves.
SOMERSET					
Redd, James	1	1	2		
Chapman, Jno.	1	1	5		
Chapman, William	1		5		
Hazell, Jno.	1	1	4		
Kinter, Geo. Senr.	1	1	2		
Onstole, Henry	1	4	1		
Shuster, Samuel	2	1	4		
Messinger, Daniel	2	3	1		
Lyda, Jno.	3	1	2		
Booher, Michael	1		2		
Rose, Isaac	1	4	2		
Booch, Margaret	4		2		
Booch, Jacob	1	2	5		
Greenlee, Jno.	1	3	2		
Lyda, James	1	3	3		
Ault, Frederick	1	1	3		
Decker, Catharine		3	1		
Shuster, Morgaret	1	1	3		
Ault, Frederick, Jur.	1		2		
Ault, Andrew	1		2		
Swickard, Daniel	1	2	1		
Myers, Michael	2	1	2		
Kintner, Adam	1		2		
Swickard, Martin	1	3	4		
Swickart, Daniel, Jur.	1		2		
Myers, Geo. Jur.	1		2		
Cregglebaugh, John	1	2	5		
Wilhelm, Geo.	2	1	2		
Mizner, Peter	1	4	1		
Myers, Geo. Senr.	1	4	4		
Study, Jno.	2	3	4		
Sarter, Peter	1	3	4		
Rooper, Phillip	2	4	5		
Preston, Barnett	1	4	1		
Johnston, Robert	1	5	1		
Means, Joseph	2		3		
Morrison, Robert	1	2	2		
Armstrong, Thos.	1	3	3		
Friend, Geo.	1	3	4		
McCulloch, Jno.	3	2	3		
McCurdy, Racheal			4		
Forward, Jacob	1	2	4		
Flowers, James	1	1	2		
Cox, Joseph	1		2		
Miller, Andrew	1	3	4		
Carrell, Hercules	1	1	3		
Smith, Adam	1	1	3		1
Wilson, Joseph	1	3	1		1
Jones, Levi	2	1	2		
Sock, Jacob	1	1	2		
Stevenson, Daniel	1	1	3		
Neblack, William	1	3	4		
Carrell, Daniel	1		4		
Burkhammer, Martin	1	1	4		
Shippens, Geo.	1	1	4		
Shimps, Geo.	1	1	4		
Wallace, Jno. Jur.	1	2	2		
Wallace, Jno.	2	4	2		
Mizner, Conrod	1	1	2		
Bradin, James	1	1	7		
Dawson, James	1	3	5		
Campbell, Rosannah	1	1			
Morrow, Chas.	2		3		
Miller, James		2	3		
Ferguson, Mary	2	2	3		
Fryer, Jno.	5		4		
McElvain, Geo.	1		2		
McElvain, Greer	1		2		
Barnett, Jno.	2	2	3		
Ault, Jacob	1	1	2		
Davis, Joshua	1	3	4		
McMillan, Geo.	1		3		
Cravin, Fanney	1	2	6		
Huffman, John	1	3	4		
McLory, Chas.	1	2	4		
Mortin, Edward	3	1	3		
Ammon, Jacob	2		2		
Ammon, Conrod	1	4	2		
Antt, Felty	2		4		
Hill, John	1	3	2		
Johnston, John	1		1		
Burt, Joseph	1	2	4		
Luchey, Robert	1	1	6		
Redd, Daniel	1	3	7		
Kelly, Francis	1		4		
Smith, David	1	2	2		
Stockton, John	1		2		
Mosser, Samuel	1		2		
Black, Geo.	1		1		
Bently, Shovbear	1	4	2		6
Pile, Amos	1	4	1		
Cook, Jeremiah	1	1	4		
Thompson, William	1	1	1		
Read, James	1	1	5		
Young, Daniel	1	2	4		

SOMERSET

Name of Head of Family	Free white males of 16 years and upward, including heads of families	Free white males under 16 years	Free white females, including heads of families	All other free persons	Slaves
Rolling, Henry	1	4	3		2
Laughlin, Matthew	2	2	4		2
Sheppard, Thomas	2	2	4		
Faulkner, Elizabeth	2		6		
Taylor, Robert	1	4	4		
Stillwell, Elias	1	2	4		
Lutz, Christian	1		4		
McCleary, Joseph	1	1	1		
Allman, Nezar	1		2		
Newkirk, Abm	1	1	2		
Newkirk, Isaac	2		2		
Newkirk, Henry	1	1	1		
Morton, Joseph	1		1		
Riggs, Jno	1	4	3		
Wallace (Widow)			4		6
Wallace, Nathl	1		4		
Wallace, William	1	2	5		5

STRABANE

Name of Head of Family	M 16+	M <16	Females	Other	Slaves
McCready, James	1	2	3		
Bradford, James	1	1	5		
Montgomery, Jno	2		3		
Bradford, Jean	2		3		
Riddle, David	2	1	4		
Hughes, James	2	4	6		1
McDowell, John	2	1	3		
Steen, Mattw	1	3			
Laughlin, William	1	2	6		
McComb, David	1	2	4		
Sutherland, Jno	2	2	6		
Johnston, Wm	3	4	5		
Campbell, Wm	2		1		
Young, Robert	2	1	1		
Linn, James	1	2			
Merrick, Daniel	1	2	2		
Wright, John	1		1		
Purse, James	1	2	5		
McWhister, Moses	3		3		
McGlumphey, John	2	1			
Peas, Andrew	1		1		
McDowell, James	1	2	4		
Hannah, James	1	4	1		
Herring, James	1	3	1		
McNaisy, Thos		2			
Moore, James		2	1		
Dehaven, Edward	4	1	1		
Jordan, William	4		4		
Thompson, William	2	5	4		
Anderson, Robert	1	4	2		
Peas, Nicholas	2	1	4		
Barnett, Ezekiel	3	5	6		
Scott, James	1		5		
Vinneman, George	3	5	2		
Vinneman (Widow)	1		2		
McClean, James	1	1	4		
Leiper, Samuel	2		4		
McClean, Jno	3		4		
Blakney, James	1	2	6		
Scott, Wm	1	1	3		
McDowell, John	1	3	3		
Lucky, Andrew	1		5		
Adams, William	1	2	4		
Simpson, James	1	2	3		
Gillmore, James	1	5	2		
Hindman, James	1	2	2		
Reed, William	2	2	5		
Shannon, Arthur	3		4		
McMullin, Revd John	3	3			
Dickson, Thos	1		4		
Wallace (Widow)	2				
Bowman, John	1	1	3		
Gilliland, William	2	5	5		
Burdoe, Nathaniel	1	2	5		
Ewings, James	1	1	2		
McClure, Andrew	1	4			
McDowell, Agnes			6		
Early, Thos	1	1	6		
Wiley, William	3	1	7		
McDonald, John	1	2	6		
Haynes, Josiah	1	2	6		1
Ryan, Andrew	2	1	3		
Wiers, William	2	2	4		
Gibson, William	1	2	3		
Riddle, Joseph	2	3	2		
Montgomery, William	1	2	4		
McComb, George	1	2	3		
Taylor, Henry, Esqr	1	6			
Watt, Jno	1		5		
Scott, Josiah	4	5	4		
Seaman, William	1	3	3		
Clark, Aron	1	3	1		
Seaman, Joseph	1		3		
Hunt, Aron	1		3		

STRABANE

Name of Head of Family	M 16+	M <16	Females	Other	Slaves
Richmond, John	1	1	1		
Titton, John	1	1	5		1
Gusea, Benjamin	3		5		2
Toland, John	1	1	2		
Campbell, Daniel	1	3	2		
Offard, Hugh	1	1	2		
Riddle, Samuel	1		1	2	
Gordon, George	1	4	2		
McClean, Hugh	1			2	
Little, Nicholas	4	1	4		
Little, John	1	1	1		
Curry, John	1	1	5		
Hawthorn, William	1	1	3		
Cotton, John	1	1	5		
Cotton, Hugh	2	1	4		
Cotton, William	1	1	2		
Millegan, James	1	1	2		
Workman, James	2	1	7		
Steel, James					
Huston, William	4	1	4		
Shively, Jacob, Jur	3	1	1		
Anstote, Nicholas	1		2		
Steward, John	1	2	2		
Madman, James	1	5	1		
Meetkop, Veach	1	3	4		
Martin, Jno	1	3	4		
Urie, Jno	1	2	3		
Greenlee, Archibald	1	2	3		
King, Jno	1	3	2		
Brown, James	2	3	3		
McKee, Andrew	1	4	3		
Patterson, Arthur	2	5	4		
King, Samuel	2	2	3		
Young, James	2	2			
Mercer, William	2	4	2		
Mercer, Jno	1		1		
White, Geo	1	1	2		
White, Nathl	1	2	2		
White, Jno, Senr	3	1	2		
White, Samuel	2	1	3		
White, James	1		1		
White, Patterson	1		3		
McKitrick, Jno	1	3			
Norris, Matthew	1	1	6		
Norris, William	1	1	3		
Kelly, William	1	3	4		
Davis, Thomas	2		2		
Holmes, Henry	1	1	5		
Silex, Samuel	1	5	4		
Smith, Ludwick	1	3	5		
Kerr, Thos	2		2		
Biggan, Hugh	3	3	4		
McMurdie, James	2	1	2		
McBratney, Robert	1		4		
Mundle, Jno	1	5	3		
Docke, Robert	2	1	2		
Lock, Mary			3		
Hogshead, Jno	1	2	3		
Black, Robert	3	2	4		
Darby, Patrick	1	4	1		
Dickenson, Joshua	2	3	4		
Martin, Joseph	1		—		
Feely, Thomas	1	2	5		
Dill, Thomas	1		2		
McEwin, Thos	2	1	4		
Mays, Thos	1	2	3		
Shannon, Robert	1	2	4		
Fryer, Leanard	3		1		
McMillan, Samuel	1	2	3		
McDowell, Agnes		2	4		
Chambers, James	3	2			
Clemmens, Nicholas	1	1	3		
Fitts, Wm	2		4		
Lewis, John	2	2	3		
Sittsker, David	1		3		
Parramore, Jno, Ser	1	1	3		
Parramore, Jno, Jur	1	3			
Parramore, Nathl	1	5	1		
Ralph, Thos	1		2		
King, Ralph	1		2		
Kinney, Wm	1	3	2		
Simpson, Alexander	1	2	2		
Melony, Jno	1	2	4		
Flnk, Gasper	2		2		
Hamilton, Thos	3	1	4		
Sutherland, George	1	2	2		
McConneney, Jno	2	2	7		
Bucchannon, James	1				
Hamilton, Robert	1		1		
Hamilton, David	3	4			
Ronsy, James	1		2		
Mercer, Robert	1		4		
Johnston, Abm	1	2			

STRABANE

Name of Head of Family	M 16+	M <16	Females	Other	Slaves
Parramore, Thos	4	2	7		
Parramore, Jonathan	1	1	1		
Ralph, Samuel	1		1		
Rankin, Thos	4		2		
McDowell, Jno	4	3	2		
Westley, Burrows	1	4	2		
Spivey, Jno	3	4	4		
McDonald, James	2	1	3		
Penticost, Dorsey	2	1	3	5	1
Orr, William	2		5	1	
Kerr, Jno	3	1	1		
Kerr, James	5	1	4	1	2
Edgington, Jesse	2	1	4		
Bowers, Robert	1	1	2		
Ferguson, Henry	3	4	2		
Holmes, Francis	2	1	4		
Crouch, Robert	1	3	6		
Betts, Michail	2		2		
Ingles, Jno, Senr	2		2		
Stephens, Jehu	1	2	3		
Miller, David	2	2	2		
Vann, Jno	3	2	4		
Erth, Lonard	3	3	2		
Gillespie, Geo	3	3	2		
Hazlett, John	2		2		
Campbell, Joseph	5		2		
Forbes, Hugh	1	2	3		
Jolly, James	2		4		
Blackmore, Nathl	2	3	2		
Murdock, Jno	2	1	2		1
Rankin, Jno	4	1	2		

CANTON (formed 1791) from STRABANE

Name of Head of Family	M 16+	M <16	Females	Other	Slaves
Cravin, James	1	3	5		
Woodard, Thos	1		1		
Roberts, Nancy		1	2		
Carter, Daniel	1		3		
McComb, William	2	3	5		
Clark, Joseph	1	1	6		
Bass, Edward	1	1	2		
Carrol, Edward	1		2		
Ridgeway, James	3		2		
Brownlle, John	1	2	5		
Scott, Arthur	1		2		
Ralstone, James	1	2	2		
Martin, Joshua	1	3	4		
Mitchell, Mary		2	2		
Runnion, Abner	1	1	3		
Young, James	1	1	1		
Markland, Mattw	1	1	3		
McPherson, Alex	2	1	1		
Leet, Danl	1	1	2		
Seams, Jabis	1		2		
Shively, Jacob	1	3	2		
McKibbon, James	1		2		
Stoner, Jacob	2		6		
Polk, Samuel	2	1	9		
Sherrard, William	2		9		
Nichols, Thomas	1	2	2		
McQuiston, Jno	1		2		
Huston, Jno	2		3		
Huston, James	1	3	7		
Dickey, Samuel	1	3	4		
Nichols, Andw	1	3	4		
McCleary, George	1		2		
Clark, Samuel	3		2		
Wilson, Thos	4	4	2		
Ferguson, Jno	3	1	2		
McGowan, Jno	1	1	2		
Hannah, Samuel	1		2		
Porter, Joseph	1		4		
Brice, James	1	3	4		
Howlett, James	1	2	4		
Ralstone, Jno	1	1	4		
McGowen, William	1	3	4		
McGowen, Robert	1	1	3		
Slamkin, William	1	1	3		
Bell, Robert	1	1	3		
Ralstone, James	1		2		
Johnston, William	2		1		
Johnston, John	1		1		
Wiley, Robert	1	1	5		
Watt, Joseph	1		2		
McGarvay, Francis	2	1	3		
Aclin, Joseph			2		
Huggins, Edwd					1
Wilson, Jno	3	2	3		
Kerr, Danl	1		2		
Kerr, Mary		2	1		

STRABANE (CANTON)

NAME OF HEAD OF FAMILY.	Free white males of 16 years and upward, including heads of families.	Free white males under 16 years.	Free white females, including heads of families.	All other free persons.	Slaves.
Faugher, Jno	1	2	2		
McConkey, James	2	5	2		
Richmond, John, Senr	2	5	5		
Snowden, Jos	3		2		
Snowden, William	1		2		
Snowden, David	1	3	2		
Simpson, James	1	2	2		
Trueax, David	1	2	2		
Alexander, William	1		3		
Hainey, Matt	2	2	4		
Alexander, Hector	2	2	4		
Wolf, Jno	1	5	5		
Mavis, Henry	2		3		
Mavis, George	2	1	4		
Clendennan, John	1	3	6		
Clark, David	1	2	4		
Irvine, David	4	2	5		
Ross, James, Esqr	2				1
Miller, Alexander	2	3	1		
Falconer, Wm	7	1	4		
Brown, James	1		4		
Jolly, Elisha	1	1	2		
Runnion, Stephen	1	3	4		
Miller, Thomas	4	2	4		
Reed, Samuel	1		2		
Baird, John	2	3	3		
Gliff, Patk	1	1	2		
Gabby, James	1	2	5		
Wilson, James	1	3	5		
Braddock, Jno	1	2	7		
Dickeson, Richard	1		4		
Templeton, Jno	2	3	4		
Been, Jno	1	1	4		
Hart, Jesse	4	1	3		
McCarmick, George	2	3	5		
Coe, Philip	1	2	2		
Hainey, William	2	2	5		
Leet, William	1	1	3		
Dinnen, Jno	2		2		

STRABANE (CANTON)

NAME OF HEAD OF FAMILY.	Free white males of 16 years and upward, including heads of families.	Free white males under 16 years.	Free white females, including heads of families.	All other free persons.	Slaves.
Dye, Enoch	2	2	7		
Smith, Jno	4		2		
Osburn, Joseph	1		2		
Leet, Isaac	3	1	2		
Mashman, Jno	1	3	1		
Forbes, William	1	2	2		
Forbes, William, Junr	1	1	2		
McCullouch, William	1	1	8		
Knox, Robert	1		1		
Leaman, Jno	1	1	3		
Lattimore, James	1	2	2		
Browlee, James	1	3	6		
Sherrard, Leanard	1	5	5		
Wylie, Hugh	1		1	1	
Stogdale, Robert	3	2	3		
Moore, Jno	3	4	3		
Brownlee, Wm	1	5	7		
Anderson, Joshua	3	2	7		
Cunningham, Robert	1		1		
Cunningham, James	2	1	5		
McConnel, James	1	1	5		
Early, William	1	1	7		
Hamilton, Robert	1	2	3		
Moody, Peter	1	2	3		
Baird, Absalom	2	4	3		
Slatten, Samuel	1	2	2		

STRABANE (WASHINGTON TOWN)

NAME OF HEAD OF FAMILY.	Free white males of 16 years and upward, including heads of families.	Free white males under 16 years.	Free white females, including heads of families.	All other free persons.	Slaves.
Blackmore, Sarah	1		3		1
Lyttle, Alex	1	1	4		
McMichael, Jno	2	1	2		
Hughes, Jno		5	1		
Black, Samuel	3		1		
Boyer, Leanard	2	1	2		
Brynard, Bernard	1		5		
McNaught, Elizabeth			3		
Valentine, Chas	1	1	3		

STRABANE (WASHINGTON TOWN)

NAME OF HEAD OF FAMILY.	Free white males of 16 years and upward, including heads of families.	Free white males under 16 years.	Free white females, including heads of families.	All other free persons.	Slaves.
Cunningham, Alexander	1	2	1	1	
Scott, Thos, Esqr	3	4	10	2	2
Redick, Jno	1	4	2		
Purviance, Jno	3	6	2		
Blakney, Gabriel	2	1	2		
Beer, Alexr	3	1	2		
Reddick, David, Esqr	1	2	3		1
Wilson, James	1	2	4		
Husti k, Jno	1	1	1		
Kerr, Wm	1	2	3		
Stewart, Samuel	1	2	3		
Chambers, James	1	1	3		
Redick, Sarah			3		
Hoge, Jno, Esqr	2	1	2	1	
Workman, Hugh	5		2		
Baird, Samuel	2	2	4		
Shannon, Samuel	2	3	8		
Bradford, David, Esqr	3	1	4		2
Wilson, Hugh	3	1	4	2	
Acheson, John	4		3		
Acklen, Samuel	1	2	4		
Swearingen, Andw	2	2	5		1
Marshal, James, Esqr	2	2	5		
Mutkirk, William	1	1	4		
Dodd, John	4	3	3		1
Addison, Alexander, Esqr	1		3		
Marshal, William	2	4	3		
Jefferys, Thos	1	1	1		
Willson, Jas, Jur	1	1	4		
Moreland, George	1	1	2		
McCandless, Robert	1		1		
Clark, Samuel	3	2	2	1	
Means, Hugh	5	4	3		
Stokely, Thos	1		3		
McGowen, Thos	2				
Morris, Robert	1		1		
Blaqueath, Cyrus	2		3		
Moody, Daniel	2	2	4		
McCully, Patrick	1	4	1		

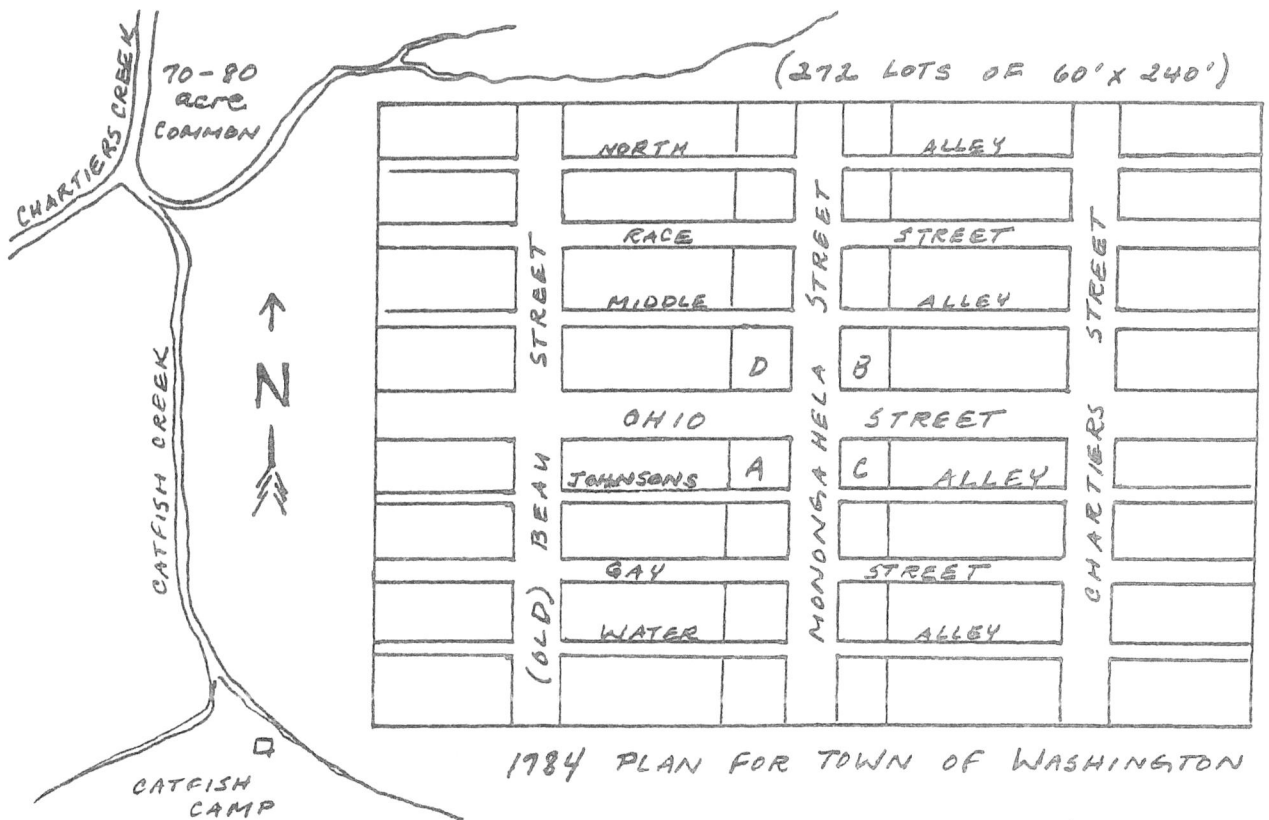

1784 PLAN FOR TOWN OF WASHINGTON

KKZ 1988

CUMBERLAND

NAME OF HEAD OF FAMILY	Free white males of 16 years and upward, including heads of families	Free white males under 16 years	Free white females, including heads of families	All other free persons	Slaves
Allen, Moses	1		2		
Anderson, Chandler	3	1	1		
Anderson, Charles	1	2	1		
Anderson, Daniel	2	1	2		
Anderson, James	1	1			
Anderson, Richard	1		2		
Armstrong, John	2	5	2		
Armstrong, Abm	1	4	6		
Adamson, Joseph	3	1	3		
Adamson, James	1	1	1		
Allison, James	1	6	3		
Argo, William	1				
Adamson, John	3	1	4		
Boardman, Robert	1		1		
Reessen, Aron	1		1		
Ball, Joseph	1	3	4		
Beedle, Everard	1		3		
Boner, William	1	3	3		
Brown, John	1	4	3		
Barns, Job	1	1	3		
Blacklidge, Margaret	5	1	2		
Boreman, Jno	1	1	2		
Blacklidge, Enoch	1	2	3		
Bowman, John	1	1	2		
Brown, Thos	1		3		
Blaney, Jacob	1	4	4		
Blair, James	1	4	1		
Bailey, Elexious	2	1	5		
Bussin, Edward	1	5	2		
Booze, Henry	1		3		
Buskirk, Samuel	1		3		
Buskirk, George	1	1	1		
Broockover, John	1	2	1		
Brooks, Joseph	1		1		
Brant, Joseph	1		2		
Clark, Elizabeth		3	1		
Carter, Richard	1	4	4		
Cline, Jacob	4	2	3		1
Cree, Wm	1		5		
Crossly, Robert	1	1	1		
Cox, Geo	1	1	2		
Crawford, William	2	1	6		1
Crawford, John	2	7	3		
Crawford, Oliver	2	1	5		
Coons, Michael	2	6	7		
Cockran, Alex	1	1	3		
Carmichael, James	2	1	3		3
Cree, Robert	1		3		
Cree, Robert, Jur	1		4		
Cree, James	1	1	2		
Cain, John	1	1	3		
Carter, Joseph	2	1	2		
Cragoe, Thos	1	3	4		
Curtis, Robert	1	1	4		
Carter, Thos	1	3	3		
Catchem, Phillip	1	1	2		
Crago, James	1	1	1		
Crago, Robert	1	2	2		
Clawson, Jno	1	1	2		
Simmons, James	1		2		
Conner, John	1				
Eaton, William	1	1	4		
Carns, James	1		1		
Davis, John	1	2	4		
Davis, Azariah	1	3	4		
Davis, Stephen	3		2		
Dunn, Isaac	1	2	4		
Dickison, Jesse	1	1	2		
Dalrimple, Joseph	1	2	5		
Davidson, William	1	2	2		
Davis, William	1	9	2		
Dollison, William	1		3		
Eagan, James	1	1	2		
Eagan, Barnett	1	2	2		
Estall, Daniel	1	2	7		
Estall, Silas	1	1			
Eastwood, Joseph	1				
Fordyce, Samuel	2	2	2		
Fox, Peter	1				
Flannegen, James	3	2	4		1
Flannegen, John	2	2	4		
Flannegan, Elias	1	3	5		
Fordyce, James	1	1	2		
Finley, Alexander	1		1		
Gwyn, Joseph	1	2	1		
Green, John	1		1		
Gately, Thos	1		1		
Grigg, Geo	1	2	2		
Grigg, Richd	1	3	1		
Gillespy, Henry	1		1		
Garwood, Median	2	1	7		
Grary, Joel	1	3	4		
Gardner, James	1	1	2		
Kentner, William	1	3	5		
Holden, Jno	1	3	2		

CUMBERLAND

NAME OF HEAD OF FAMILY	Free white males of 16 years and upward, including heads of families	Free white males under 16 years	Free white females, including heads of families	All other free persons	Slaves
Hibbs, Aron	1	3	2		
Hibbs, Lacy	1	1	1		
Harden, Savil	1	2	2		
Harboug, Thos	1	3	4		
Hickman, Robert	1	1	3		
Haynes, Aron	1	1	2		
Heaton, John	1		1		
Hannah, Francis	1	2	3		
Hartman, Adam	1	6	3		
Hoge, Solomon	1	2	6		
Holley, Samuel	1	1	2		
Hughes, James	4	2	5		2
Hughes, James (Black Smith)	2		7		
Hughes, Thomas	2	2	5		3
Holton, Jno	2	3	4		
Hale, William	3	1	3		
Henderson, James	1	1	5		
Herrod, William	2	1	4		
Heaton, Isaac	2	4	3		
Hill, Jno	1	1			
Hartman, Geo	1		1		
Hannah, James	2		1		
Hiller, William	1	1	4		
Ingledue, Thomas	1	2	3		
Ingram, Elijah	1	2	5		
Irael, Isaac	1	4	2		
Johnston, Cornelius	1	2	2		
Johnston, Nicholas	1	2	1		
Johnston, John	1	6	1		
Jamison, Alexander	3		6		
Jackson, Samuel	1	1	3		
Jonas, John	1	2	3		
Jones, Michael	1	2	3		
Johnston, Hugh	1	3	1		
Knight, John	1		1		
Kelly, Robert	1		5		
Kerby, Joseph	1	3	2		
Kerby, Richard	1	1	2		
Leanard, Lott	1	1	7		
Livingood, Peter	1	1	2		
Lewis, Andrew	3		4		
Lewis, Robert	1		2		
Linsay, Jacob	1	1	5		
Lewis, John	1		2		
Lemon, Benjamin	1	3	4		
Lowry, Josiah	1	2	1		
Longacre, Daniel	1	1	1		
Luzader, Abraham	1	1	3		
Little, Michael	1	5	2		
Lockey, Hugh	1	1	2		
Morrow, Charles	2	1	3		
McLeland, Andrew	3	1	4		
McLeland, Andrew, Jur	1		2		
McLeland, Robert	1	1	3		
McLeland, Robert, Jur	1	1	3		
Morris, Ezekiel	2	3	7		
Morris, Robert	3	1	2		
Maratta, Jas	1	2	2		
Myers, Peter	2	3	2		
Martin, Thomas	1	1	2		
Masters, Moses	1	1	4		
McElroy, William	1	1	1		
McCartney, Michael	1	1	2		
McElroy, Jno	1	2	2		
Moore, Jno	1	3	4		
Moore, Saml	1	1	5		
Moore, William	1	1	2		
Mustards, Wm	1	4	2		
McDowell, Wm	2	1	3		
Murdock, James	3	5	4		
Murdock, Daniel	1		6		
McLeland, James	1	1	2		
Myers, George	2	1	4		
Martin, Patrick	1	2	2		
Murdock, Danl, Jur	1	2	1		
Manning, John	1	2	2		
Maxer, William	1	2	4		
McClean, Abm	1	1	4		
Miller, Mattw	1	1	1		
Moore, Ezekiel	1	1	2		
McKean, Robert	1	2	3		
McCoy, George	1	2	1		
Moore, John	1	5	11		
McLughlin, Ann		1	3		
McGomery, Wm	1	1			
Mills, Amos	2		3		
Morrison, Jane	1	2	3		
Nevitt, Philip	2	2	4		
Newland, George	1	2	4		
Newland, Richard	1	2	2		
Newland, Jno	1	2	2		
Nichols, John	1	1	2		
Nichols, Richard	1	2	4		

CUMBERLAND

NAME OF HEAD OF FAMILY	Free white males of 16 years and upward, including heads of families	Free white males under 16 years	Free white females, including heads of families	All other free persons	Slaves
Prior, Timothy	1	2	3		
Prior, John	1	2	3		
Porter, Robert	2	4	2		
Pugh, William	1		5		
Pigman, Jesse	1	1	2		
Pribble, Thomas	1	1	2		
Pribble, Thos, Jur	1	1	1		
Pribble, Job	1	1	1		
Pribble, Rueben	1	3	4		
Prior, Isaac	1	2	2		
Purtee, John	1	2	2		
Perone, Obadiah	1	5	3		
Perkins, William	1	3	2		
Parker, James	2	1	3		
Prior, Nathan	1	2	3		
Plummer, Elisha	1	2	2		
Quintain, Isaac	1	1	2		
Roseburry, Mathias	2		1		
Anderson, Daniel	1	2			
Moore, Pat	1	1	2		
Morris, John	1	2	3		
Wright, Lucy			3		
White, Rachael			3		
Whitlactch, Thomas	1	1	2		
Whitlatch, Chas	2		2		
Wood, Danl	2	1	2		
Newland, John	1	1	2		
Vensicle, Saml	1	1	3		
Rose, John	1	2	1		
Pipanges, John	1		2		
Riley, James	2	1	4		
Rude, Andw	1	1	3		
Reese, Jno	1		2		
Reese, Jno	1		1		
Roberts, Edward	2	1	2		
Randell, David	3	4	4		
Roach, Thos	1	3			1
Rose, Ezekiel	1	2	2		
Johnston, John	4	1	2		
Reinhart, Joseph	1	1	4		
Ramsay, Chas	1	3	5		
Roseberry, Chas	1	1	2		
Rockhold, Charles	1		2		
Reed, Joseph	1		2		
Rush, Jesse	1	1	2		
Ruggles, James	1	2	3		
Stiles, Stephen	1	2	3		
Simonton, John	2	1	3		
Stewart, James	2	1	3		
Stewart, Daniel	2	1	2		
Smith, Noah	1	5	2		
Sears, Josiah	1	2	2		
Seaton, James	1	4	4		1
Seaton, Francis	1	4	2		
Seaton, Elizabeth			2		5
Swan, John	1	1	5		6
Swan, Charles	1	4	5		
Swan, Richd	1	2	2		
Swan, William	1	2	2		
Sedgwick, Thos	2	4	2		
Strawn, Jacob	1	3	6		
Strode, Samuel	1	3	7		
Strawn, John	1	8	7		
Scratchfield, William	1	2	3		
Scarfield, Absalom	1	2	3		
Scratchfield, Arthur	1	2	2		
Shepherd, William	1	6	4		
Stevenson, William	1	2	3		
Stephenson, Hugh	3	2	3		
Scott, Abm	1	4			
Smith, Jacob	1	5	4		
Smith, Benja	1	3	5		
Stewart, John	1	3	1		
Santee, George	1	3	4		
Shelby, Evan	1	1	1		
Stiles, William	1		1		
Spencer, John	1	3	1		
Edwards, Thos	1	3	3		
Thoroughman, Wm	1	1	3		
Thoroughman, Saml	1	1	2		
Thoroughman, Thomas	1		3		
Teagarden, Geo	1	8	3		
Aikens, Gabriel	1		1		
Barns, Zachariah	1	1	1		
Blackstad, William	1				
Bowman, Benjamin			2		
Clevinger, Isaiah	1		1		
Driver, John	1	1	1		
Dunn, Samuel	1		1		
Evans, David	1	1	1		
Foster, John	3	1	1		
Gregg, Levi	1		2		
Heerdman, Abel	1		1		
Hull, Nathl	1	1	1		
Hill, Saml	1	2			

CUMBERLAND

Name of Head of Family	Free white males of 16 years and upward, including heads of families	Free white males under 16 years	Free white females, including heads of families	All other free persons	Slaves
Thomas, Saml	1	3	3		
Thomas, Ellis	2	2	2		
Tomlinson, John	1	2	5		
Tater, John	1	1	2		
Lewis, David	1	1	2		
Leeman, James	1	1			
McLeland, John	1	1	1		
Masters, Henry	1	1	2		
Varts, Francis	1	2	6		
Veal, David	1	2	4		
Vetch, Nathan	1	2	4		
Villars, John	1	2	7		
Vanmetre, Henry, Esqr	2	3	6		
Vanmetre, Joseph	1	4	4		
Vanmetre, Jesse	1	1	3		
Vanmetre, Absalom			3	4	
Vanderoen, Hezekiah	1	1	4		
Valentine, Amos	1	1	1		
Vinsicle, Zachariah	1	1	4		
Wise, Thomas	1	1	3		
Whitelatch, William	1	1	3		
Wood, Benjamin	2	3	5		
Wright, Benjamin	2	1	2		
Wootham, Shem	1	1	1		
Williams, George	3	2	1		
Wells, William	1	4	3		
Wright, Thomas	1	1	3		
Wootham, Peter	2	6	2		
McIntosh, John	1	1	1		
Miller, James	1		1		
McCann, John	1	2	1		

FRANKLIN

Name of Head of Family	Free white males of 16 years and upward, including heads of families	Free white males under 16 years	Free white females, including heads of families	All other free persons	Slaves
Sellars, Christian	1	3	5		
Slater, Thos	2	2	5		
Stewart, Hezekiah	1	2	3		
Scott, Jno	1	2	3		
White, David	2	3	4		
Bowers, Rachel		2	2		
Hickman, William	1	1	2		
Adkins, Chas	2	1	2		
Stien, Alex	1	4	4		
Mirandy, Samuel	1	3	2		
Sellars, Leanard	1	2	2		
Gooden, Thos	1		1		
Morris, Caleb	1	2	1		
Huffman, George	1	2	2		
Markens, Samuel	1	1	2		
Love, Leanard	1	2	3		
Sellars, John	1	2	2		
Deval, Daniel	1	4	4		
Pratt, Jno	2	2	1		
Lewis, Robert	1	4	3		
Freeland, James	1	2	3		
Sayers, William	2	3	1		
Kerge, Geo		2	1		
Dillon, Peter	2		2		
Eaton, Thos	1		1		
Maple, William	1	2	1		
Davis, James	2	2	2		
Archer, Jacob	1		2		
Leakins, Joseph	1		4		
Leakins, Samuel	1	4	2		
Aldridge, Jno	1	1	1		
Hayns, Daniel	1	3	3		
Cummins, Andrew	1	2	3		
Wood, Jno	1	4	3		
Kent, Thos	1	4	2		
White, Solomon	1	2	2		
Peckenpough, Geo	2	2	2		
Ross, Reuben	1	1	1		
Cowen, William	2	4	4		
Raper, Leanard	1	3	2		
Vanasdale, Cornelius	1	1	2		
Craig, John	1	3	1		
Morris, Archibald	1	3	2		
Wells, Thomas	1	3	5		
Potter, Jno	2	6	5		
Fee, Thos	1	4	3		
Fee, Thos, Jur	1	2	1		
Fee, William	1	1	1		
Ingram, Arthur	1	4	4		
Ingram, William	1	3	4		
Bryan, Jno	2	2	4		
Carrol, Geo	1	2	4		
Carrol, William	1	4	2		
Simmerman, Abm	1	1	1		
Archer, Elizabeth	1	1	2		
Grogan, Lawrence	1	2	3		
Barker, Abm	1	3	3		
Parker, Jno	1	3	1		
Ankrim, Mathw	1	3	4		
Gordin, Jno	1	4	4		
Hughes, Nathl	1	4	4		
Knight, David	2	4	5		
Ankrim, Richd	1	2	2		
McCoy, William	1	1	3		
Brown, Mary		1	3		
Devall, Jno	1	3	4		
Devall, Leanard	1		1		
Devall, Danl	1	1	2		
Bradford, Robert	1	2	3		
Knotts, Ann		3	4		
Dolson, Alex	1	2	2		
Devall, Conrod	1	3	2		
Levingood, Peter	1	3	2		
Sellars, Geo	1	3	4		
Dally, Peter	1	3	4		
Hathaway, Samuel	2	3	3		
Hathaway, William	2	6	3		
Rhinehart, Thos	1	5	3		
Rhinehart, Thos, Senr	1	5	2		
Delany, William	1		2		
Rhinehart, Bernard	1	4	2		
Rhinehart, Sarah		2	3		
Smith, Thomas	2	8	3		
Smith, Jno	1	4	4		
Smelly, Jacob	1	2	2		
Seals, James	1		5		
Gorral, Robert	1	5	5		
Gray, David	1	6	4		
Gray, Jno	2	2	1		
Archer, James	2	4	5		
Archer, Joseph	1	3	3		
Whealy, Jno	2	4	2		
Whealy, Jno, Jur	3	8	5		
Whealy, Elijah	1	2	2		
Loss, Moses	1	1	2		

GREENE

Name of Head of Family	Free white males of 16 years and upward, including heads of families	Free white males under 16 years	Free white females, including heads of families	All other free persons	Slaves
Alley, John	1	2	2		
Asher, Anthony	1	2	5		
Anders, John	1	2	3		
Badcock, Andw	2	2	4		
Belshas, James	2	3	4		
Burtnett, Adam	2	2	4		
Baker, Roger	1	1	4		
Brown, Andrew	2	3	6		
Blake, Nicholas	1	3	3		
Baker, Nicholas	2	3	5		
Brown, Thomas	1	4	3		
Burns, Michael	1	4	5		
Burt, William	1	2	3		
Bowers, John	1	2	3		
Bowers, Jacob	1	3	3		
Bradford, John	1	3	3		
Bradford, James	1	3	3		
Boyistons, Geo	1	2	3		
Boyistone, David	1	2	4		
Boyis, William	1	1	2		
Brittain, Jane		2	4		
Breckin, William	2	4	3		
Bushill, Barbara		2	3		
Baldwin, John	1		1		
Comston, John	1	5	3		
Cannon, Richd	1	5	5		
Callwell, William	1	2	4		
Kimble, Leanard	1	3	2		
Curby, Elizabeth		3	2		
Cain, Edmund	1	2	4		
Callwell, Elverton	1	2	6		
Campbell, Obadiah	1	5	3		
Corbley, The Revd Jno	1	1	5		
Crawford, Alexr	1	2	6		
Colvin, Geo	1	1	4		
Chaffin, William	1		1		
Chaffin, John	1	3	4		
Campbell, Dugal		3	4		
Clegg, Alexr	1	1	1		
Clevinger, Zachariah	1	3	6		
Davis, Jonathan	1	3	4		
Drake, Joseph	1	1	3		
Douglass, Thomas	1	1	3		
Douglass, Timothy	1	2	3		
Dougherty, James	1	3	2		
Davis, Ignatious	1	3	2		
Dougherty, Elizabeth		1	2		
David, Henry	1	1	4		
Davis, Benjamin	1	2	4		
Dimond, Daniel	1	1	2		
Dye, James	1	1	2		
Dye, Andrew	1	4	4		
Dye, Eliz	1	1	1		
Dawson, Alexr	1	1	6		
Dobbins, John	1	2	2		
Delinges, Augustine	1	3	2		
Dixon, Stophel	1	2	2		
Derrough, Henry	1	2	5		
Davis, John	1	2	2		
Evans, David	1	2	2		
Edwards, Thomas	1	2	1		
Edwards, Samuel	1	1	2		
Evans, James	1	1	2		
Eddy, John	1	2	6		
Eddy, Isaac	1	2	2		
Rogers, William	1	1	3		
Irvine, William	1	2	1		
Irvine, Richd	1		2		
Evans, John		1	4		
Evans, Jesse	1	1			
Enoch, Catharine			2		
Enoch, John, Senr	1	2	2		
Flowers, David	1	5	6		
Flowers, Thos	1	2	5		
Flowers, Aron	2	2	4		
Fos, John	1	2	4		
Freeland, Robert	1	5	4		
Freeland, Benjamin	1	8	5		
Fricks, Henry	1	2	3		
Frick, Henry, Senr	1	8	2		
Gappin, Zachuriah	2	2	3		
Huston, Paul	1	1	4		
Huston, John	1	1	3		
Hazlett, John	1	3	3		
Harr, John	1	3	6		
Huston, William	1	4	6		2
Hide, Samuel	2		3		
Hobbs, Henson	1	2	3		
Hobns, Solomon	1	1	4		
Hardy, Thomas	1	1	1		
Huggins, William	1	1	1		
Hannah, Matthew	1	1	4		
Hannah, James	1	2	1		
Holmes, Thomas	1	2	1		
Howard, Samuel	1		1		
Howard, Jno					

GREENE

Name of Head of Family	Free white males of 16 years and upward, including heads of families	Free white males under 16 years	Free white females, including heads of families	All other free persons	Slaves
Hallman, Thos	1	3	3		
Herrod, Jno	1	2	1		
Howard, Cornelius	1		3		
Gallop, Jesse	1		1		
Woodman, Samuel	1	1			
Miller, Benjamin	1		1		
Miller, James	1	1	2		
Drake, Chas	1	1	2		
Flowers, Samuel	1	2	2		
Hickson, Benjamin	2	1			
Smith, John	1				
Gappin, William	1	1	1		
Gappin, Stephen	1	2	2		
Gappin, John	1				
Jones, Robert	1	1	4		
Jordan, Jacob	1	2	2		
Morgan, James	1	4	5		
Jones, Amos	1	4	2		
Ives, Richard	1	1	2		
Johnston, Bailey	1	1	2		
Jones, Mary		3	4		
Jenkens, Aron	1	5	3		
Jamison, William	2	1	2		
Johnston, Thomas	1	1	1		
Jackson, Jesse	1	2	1		
Jackson, Henry	3	3	5		
Johnston, Henry	1	3	4		
Knox, James	2	4	4		
Gillchriest, Hans	1	1	3		
Knox, Samuel	1	4	4		
Knobs, Solomon	1	1	2		
Kidd, Nathl	1	4	3		
Kitch, Jno	1	5	5		
Moore, Daniel	1	2	1		
Shalby, Jnthn	1				
Bellman, Christian	1	2	1		
Ross, Robert	1		1		
Ross, John	1	1			
Bartholemew, Jno	1		2		
Stewart, James	1	2	1		
Rankin, Geo	1				
Elegy, Nicholas	1	2	2		
Garretson, Jacob	1	2	1		
Alley, Thos	1		2		
Knotts, William	1	1	5		
Kenner, Boston	1	3	3		
Knotts, Benj	2	2	4		
Leaton, Samuel	1	1	2		
Long, Noah	1	3	2		
Leaton, William	1	5	3		
Long, David	2	3	6		
Long, Thos	1	3	3		
Launce, Jno	1	7	3		
Long, Gideon	1	2	3		
Lettimore, Jno	1	4	5		
Lewis, Phillip	1	3	1		
Launce, Andw	1	1	5		
Long, Jeremiah	1	3	5		
Long, Jno	1	4	4		
Livingood, Jacob	1	2	4		
Lemly, Geo	1	4	5		
Lemly, Jacob	1	1	2		
Maple, Benjamin	1	1	3		
Mannon, Samuel	1	2	1		
Alley, John	1	1	2		
Gastin, Samuel	1		2		
Livingood, Benjamin	1	2	1		
Eddy, William	1	1	2		
Eddy, Alexr	1	2	1		
Levi, Martin	1	1	2		
Six, Jacob	1	2	3		
Six, Lewis	1		2		
Glascow, Stephen	1	1	2		
Chaffin, Jno	1	2	1		
Pollock, Oliver	1		2		
Thomas, John	1	2	2		
Davis, John	1	2	2		
Roberts, William	1	1	2		
Lemons, James	1	2	1		
Jackson, William	1	1	3		
Prickett, Jno	1	1	2		
Evans, Zachariah	1	2	4		
Evans, John	1	3	2		
Miller, Jno	1		2		
Mundle, Abner	1	2	4		
Munde, James	2	4	2		
Moore, Jno	1	2	6		
McCraken, Alexander	1	1	4		
McCoy, William	1	3	2		
McKinnon, Joseph	1	1	2		
McClurg, Jno	1	1	3		
McDowell, Chas	1		2		
Moore, Philip	1	1	1		
Freckels, David	1		2		
Freckels, Nathan	1				

GREENE

Name of Head of Family	Free white males of 16 years and upward, including heads of families	Free white males under 16 years	Free white females, including heads of families	All other free persons	Slaves
Frazer, Joseph	1	2	2		
Frazer, Joseph	1	2	4		
Furt, Francis	1	3	3		
Furt, Benjamin	1	4	2		
Fulner, Henry	1	2	2		
Fast, Joseph	1	1	4		
Fast, Christian	1	4	3		
Garwood, William	1	3	5		
Gillmore, Matthew	1	4	2		
Strain, Gilbert	1	1	1		
Garwood, Jonathan	1	2	2		
Gerrard, Isaac	1	2	5		
Gerrard, Jonathan	1	2	3		
Garrard, Justice	1	2	4		
Gasten, Benjamin	1	1	1		
Jameson, William	2	1	4		
Gustis, Jeremiah	2	1	4		
Garrison, Leanard	2	4	3		
Glascow, Jno	2	4	3		
Garrison, Frederick	1	1	2		
Garner, Adam	1	2	3		
Grimes, William	1	5	2		
Grimes, Richard	1	1	1		
Nevitt, Jno	1	1	2		
Nowland, John	1	1	1		
Preston, Jonathan	1	1	5		
Parker, Samuel	1	1	4		
Patterson, James	1		2		
McKnight, Wm	1	3			
McKnight, Ezekiel	1				
Passover, Geo		2	3		
Pollock, Jno	1	3	1		1
Pickenhough, Peter	1	2	3		
Ranken, Joseph	2	3	2		
Williams, Paul	1	1	3		
Robinson, Susannah	1	1	1		
Roberts, John	1	3	4		
Rutter, Jno	3	3	4		
Ross, Jno	1	1	4		
Rhinehart, Danl	1	3	2		
Robbins, William	1	2	5		
Stone, Elias	1	2	6		
Sutton, Ebenezar	1	2	2		
Savery, Jno	2	1	1		4
Stone, James	1	1	4		
Shroyer, John	1	3	2		
Shoemaker, Adam	1	3	2		
Snover, Henry	1	1	4		
Shriver, Jacob	1	3	2		
Shriver, Jno	1	2	2		
Stewart, Elijah	3	4	3		
Shelby, David	3	2	3		
Statton, Joseph	1	4			
Subzer, Lewis	1		2		
Subzar, Geo	1	3	1		
Subzar, Frederick	1		1		
Sutton, Stephen	1	1	1		
Sutton, Benjamen	1	4	4		
Morrison, Robert	1	2	4		
Mills, Samuel	1	1	2		
McMullen, Richard	1	2	5		
McKee, Jno	1	2	5		
Morris, Jonathan	3	6	9		
McDowell, Thos	1	2	1		
Mills, Jno	1	1	3		
Martin, Thos	1	1	3		
Masters, William	1	4	6		
McKelby, John	1	3	3		
Myers, Frederick	1	2	3		
McMullin, James	1	2	3		
Morris, Joseph	1	3	3		
Morris, Levi	1	2	1		
Maxtell, Daniel	1	2	2		
Montgomery, Robert	1	3	4		
Maryfield, Samuel	1	3	2		
Rutter, George	1	1	2		
Drake, Lewis	1	2	2		
Drake, Mannon	1	3	1		
Mundle, Andrew	1	1	1	2	
Allison, Abner	1	1	2		
Gillkeese, Geo	1	2			
Lewis, William	1	1	1		
Knotts, Jno	1				
Daniel, Michael		2	2		
Christ, Geo		2	2		
Donald, John	2	1	3		
Morgan, Temperance	2	1	4		
Morris, Geo	1	5	2		
Myers, Andw	1	1	2		
Marshall, Samuel	1	1	2		
McFarlane, Jesse	1		3		
Minor, John, Esqr	1	3	4		2
Minor, William	3	2	5		3
Six, Margaret		3	1		
Six, Henry	1	1	3		

GREENE

Name of Head of Family	Free white males of 16 years and upward, including heads of families	Free white males under 16 years	Free white females, including heads of families	All other free persons	Slaves
Terrance, William	1	2	6		
Thompson, John	1	1	2		
Teaboe, Geo	1	1	3		
Truloch, Thomas	1	2	3		
Terrance, Samuel	1	1	4		
Villery, David	2	1	4		
Vernes, Jno	3	5	4		
Williams, William	1	3	4		
Worley, Brice	1	2	3		
Wolf, Geo	1	1	2		
Hawkins, Peter	1		1		
Hawkins, Samuel	1	3	3		
Westbrook, William	1	1	1		
Watters, John	1	2	3		
Woodmsey, James	1	3	5		
White, Israel	1	3			
White, Isaac	1				
White, Thomas	1	1			
Baldwin, Benjamin	1	3	4		
Chaffin, Thos	1	1	3		
Perkins, Samuel	1	1	2		
Belcher, Elijah	1		2		

MORGAN

Name of Head of Family	Free white males of 16 years and upward, including heads of families	Free white males under 16 years	Free white females, including heads of families	All other free persons	Slaves
Hays, William	2	2	4		
King, Joseph	1	1	2		
Parson, Daniel	1		2		
Chedester, Holdridge	1	2	2		
James, William	1	1	4		
Shorter, Geo	1	1	2		
Reese, John	1	4	1		
Meeks, Nathan	1	6	3		
Gray, Andw	1	1	2		
Miller, John	1	3	2		
Swart, Phillip	2	2	2		
Crain, Daniel	1		3		
Wright, Lewis	1		3		
Crain, Silas	2	3	4		
Brown, Paul	1	4	4		
Ross, William	1		3		
Lines, Benjamin	1	3	2		
Jewell, Seth	1	2	2		
Limes, Solomon	1	5	3		
Murford, Benjamin	1	3	4		
Weakly, Thomas	1	4	1		
Lunback, Nicholes	1	1	2		
Browbury, Andrew	1	1	2		
Carey, Abel	1	6	2		
Fulton, Israel	1	2	3		
Martin, Jno	2	3	4		
Timmons, Jean	2		5		
Timmons, Levi	1		2		
Mintor, Daniel	1		5		
Millegan, William	1	2	5		
Robinson, John	2	1	2		
McGiffon, Nathl	2	2	2		
Millegan, James	1	5	3		
Tix, Henry	1	6	3		
Adamson, Thomas	1		2		
Busson, Aron	3	2	2		
Hoge, George	1		5		
Darnal, Peter	1		3		
Seal, James	1		2		
Seal, Joseph	1	5			
Morris, Richard	1		2		
Wead, Nathan	1		3		
Chambers, Smith	1		3		
Pounds, Samuel	2	2	4		
Bell, Nathan	1	1	4		
Howard, Jordan	1	1	2		
Ross, Timothy	1	1	2		
Lutes, Geo	1	4	3		
Smith, Dennis	1	3	2		
Stewart, Joseph	1	3	3		
Julen, Isaac	3	4	5		
Cox, Michael	1	3	3		
Case, Joseph	1		3		
Holloway, Saml	1	3	1		
Johnston, Isaac	1	5	2		
Briston, James	1	2	6		
Ross, Jno	1		2		4
Parker, Stephen	1		3		
Parker, Jesse	1	1	4		
Patterson, Thomas	2	5	2		
Denham, Nathaniel	2	6	2		
Shelvy, David	2	2	2		
Leanard, Zaba	1	1	2		
Leanard, William	4	3	2		
Lowry, John	1	2	5		
Cooper, Nathan	1	2	6		
McGill, Robert	1				
Heaton, Miles	1	3			
Cleaton, Elizabeth	1		3		
Hook, James	3	4			

MORGAN

NAME OF HEAD OF FAMILY.	Free white males of 16 years and upward, including heads of families.	Free white males under 16 years.	Free white females, including heads of families.	All other free persons.	Slaves.
Reese, John	1			2	
Prong, Stophel	1			5	
Grooms, Solomon	1	3	4		
Beeman, Peter	1	4	1		
Smith, Andrew	1	1	1		
Smith, James	1		1		
Martin, Zephaniah	1	2	3		
Martin, Jno	1	2	3		
Belles, Nathan	1	3	3		
Arnold, Jno	1		1		
Lolle, James	1	1	4		
Young, Philip	1	1	4		
Ball, William	1	3	3		
Moore, Christian	1	2	3		
Stogdon, James	1		2		
Hill, Thos	2	1	2		
Wise, Adam	1	2	2		
Wilson, Samuel	1	3	2		
Arnald, Abm	1		2		
McDowell, Andw	1	1	2		
Johnston, Zephaniah	1		2		
Coleman, Joel	1	3	5		
Herrod, Levi	1	3	2		
Johnston, David	1	3	2		
Polson, Geo	2	3	3		
Burgh, Jacob	1	4	5		
Bills, William	1	2	1		
Bills, John	2	1	3		
Enoch, Henry	1		4		
Hull, Zachariah	1	3	2		
Stull, John	1	2	4		
Heaton, Daniel	1		4		
Pitnid, Nathl	1	1	4		
Dote, Anthy	1		1		
Ball, Davis		3	1		
Woodrough, Stephen	1		4		
Stiles, Rachael			2		
Huttenfield, Phobe	1	2	2		
Mills, Joseph	1	3	5		
Cowplane, Caleb	1	1	6		
Trumph, John	1	1	3		
Rush, Jacob	2	6	1		
Headle, Samuel	1	1	1		
Dunn, Benagey			1		
Dun, Sarah			1		
McEwen, James	1	3	2		
Batten, Margaret	1	1	1		

MORGAN

NAME OF HEAD OF FAMILY.	Free white males of 16 years and upward, including heads of families.	Free white males under 16 years.	Free white females, including heads of families.	All other free persons.	Slaves.
Brown, Abner	1	3	1		
Casto, David	1	2	1		
Biggs, Abigail	3	1	1		
Brown, Abner, Senr	1		1		
Bell, Benjamin	1	1	1		
Timmons, Nicholas	1				
Mills, John	1	2	3		
Jail, Samuel	1	2	2		
Bell, James	1	5	4		
Jennings, Cyrenas	1	1	2		
House, Samuel	1	3	3		
Lee, William	2		3		
Lee, John	1				
Ross, Henry	1		3		
Ross, Robert	1		2		
Bell, Abel	2		7		
Wolverton, John	1	1	1		
Crain, Caleb	1	4	4		
Clark, Israel	1	2	2		
Bell, Nathaniel	1		1		
Wright, William	1	1	4		
Wolverton, Thos	1	3	2		
Eaton, Jonah	1	5	2		
Davis, James	2	2	2		
Davis, James, Senr	1	1	2		
Parker, David	2	3	1		
Smith, Ralph	1	6	3		
Flecher, Thomas	1		2		
Ball, Grace		1	1		
Lucey, Samuel	1	2	3		
Heaton, John	1	2	4		1
Heaton, Isaac	4	2	5		1
Heaton, Henry	1		2		
Lucy, Eleazar	3	2	2		
Moore, Thomas	3	5	3		
Allen, Thomas	2	1	4		
Case, Samuel	1		2		
Heaton, William	1		2		
Heaton, David	1	2	1		
Hays, George	1	1			
Smith, Jacob	1				
Gayman, Daniel	1		1		
Gayman, Daniel, Jur	1	1	2		
Davis, Isaac	1	1	1		
Daine, William	1		2		
Daine, Ebenezar	1	1	2		

MORGAN

NAME OF HEAD OF FAMILY.	Free white males of 16 years and upward, including heads of families.	Free white males under 16 years.	Free white females, including heads of families.	All other free persons.	Slaves.
Futton, John	4	1	4		
Ross, Tichabad	1	4	4		
Futton, Robert	1		5		
Clark, Thos	1	3	2		
Clark, William	1		2		
Smith, Abraham	1	3	5		
McKewan, John	1	1	2		
Jewell, Samuel	1	2	4		
Casto, Andrew	1	2	2		
Wortham, Nicholas	1	1	4		
Young, Andw	1	1	2		
Dickeson, Jesse	2	2	2		
Lines, John	1		1		
Butts, Michael	1	2	2		
Jordan, Joshua	1	4	4		
Stickel, Philip	1	1	5		
Need, Jacob	1	4	5		
Arnold, Daniel	3	1	2		
Arnold, Daniel	1	3	3		
Arnold, David	1		3		
Vollery, Jacob	1		1		
Thomas, Sarah		5	5		

RICHHILL

NAME OF HEAD OF FAMILY.	Free white males of 16 years and upward, including heads of families.	Free white males under 16 years.	Free white females, including heads of families.	All other free persons.	Slaves.
Archer, Simon	1	2	4		
Pope, Samuel	1		1		
George, Samuel	1		2		
Statten, William	2		2		
Kennedy, John	1	2	3		
Braddick, Francis	1	4	5		
Bradock, Ralph	1	1	4		
Harris, Lawrance	1	1	1		
Hunton, Isaacher	2		1		
Granden, Edward	1	1	3		
Bates, Epm	2	4	4		
Bean, Elias	2	3	3		
Crow, Jacob	1	1	7		
Wharton, Robert	1	2	4		
Linsley, Zenna	1	1	3		
Farley, Andw	1	3	2		
Burns, Alexr	1	2	1		
Carrol, Edward	1	2	4		
Frazer, Andw	1	2	3		
Ryerson, Thos, Esqr	1	2	2		1

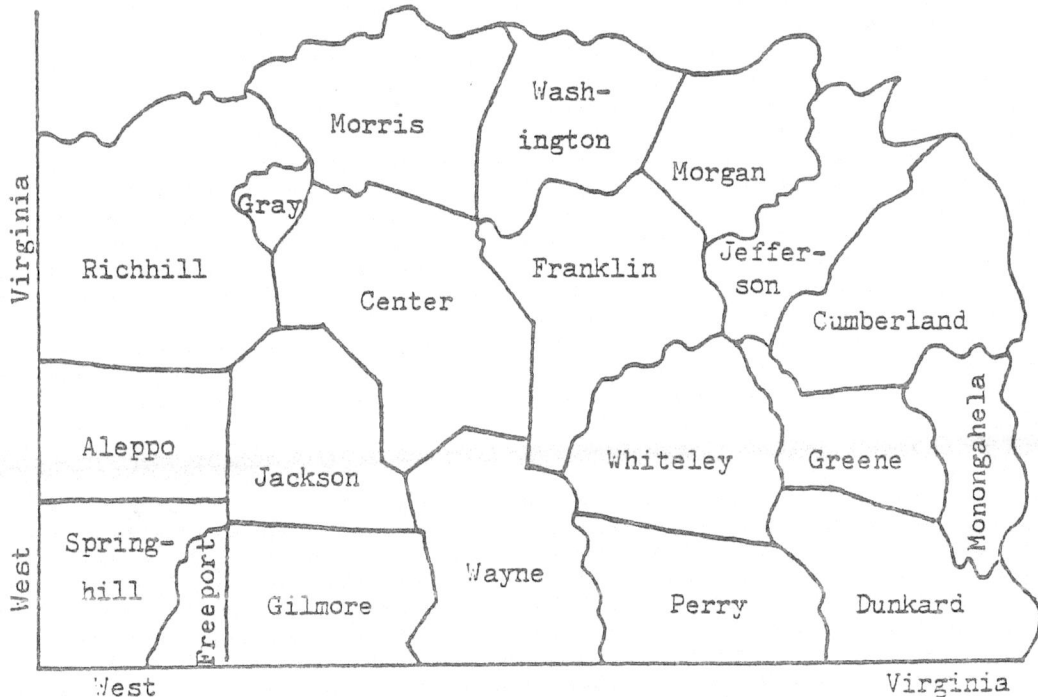

PRESENT GREENE COUNTY, PA TOWNSHIPS

KKZ 1988

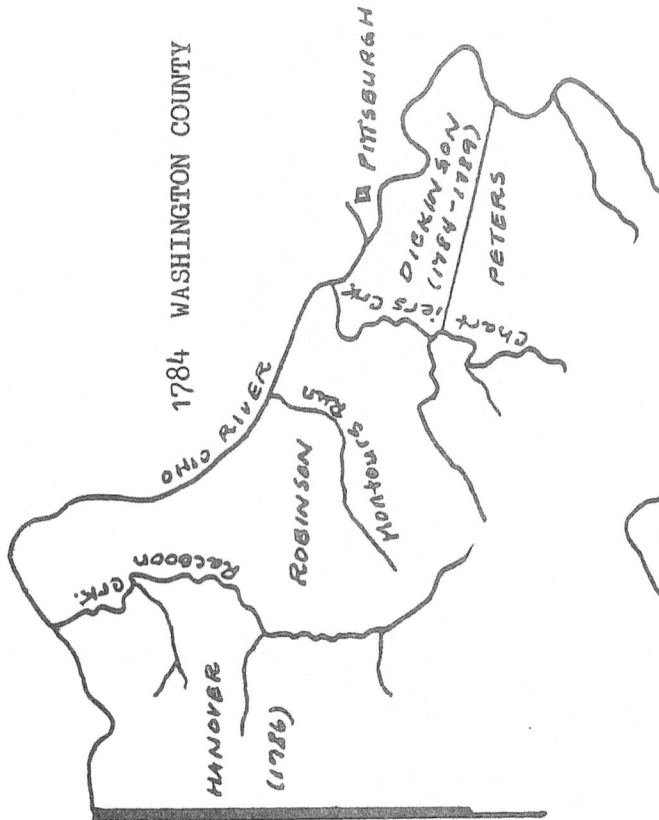

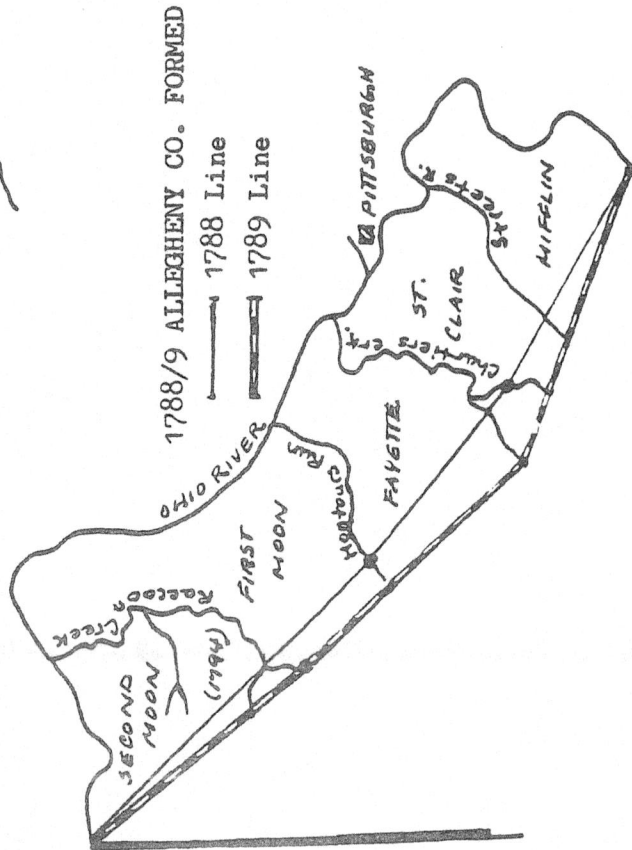

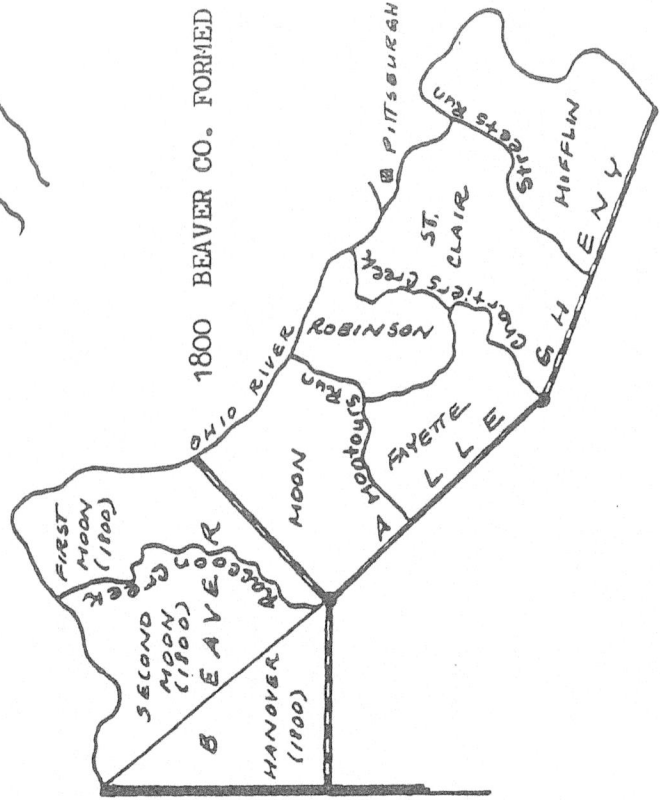

THE DIVISION OF NORTHERN WASHINGTON COUNTY, PA INTO ALLEGHENY AND BEAVER COUNTIES
(boundaries approximate)

KEY TO CODES:

1789 Washington County Tax List Code

C - Cecil Township   H - Hanover Township   R - Robinson Township
D - Dickinson Township   P - Peters Township

Allegheny County Township Code

Township Abbreviation	Number of Households by Year		
	1790*	1791	1794
Mo - Moon Township+	263	567	232
F - Fayette Township#	265		222
S - St. Clair Township	277	262	261
Mi - Mifflin Township	267	257	243
	1072	1086	1158

* estimated
+ Moon Twp. divided into First and Second Moon by 1794
# Fayette established 1789/90 but not used much until 1792

PART III: PORTION OF ALLEGHENY COUNTY TAKEN FROM WASHINGTON COUNTY

Name of Head of Family	Free white males of 16 years and upward, including heads of families	Free white males under 16 years	Free white females, including heads of families	All other free persons	1789 Wash TL
FAYETTE					
Bell, James	1	8	2		R
Boden, Joseph	1		2		
Davis, William	1	3	2		
Denny, John	1	2	2		
Hall, Robert	1	2			R
Hall, William	1		1		
Jones, Thomas	2				
Johnston, Coarl	2	5	6		
Lawless, Jas.	1	1			
Lutton, Robert	1	1	3		
McMullin, Tho.	1		2		R
McCoy, William	1	2	1		R
Marks, William	1	7	1		
McMichael, John	1		3		R
McMichael, Isaac	1		2		
McKee, James	1	2	4	2	6
McCoy, John	1		1		
Merryman, John	1	1	1		
Moore, John	1	2	5		R
Nichols, John	1	2	5		
Phillips, Samuel	3	3	6		R
Phillips, John	1		4		
Pickel, Henry	1	2	4		R
Phillips, Jonathan	2	5	2		
Riddle, Samuel	1	2	1		
Spear, Alexr.	1	3			
Scott, John	1		3		R
Stewart, William	1	1	2		R
Sharp, Nehemiah	3	4	2		R
Stevenson, John	1	2	1		R
Thornsberry, Thos.	1		2		R
Wolf, Adam	1		3		
Willis, Geo.	1	2			
White, Joseph	1		2		
Young, Matto.	1		1		
Wagstaff, Wo.	1		3		
McHerron, Jno.	1	1	3		
Porter, Tho.	2	3	2		R
Quigley, James	1	3	6		R
McCurdy, Alexr.	2	2	4		R
Nichols, Wo.	1	3	5		
Faulkner, David	1	3	2		
McMahon, Robert	1	3	5		
Quinn, Edward	2	3	5		
Wright, James	2		1		
Murphy, William	1	2	3		R
Johnston, Andrew	1	3	3		R
McCoy, James	1	3	3		
Scott, James	1	2	3		R
Young, Tho.	1	5	3		R
Cox, Tho.	1	2	1		R
Hall, William	1	3	1		
Piercall, Benj.	1	3	4		
Taylor, Wo.	2		4		R
Bayles, Jno.	2	1	1		
Bayles, Geo.	1	1	1		
Neely, Samuel	1	4	4		
McCoy, Margaret	1	3	3		
McCoy, John	1		2		
McCartny, Alexr.	1		2		
Collins, John	1		4		
Allen, James	1	1	4		
Aga, Frederick	1	1	5		

Name of Head of Family	Free white males of 16 years and upward, including heads of families	Free white males under 16 years	Free white females, including heads of families	All other free persons	1789 Wash TL
FAYETTE					
Alexander, Tho.	1	1	2		
Boyd, Robert	1	2	5		R
Boyd, Tho.	1	1	7		
Boyd, Peolly	3	2	3		R
Barns, John	2	3	4		
Burwell, Epo.	2		4		
Bond, Hugh	1	2	6		R
Criswell, Jos.	1		1		
Cockran, Alexr.	1		3		
Cockran, Wo.	1	1	3		
Chambers, Jas.	1		2		
Dennis, Bartly	1	3	2		R
Dinsmore, James	1	2	5		
Dinnahoo, William	1	2	3		R
Ewings, James	4	2	5		Rj
Evans, Walter	1		2		
Ewings, Saml.	1	3	4		R
Ewings, Alexr.	1	3	1		R
Frazier, Jonthn.	2	1	5		
Fink, Andr.	1	5	3		R
Frazier, Jno.	1		3		
Gossitt, Jno.	1	2	1		
Grimes, Abo.	1	2	3		
Gray, Alexr.	2	2	3		
Holmes, Obadiah	1	1	1		
Herrod, Andrew	2	1	1		R
Hickman, Adam	1	4	2		
Hickman, Peter	2	1	1		
Heddon, Robert	1		2		
Herrod, Epo.	1	2	2		
Jones, Epa.	1	4	3		
Jackson, Geo.	3		1		R
Kelso, Geo.	1	5	2		
Kelso, Jno.	1	5	2		
Kirkpatrick, James	1	4	2		R
Kirkpatrick, William	1	1	1		
Kelso, Jno.	1	1	1		
Lush, Wo.	1		1		
Link, Jos.	1	2	1		
McKinzie, Kenith	3	1	1		
McDate, ———	1		1		R
McGregor, Matt.	1	1		1	R
McAdoo, Jno.	1				R
McGregor, William	1		4		R
McClelland, Alexander	2	1	5		R
McVay, Wo.	2	1	4		R
McCandless, Wo.	2	2	4		R
McElhany, Jno.	1	1	1		R
Morgan, Hugh	2		2		
Middlesworth, Abo.	2		2		
McGregor, Jno.	1	3	2		
Marutta, Jno.	1		2		
McCarmick, Samuel	1	1	2		
Miller, Jno.	1		3		
McBride, Archo.	1		3		
Morgan, Saml.	1	2			
Milte, Jno.	1		3		
Millar, Jas.	1		2		
McLaughlin, Wo.	1	3	3		
McKewan, Saml.	1		3		
Noble, Henry	1			4	
Nesbitt, James	1	2	3		
Pinkerton, Alexr.	2	4	3		
Porter, Wo.	4		1		

Name of Head of Family	Free white males of 16 years and upward, including heads of families	Free white males under 16 years	Free white females, including heads of families	All other free persons	1789 Wash TL
FAYETTE					
Patridge, Jos.	2		3		R
Potter, Henry	2		2		
Potter, Joseph	1		1		
Quillan, Ambrose	1	1	4		R
Quigley, James	1	3	5		
Richardson, James	3	3	1		
Rollinson, Richd.	1	1	1		
Rammage, Robert	1	3	1		
Reed, Tho.	1	1			C
Roseberry, Jno.	1	1			
Roseberry, Jno.	1		1		
Roseberry, Isaac	1				
Smith, Tho.	1				
Short, Martin	1		2		R
Stevison, William	1	2	4		R
Booth, Daniel	1	4	6		
Shoemaker, Michael	1	2	4		R
Shrode, Henry	1	2	2		
Shrode, Jacob	1				
Sutton, Wo.	1				
Sprowl, Hugh	1		1		
Smith, Jno.	2				
Thornsberry, James	1				R
Turner, William	4		3		R
Tucker, William	2		2		
Tucker, James	1	2	2		
Valandingham, Geo.	1	2	4		R
Ulery, Henry	1		7		R
Walker, Isaac	1	1	1		
Wilkison, Jno.	3		6		R
Walker, Gabriel	2	1	4		R
Walker, Jno.	1		5		
Williams, Wo.	2	3	4		R
Walrub, Geo.	1		8		R
Wilson, Geo.	4		2		
Wilson, Samuel	1	1	7		R
West, Gasper	2	2	3		R
Witherspoon, David	1	1	3		R
Wood, Jno.	1		5		R
Wright, Jeremiah	1	2	4		R
Johnston, John	1	1	1		
Rector, Daniel	1	2	1		
Loring, John	1		1		
McClennahan, Hugh	1				
Middleswart, Henry	1	2	4		
Kerr, Jas.	1				
Johnston, Jos.	1	3	4		
Walker, William	1	3	4		R
Logan, William	1	1	3		
Cunningham, Jonathan	1	3	3		
Lewis, Tho.	1		3		
Thornsberry, Tho.	1	3	4		
McMichael, Isaac	1	3	4		
McMichael, Jno.	1		3		
McCarty, Wo.	1	1	5		
Turner, Jno.	1	3	2		
Moore, James	1		3		
Ewing, Geo.	1	1	3		
Biney, John	1		3		
Ewing, John	1	2	1		R
Short, John	1		4		R
Inggs, Jas.					

125

FAYETTE

Name of Head of Family	Free white males of 16 years and upward, including heads of families	Free white males under 16 years	Free white females, including heads of families	All other free persons	1789 Wash TL
Thomson, Samuel	1		1		
Thomson, Benjamin	2				R
M'Elhany, John	1		4		R
Stewart, Jos	1	1	3		R
Hannah, Thos	2	3	7		R
Jeffery, Saml	2	3	4		R
M'Bride, Henry	3		2		R
Pierce, Daniel	1	1	4		
Hinds, Joseph	1	3	4		
Ewings, William	1	3	3		
Abbeny, James	1		3		
Shrode, John	1	1	3		
Simcock, Samuel	1	5	2		
Short, John	1	2	6		R
M'Cart, Jno	1	2	2		R
Long, Geo	1		1		R
Link, Daniel	1	2	1		R
Walker, Jas	1	4	5		
Link, Adam	1		3		
M'Carmick, Saml	2	3	4		R
Walker, Joseph	1	3	5		
Whiteside, James	1	4	1		
English, Saml	1		1		R
Hinson, Jacob	3	2	4		R 1
M'Vay, Benjo	1	2	2		
Adams, Jacob	1	2	2		
Meratto, Daniel	1	1	1		
Dobbins, John	1	1	3		
Webster, Samuel	1	3	1		
Herrod, Geo	1	1	1		
Morgan, Jno	1	1	2		
Brice, Wm	1	1	4		
Alexander, Saml	2	1	3		
Hill, Geo	1		2		
Davis, Basil		4			
Cockran, Alexr	1		4		
Alexander, Matthew	1				R
Stewart, William	1	2	1		
Hobblen, Cutlip	1	1	1		
Adams, Wm	2		2		
Johnston, John	1	3			
Martin, Jonth	1		4		
Larrimore, John	2	1	2		
Evans, Hugh	1		2		
Armstrong, Jno	3		8		
Boyce, Richd	2	1	2		
Roly, William	1		2		
Lesnett, Christian	4	1	2		
Thomson, John	1	1	3		
Brackenridge, James	1	3	2		
Gilison, Geo	3		7		
Masters, Stephen	2	3	2		
Crail, Tho	2	1	5		
Short, Richd	2		2		
Williams, William	1	2	2		
Carter, Barney	1	2	1		
Hays, Robert	2	1	1		
Reed, David	1	1	5		
M'Gowen, John	1	3	2		
Aur, John	1		3		
Lisle, William	1	3	2		8
Craig, Isaac	1				
Grimes, Mathew	1				
Nevill, Presley	3	2	4	1	P 9
Baker, Jno	1	2	1		R
Baker, Geo	4				

MOON (FIRST)

Name of Head of Family	Free white males of 16 years and upward, including heads of families	Free white males under 16 years	Free white females, including heads of families	All other free persons	1789 Wash TL
M'Coy, David	1	1	2		R
Cheny, John	1		2		R
Lafarty, William	1	2	4		
Blair, Jno	1	3	4		
Montgomery, Hugh	1	2	2		
Hillman, Jas	2		2		
Hillman, Jas, Jur	1		1		
Kennedy, Saml	1	3	1		
Thompson, William	1		4		R
Clifford, Jno	1	3	6		R
Drake, Ed	2		2		
Cunningham, Thos	1		2		
M'Daniel, Christopher	1				
Anderson, Norman	1		2		
Lawrence, Isaac	1	2	2		R
Justice, Isaac	1	4	3		R
Blunt, Andw	1	4	3		R
Lawrence, Phil	3	2	3		R
Barns, Thos	1	4	3		
Woods, Wm	2	1	5		R
Blunt, Rachl	1		3		R
Veesy, Elijha	1	4	5		R
Hart, Jno	2		3		R
Robinson, Jos	2				R
Kierr, Jos	1	1			

MOON (FIRST)

Name of Head of Family	Free white males of 16 years and upward, including heads of families	Free white males under 16 years	Free white females, including heads of families	All other free persons	1789 Wash TL
Huster, Thos	1	3	2		R
Jordin, Jas	2	3	3		R
Hill, Jno	2	5	3		R
Fenasin, Jno	1	1	3		
Euclit, Thos	1	1	5		R
Elliott, Geo	1		5		R
Guy, William	3	2	6		R
Tompeon, Thos	1	2	3		R
Meek, Jacob	2	5	5		R
Sproat, Thos	6	5	4		R
Galbraith, Wm	1		4		R
Barns, Peter	1	2	4		R
Miller, Saml	3	1	4		R
Lea, William	2		3		R
Galbraith, David	1	1	1		
Chambers, Thos	1		2		
Pollard, John	2	1	2		
Kerr, Jno	2		5		R
Dumer, Adam	1	4	6		R
Inman, Ezekiel	4	2	3		
Patterson, Joseph	1		4		R
Mitchell, Joseph	2		4		
Drybread, Andrew		1	2		R
Lowry, Wm	1	2	2		R
Smith, David	1	2	2		
Parks, Jas	2	1			R
Louder, Thos	1		1		R
Rougan, Hugh		3	5		R
Sutton, Wm	2		1		R
Reddeck, Wm	2	2	2		R
Veal, Jno	1	4	3		R
Hare, Robt	2	2	2		R
Forbes, Wm	2	4	2		R
Worley, Jno	1		2		
Folks, William	3	1	4		R
Crooks, Henry	2	1	3		R
Greenlee, Robert	2		5		R
Hull, Samuel	1	5			
Springer, Mathias	1		4		
Rearden, Henry	1	1	2		
Hill, Thos	1				
M'Cullough, James	1				
Grant, Jonathan	1	1	3		R
Wilson, Samuel	3	3	3		R
Johnston, Saml	2		4		
M'Ginnis, Hugh	2		2		
Springer, Michael	1				
Folks, Geo	1		2		R
Morgan, Chas	1	5	4		R i
Stewart, James	1	2	4		R
Dunn, Hugh	1	5	3		
Powell, Robert	1	5	2		R R
Stewart, Joseph	1	7	2		R R
Burns, Alexr	1	2	4		
Crooks, Henry	3	2	3		R
Cunningham (Widow)		2	2		R
M'Cullough, William	3	2	6		R
Ewing, Saml	1		6		
Read, Andrew	1	1	3		R
Cavet, Patrick	1	2	2		
Boyce, James	3	1			
Mattocks, Elijah			2		
Swimm, Jesse			2		
M'Connel, William	1	8			R
Wheeler, John	1	3	2		R
Sheen, Timothy	1	2	1		R
Bleenk, Jno	1		3		
Meloney, Samuel	1	1	5		R
Rearden, Thos	1	5	7		R
Morrison, James	1	4			R
Read, William	2		3		R
Read, John	2	2	3		
Lindsay, Josiah	2		3		
Hoge, Thos	1	1	2		
M'Adoo, Andrew	1				
Carter, Peter	1	2	4		
Ansley, Jas	2	5	5		
White, James	1	1			
Agnew, William	1				
Douglass, William	1				
George, John	3	3	3		R
Maxfield, William	1	3	8		
Sodard, James	1	3	5		
Crowley, James	1	4	7		R
Roarden, Thos	1	5	3		R
Lowrie, Jas	1	2	3		
Skeon, Henry	1	2	2		R
Boyce, Jno	2	2	8		R
Scott, James	1	3	3		
Swimm, Jno	1	3	3		
Cavitt, Thos	3	3	1		R i
Rearden, Jno	1	2	7		R
M'Connel, William	1				
M'Kinly, Andrew	1				
M'Carmick, Pat	1				

MOON (FIRST)

Name of Head of Family	Free white males of 16 years and upward, including heads of families	Free white males under 16 years	Free white females, including heads of families	All other free persons	1789 Wash TL
Field, Lawrence	1	2	8		
Welsh, Felix	1	5	4		
Powell, Robert	1	5	1		
Donn, Hugh	1	3	2		R
Moore, Jno	1	3	2		R
Williams, Chas	1				
Sampson, Thos	1	2	4		
Clark, Jacob	1	2	4		
Bruce, Chas	2				R 3
Green (Widow)		1	3		
Lennox, Chas	1		2		
Woods, William	2		2		
Ireland, John	2	1			Hc 2
Kennedy, Matthew	2				
Speers, Alexr	1				
M'Conuel, Saml	1				
Husler, Thos	1	2	2		
Bleenk, Jno	1		2		
Sliddam, Zachariah	1		2		R
Johnston, Jas	1	2	4		R
Calwell, Jas	1	1			R
M'Connehoe, Thos	1		2		
Hillman, Jno	1		1		
Warden, James	2	2	4		R
Wolf, John	2	4	5	F	R
Rodgers, Jeremiah	1	3	4		R
M'Cormick, Benjamin	1		3		R
M'Carmick, Jas	1	1	3		R
Miller, James	1	3	2	F	
M'Curdy, Samuel	1		4	F	R
Smith, Jno	1	2	4	F	R
Galbraith, Jno	1	2	1	F	R
Galbraith, Jas	1	1	2	F	R
Loudon, Thos	1	1	1	F	R 4
Meeks, Joshua	1		1		
Gray, Moses	1	4	2		
Morrison, James	1	4	1		
Setton, Jno	2		1		
Lowry, Wm	1	1	2		R
Parks, James	2	2	3		
Scott, Joseph, esqr	2	2	3	F	R
Riley, Geo	1				
Veal, Solomon	1	4	3		
Wright, Mich	1	1	3		1
Woods, Jno	1	1	5		
Stimson, Jno	1		2		R
Wiley, Jacob	1	2	2		
Woolery, Henry	1		7		
English, Thos	1		2		
Marshal, Jno	1				
M'Kinley, Andrew	1				
Johnston, Hugh	1	2	1		R
Reed, Alex	1	1	2		R
Lusk, Jno	1	1			
M'Minn, Robert	2	1	6		R
Smith, Jno	2		3		R
Gray, Alexr	1		3		
Abercomby, Jno	1				
Peeples, William	1		2		R
M'Laughlin, Wm	1	3	5		R
Gordon, Wm	2	5	3		R
M'Candless, Alexander	2		1		R
Kelso, Jno	1	3	4		R
Clark, Robert	1	3	4		R
Hepner, Jacob	1	2	5		R
Hull, Hugh	1		1		R
Records, Phil	1	1	4		
Walker, Edwd	1				

MOON (SECOND)

Name of Head of Family	Free white males of 16 years and upward, including heads of families	Free white males under 16 years	Free white females, including heads of families	All other free persons	1789 Wash TL
Poe, Andrew	1		7		R
Eaton, James	1	2	1		1
Elliott, Elias	1		2		
Kennedy, James	2		3		H
Todd, James	1	1	2		H
Little, William	1		2		H
Park, Samuel	1		3		
Cain, Jno	1	6	3		H
Hoge, Thos	1	2	1		
Harsha, William	1		4		
Calhoon, Noble	1		2		
Caughhey, Samuel	1	2	4		H
M'Elhany, Geo	2	2	4		
Park, Robert	2	2	3		
Haga, Jas	2	1	2		
Adams, Jno	1		4		H
Bryan, Henry	1		2		
Rutherford, Saml	1	1	12		H
Hook, Mathias	1	1	12		H
Hook, Jno	1		1		
Ackels, Arthur	1		3		
M'Cawn, Christopher	1	1	3		

NAME OF HEAD OF FAMILY.	Free white males of 16 years and upward, including heads of families.	Free white males under 16 years.	Free white females, including heads of families.	1789 Wash TL
MOON (SECOND)				
Potts, Jonas	2	1	1	H
Reed, Thos	3	4	3	H
Chrisley, Michl	2	4	5	H
Wetherow, Jno	1	3	5	H
Gallant, Patk	1		4	H
Graham, Hugh	1	2	5	H
Roe, Jas	1	1	2	
English, Jno	1	2	5	H
Phillis, Chas	1	3	5	H
Nelson, William	2	1		H
Nelson, Jno	1		3	
Nelson, James	1	1		
Henry, James	1	2	5	H
Calhoon, David	1	1	3	H
Glandey, William	1	1	3	H
Moore, Thos	2	3	4	H
Goe, Jos	1			
Reeder, John	2	2	2	H
Rannie, John	1		3	
Goe, Samuel	1	1	2	
Reaver, Sampson	3	1	3	H
Woods, Hugh	1	3	2	H
Campbell, William	1	2		H 1
Cragg, Henry	1			
Wells, William	1	3	4	H
Gillman, Jonathan	1	2	2	H
Bradey, James	1	2	2	H
Johnston, Joseph	1			
Rhea, Saml	1	1	2	
McCullough, Jno	1	3	4	H
Douglass, William	1	3	4	H
McCoy, Nathl	1		2	H
Bey, Robert	1	1	2	
Minmouth, David	1	1	5	
Richey, Jno	1			
Dawson, Thos	1	2	2	H
Boyce, David	2	1	1	H
Clark, Alexander	2	2	1	H
Kerr, David	1	4	5	H
Mathews, Thos	1	4	5	H
Mathews, Jas	1	6	3	H
Mathews, William	1	6	3	H
Wright, Jno	3	3	3	
Calhoon, Jno	1	2	5	H
Calhoon, Saml	1	1	7	
Laughlin, Robert	3	4	3	
Dawson, Benoni	1			
McLaughlin, Neal	1			
Parks, Saml	1			
Stocks, Thos	1			
Wetheroe, William	1		1	
Mathews, Daniel	1	2	4	
Hock, Mathew	2	1	12	
Miller, Geo	2	2	4	
Hoge, Thos	1	1		
Cahoon, Saml	1	3	4	H
Gun, Abm	1			
MIFFLIN				
Moore, James	1	4	3	D
Allison, William	1	1	1	D
McRoberts, Jno	1			D
Elliott, Jno		2	2	D
McKenzie, Jesse	1			
McKinley, Jno	1	1	2	
Stilly (Widow)	1	2	1	D
Powell, Joseph	1	1		D
McGill, Christophere	1			D
Bean, Jacob	2		1	D
Patterson, Nathl	3			DI
Cunningham, John	3			
Finch, M	1	3	1	D
Swan, Alexr	1		2	
McCarmick, James	1	3		D
Calhoon, Rob	3			
Calhoon, David	1	1	2	D
Shearer, Jno	1		5	D
McIntosh, Wm	1			
O'Neal, Chas	1	3	2	
Huey, John	3		5	
Harding, Thos	1	2	3	D
Irvine, Jas	3	2	3	D
Robinson, Saml	1			
Dunn, John	1	3	3	
Pluck, Richard	1	2		D
Gordon, Alexr	1	3		
McLeland, Jas	1			
McLeland, Jas, Jur	1	1		
McLuro, Denny	1			
McLuro, Andrew	1	3	2	
McLuro, Jno	1			

NAME OF HEAD OF FAMILY.	Free white males of 16 years and upward, including heads of families.	Free white males under 16 years.	Free white females, including heads of families.	1789 Wash TL
MIFFLIN				
McLuro, Jno	1	1	1	D
Neal, Jno	1	3	2	D
Montgomery, Geo	1	3	3	
Whitacre (Widow)	1		2	D
Leuphart, Augustine	1	1		D
McDowell, John		1	4	D
Vangelder, Jeremiah	1		4	D
McKinney, James	3		2	D
Barnett, James	3	3	4	
Thompson, Robert	1		4	D
Powell, John		3	3	
Driver, John		4	3	D
Low, Henry		2	4	D
Morrison, James	2	2	3	
Collins, Thos	1	4	6	
Wiley, Samuel	1	4	6	
Morrison, Matthew	2	1	3	
McMahon, Barny	1	1	3	
McMullin, William	1		2	
Walker, Saml	3	4	3	
Wright, William	1	4	3	
Heath, Samuel	1	1	4	
Heath, Robert	1	1		
Thatcher, James	1	1		
Braky, Andrew	1			
Graham, Doctr —	1			D
Powell, Isaac	1			
Little, Robert	3	6	3	
Bentley, Benjamin	1	3	2	
Clark, William			3	
McFarlin, Andrew	1	4	5	Pl
McDonald, Alexander	1	1	5	
Cockran, Robert	1			
McCurdy, Robert	1			
Craig, Alexr	4		3	S
Stewart, John	1	2	3	
Hall, Thos	3	4	3	
Johnston, Thos	3	3	2	
Totler, John	2		4	
Wilson, Joseph	1	3	4	
Kildoe, Thos	1	4	6	
Kildoe, James	1	6	5	
McDonald, John	1		3	F
McDonald, Thos	1	1	2	
Tannahill, Jno	1			
Tannahill, Walter	1		2	
Rigdon, William	2	1	2	S. P.
Owens, Christopher		2	3	P
Logan, Joseph		2	2	P
McClure, Denny	2		4	
Phillips, David	1		3	S.
Watson, James	1	4	3	
Murray, Jno	1		4	
Logan, Joseph	1	3	3	S. P.
Gooseborn, James		2	3	S
Riggs, Edwd		2	3	S. F.
Clark, Jno	1		4	S.
Brown, Henry	1		4	
McMullin, Thos	1			P.
Wallacre, John	1	3	3	
Hartford, Matt	1	2	4	
Wallace, Jno	1	2	5	I
McMullin, Thos, Jr	1			
Leedam, William	1		2	
Wallace, James	1	1	3	P.
Bogart, Benjamin	1		1	
Hannah, Saml	1	1		
Hannah, Saml, Jur	1		1	
Hannah, William	1		3	Fl
Boyers, John	1		1	
French, Wm	1		3	
Crawford, Thos	1	1		P
Sutton, Jas	1	1		
Hankins, Enoch	1	1	4	
Brown, Jno	1	1	1	I
McThaney, Jo	1			P.
Lisle, Chas	1	1		
Henry, Wm	1		1	
Morrow, Joseph	1		1	C.
Morrow, James	2	2		P.
Hankins, Absalom	1			
ST. CLAIR				
Lee, William	2	3	5	P
Kerr, Jno	2	1	3	
Sturgeon, Jno	1		2	
Torrence, Jno	1		2	
Blakney, Jno	1	3		
Carrol, William	4		3	Pl
Ross, Philip	3		5	
Smith, Jno	2		2	P
Matthews, Jno	1		3	
Warner, Jacob	1			

NAME OF HEAD OF FAMILY.	Free white males of 16 years and upward, including heads of families.	Free white males under 16 years.	Free white females, including heads of families.	1789 Wash TL
ST. CLAIR				
Sullivan, Chas	1	3	1	P.
Bonner, James	1		2	
Nicholson, Wm	1		1	
Cooper, Mathias	1	2	2	D
Thompson, Thos	1		3	P
Richmond, Wm	2		3	P
McConnehew, Thos	1		3	P
Watson, Thos	2	1	5	P
Steel, David	1	2	3	
Turk, William	1	2	3	
Gillmore, Matthew	1	1	3	
Moore, Jno	2		5	
Elliott, Elizabeth	1	2	2	2
Brannan, Michael	1	3	5	
Cooper, Samuel	3	1	4	
Smith, Chas	1	5	4	D
Finney, Robert	1	3	1	
Dixon, Jno	1	2	1	D
Bowsman, Nicholas	3	2	3	D
Kinkaid, Thos	2	2	4	D
Kinkaid, Jno	2	2	4	
Kinkaid, Robert	2		1	
Dougherty, Robert	1		2	
Dougherty, Wm	1	2	4	D
Fortner, Jno	1	1		
Wask, Aron	1	1	3	
Hughes, Thos	2		2	
Horshield, Thos	2		2	
Wiley, Robert	1	2	3	D.
Cool, Peter	1	3	3	D.
Herbert, Moses	1		2	
Henderson, William	1	2	2	D
Holeman, Thos	1	2	5	D.
Wallace, Geo	1	3	6	D.
Hurley, Matt	1	2	2	
Mushfrush, Michael	1	3	2	P.
Huey, Epm	1	3	2	
Wilson, James	1	1	5	
McDermott, Jos	1			
Gower, Henry	1			D.
Earr, Alexr	2			D.
Statts, James	3		4	
Depaustrenz, John Lucas				
Smith, Francis	1	3	1	D.
McClean, Angus	1	1	3	D.
Hamilton, James	1	2	1	D.
Horner, Stephel	2	2	4	D.
Cats, Geo	1		3	D.
Varner, Jno	1		3	
Patterson, Jno	2	1	4	D.
Kerr, Samuel	1			P.
Hultz, Richd	1	1	4	
McCarmick, Jno	1	3	4	P.
Hultz, Richard, Jr	1	4	1	
Gilfillan, Thos	2	2	2	
Adams, Doctr	2	2	2	P.
Parson, Thos	3	1	4	P
Bradin, Robert	3	1	4	
Jones, Thos	3	1	5	
Burns, Geo	3	1	3	
Harbert, Daniel	1	2		P.
Reno, Francis	3	2		P.
Hody, Peter	3	2	1	P.
Ewing, Alexr	3	2	1	
Abrahams, William	1	4	2	P.
Reno, William	1	1	1	
Nicholson, William	1	2		P.
Fowler, Geo	1			
McWay, Harney	1	2		
Skilling, John	1	1		
Timbrell, Isaac	1	1		
Brown, Michl	1	1	3	
Ralston, John	2	1	3	
Butler, Edward	1	1		P.
Connor, Cornelius	1	3		
Conner, Cornelius, Jur	1	1	2	
Wilson, Jno	1	3	2	
Lock, William	1	1		P.
Burk, Jno	1			P.
Lusk, Robert	1	2		P.
Murdock, Wm	1		3	
Stanning, Cornelius	2	5	6	P.
Welch, Thos	1			P.
Guy, James	1	1		
Carson, Archd	1		2	
Robb, Wm	3	2	1	P.
Wilson, Jno	1	2	1	
Churchill, Jno	1	1		
Ward, Ed	3		4	P.
Bownon, Jacob	3	2	4	P.
Mennough, Samuel	1	1	2	
Guy, Wm	1			P.
Creighton, James	1	3		

NAME OF HEAD OF FAMILY.	Free white males of 16 years and upward, including heads of families.	Free white males under 16 years.	Free white females, including heads of families.		1789 Wash TL

ST. CLAIR

Name					
Bennett, Wm	1	2	4		P.
McKnight (Widow)	1	2	3		P.
Boyd, Robert	1		2		P.
Moore, Mary Ann	2		4		
Thompson, Archibald	1	4	3		P.
Thompson, William	1	2	6		P.
Hoglen, Henry	1		1		

MIFFLIN AND ST. CLAIR
MIXED

Name					
Anderson, Jno	1	1	3	Mi	P
Allison, David	1	1	3	S.	
Allison, James	1			S.	
Andrews, Isaac	1		2	Mi	P.
Boreman, Jno & Gasper	2	2	5	S.	P.
Baker, William	1		2	Mi	
Blashford, James	1			Mi	
Boggs, William	3	1	3	S.	P.
Brody, Jas	1	3	4	S.	P.
Black, Thos	1			Mi	
Bousman, Jacob	6	4	3	S.	D.
Bently, Oswall	1			Mi	
Babb, Peter	2	2	6	S.	
Bean, Jno	1		1	S.	
Burns, Jno	2	1	1	Mi	
Biggart, Benjamin	1			Mi	
Boyer, Nathl	1			Mi	
Black, Jno	1	4	4	Mi	D.
Buck, Jos	1			Mi	
Barclay, Jno	1	2	3	Mi	D.
Babb, Jno	1		4	Mi	D.
Brenton, Thos	2	3		Mi	
Beam, Jno	2		1	Mi	
Beam, Abm	1	3	4	S.	P.
Boyd, Thos	1		2	S.	P.
Burney, Jno	1	1		S.	
Leggett, Alexr	1	3	4	Mi	D.
Louderback, Jno	1		4	Mi	
Louderback, Henry	1			Mi	
Louderback, Peter	1	4		Mi	D.
Laughlin, James	1			S.	
Long, William	1	1	1	S.	D.
Long, Josh	1	2	1	S.	D.
Lesley, Chas	2		4	S.	
Logan, Adam	1	5	2	Mi	
Leah, Jas	1	2	2	Mi	
Louderback, Michael	1	1	1	S.	
Lamb, Jno	1		1	S.	
Long, Jas	1	2	4	S.	P.
Long, Alexr	3	3	4	S.	
Lapsley, Thos	2	2	6	Mi	P.
Blair, Samuel	2	1	2	S.	P 5
Bell, John	2		6	S.	
Bell, Samuel	1	2	4	S.	
Brooks, Jas	1	1	4	S.	
Barr, Jno	1		2	S.	
Barr, Wm	1		2	S1	
Craig, Jno	1	4	2	Mi	P.
Coulter, Samuel	1			Mi	D 1
Cunningham, Samuel	1	5	4	Mi	D 1
Cockran, William	1	1		S.	
Chambers, Jos	1			Mi	
Custard, Noah	1			Mi	
Custard, Conrod	1			Mi	
Clark, Wm	1			Mi	
Custard, Benjamin	1	6	1	Mi	
Couch, Henry	1			S.	P.
Crail, Jno	1	2	4	S.	P.
Couch, Jos	1	1	1	S.	
Collins, Daniel	1	1	1	S	
Coal, Solomon	1			S	
Custard, Geo	1			Mi	
Caldoe, Thos	1	2	4	Mi	D
Cameron, Allen	1	1	2	Mi	D
Chambers, John	1	3		Mi	D.
Cully, William	1		2	S.	
Couch, Nathan	2	2	1	S.	
Conner, Jno	1	1	7	S.	P.
Conner, William	1	1	4	S.	P.
Karnahan, David	1	4		S.	
Cockran, William	5	3	3	S.	
Chess, William	2	3	4	S.	
Carr, Jno	3		3	S.	P.
Crawford, Geo	1	4	3	S.	
Draper, Jno	1			S.	
Douthett, Jno	1		2	S.	P.
Douglass, Jno	3	5	2	Mi	
Davison, Josh	1	3	2	Mi	
Dunlavey, Anthy	2	1	3	Mi	

MIFFLIN / ST. CLAIR

Name					
Irwine, Jos	2	3	6	Mi	D
Irwine, Jas	2	3	2	Mi	D
Eaton, Barnabas	1			Mi	
Elliott, William				Mi	D
Elliott, Jas	1			Mi	D.
Irvine, Archibald	2	1	1	S.	
Ferguson, Samuel	1	3	4	Mi	D.
Forsyth, Jas	1	1	2	Mi	D.
Foreman, Thos	1	2	2	Mi	D.
Fletcher, Simon	1		1	Mi	D.
Finney, Andrew	1		1	Mi	
Fulton, William	1	2	3	S.	
Fegan, Jas	1	2	3	S.	D
French, Wm	1		3	S.	
Fife, Jno, Jur	1		2	S.	
Fife, Jno	1		2	S.	P.
Fife, James	1	1	2	S.	
Fife, William	1		3	S.	P.
Fife, Jno	1	6	4	S.	P.
Friend, Isaac	3	3	4	S.	
Feree, Jacob	3	3	7	Mi	D
Foster, Saml	2	1	4	Mi	D
Forgey, Jno	2	3	4	Mi	
French, Robt	1		1	Mi	
Fife, Wm, Jur		4	2	S.	P.
Free, Jno	5	5	3	S.	
Grimes, Andw	4		2	S.	
Giffin, Wm	4	4	3	S.	
Grant, Hugh	1		3	S.	
Gill, Jas	1		2	S.	P
Glass, Saml	1	3	4	Mi	P
Galliher, Lewis	1		1	S.	
Gallaher, James	1		2	Mi	
Gaily, James	1	2	2	S.	
Gilfallin, Alexr	1	1	4	S.	
Gilmore, Jos	1	3	4	S.	D.
Gallaher, William	2		2	Mi	
Gallaher, Ebenezer	2		3	Mi	
Guttshllk, Daniel	1		3	S.	
Gordon, Jno	1	1	3	S.	P.
Gilkeson, Jas	1	2	7	S.	
Holland, Jno	1		3	Mi	
Hays, Abm	3	4	3	Mi	D.
Humbard, Jacob	1	2	3	S.	
Hucheson, Saml	1			S.	
Huffman, Lewis	1	4	3	Mi	P
Hulse, Henry, Jur	1	2	2	S.	
Henry, Wm	1	3	2	S.	
Holliday, Jno	1		1	S.	
Harris, Samuel	1	1	1	S.	
Hind, Jno	1	2	2	S.	
Hill, Adam	1		2	Mi	
Hulse, Henry, Senr	1	2	5	S.	P.
Hulse, Jos	1	2	5	S.	
Henry, Jno	1	4	2	S.	P.
Houy, William	3		3	Mi	
Harris, William	1	1	3	S.	P.
Harvey, William	2	2	4	S.	
Hargan, Michl	3		2	S.	
Jackson, Thos	1		1	S.	
Jones, Jno	1	3	2	S.	
Jewell, Robert	1	4	3	S.	
Johnston, Robert	1	4	3	S.	P.
Kermichael, Jno	1		2	S.	
Kermichael, Thos	1		1	S.	
Kerr, Geo		2		Mi	
Killen, Jno	2		4	Mi	
Kinkead, Saml	1			Mi	
Keykendall, Cobus	2	3	5	Mi	P.
Keykendall, Benjn	3		5	Mi	P.
Keykendall, Henry	1	2	2	Mi	
Keykendall, Sarah	1		3	Mi	
Kennedy, Wm	1		1	Mi	
Kinkead, Jno	1		1	S.	
Kellen, Patt	1		1	S.	
Kennedy, David	1	3	3	S.	
Kairns, Jas	1	3	5	S.	
Keen, Timothy	1	3	3	S.	
McCullen, James	2		2	Mi	D
McCully, Jno	1		2	Mi	
McCully, Robert	1		2	Mi	
McKinney, Jas	1		2	S.	
McGee, Danl	1		1	S.	
McDaniel, Archibald	1	5	3	Mi	
McKee, Jno	1		2	Mi	
McCoy, Hugh	1		3	Mi	
Morris, George	2	1	7	Mi	
McDowell, Jos	2	1	7	Mi	
Mulhullen, Jno	1		2	S.	
McKnitt, Alexr	2	3	4	S.	
McCormcek, Jno	1	3	7	S.	D
McGill, Arthur	1			S.	
Means, Robert	1	4	5	S.	D
McDonald, Robert	1			S.	
McDonald, William	2		5	S.	
McLaughlin, Jno	1		2	S.	D

MIFFLIN / ST. CLAIR

Name					
Miller, Jacob	1	3		S.	D
Metzear, Jno	1		3	Mi	D
McGuire, Danl	1	4		Mi	
McDaniel, Alexr	1		5	Mi	D
McLean, Archibald	1		1	Mi	
McElhany, Thos	1			Mi	
McMahon, Barney	1		6	S.	
Morrison, Matt	2	1	3	Mi	
McCool, Jno	1		4	Mi	
McElhany, Jno	1	3	4	Mi	
Mace, Job	1	1	4	Mi	
Means, Adam	1		2	Mi	
Muskelly, William	1		2	Mi	P.
Mantle, Geo	1	1	2	S.	
McCullough, David	1	1	2	S.	
Manners, Jno	1		5	S.	
Murphy, Edwd	1	2	5	S.	
Millar, Alexander	1	2	7	S.	
Murry, Geo	2		1	S.	P.
McCush, Samuel	1	8	1	S.	
McElway, Barney	1		2	Mi	
Minnis, Hugh	1	3	2	Mi	
Millar, Jas	1		3	Mi	
Millar, Thos	1	5	3	Mi	P.
Murray, John	1	4	4	Mi	P.
McCartney, Robert	1	2	2	Mi	P.
McKneght, Joseph	1	1	1	Mi	
Mount, James	1	1	2	Mi	
McGill, Wm	1		2	Mi	D.
McGill, Jas	1			Mi	D.
McKenzie, Jas	1	2	1	Mi	D.
McBride, James	1		2	Mi	
Morton, Geo	1	2	2	Mi	
McGowen, Chas	1	2	4	Mi	D.
Made, Jno	1		1	S.	
McElroy, David	1		1	S.	
McKee, Robert	1	3	2	S.	P.
Mullin, Jno	1	3	1	S.	
Martin, Jas	2	2	2	S.	P.
Millar, Isaac	2	4	3	S.	P.
Middlesworth, Jacob	1	1	1	S.	
McDowell, Jas	1		2	S.	
Millick, Jacob	1		2	S.	
McDermott, Archibald	2		1	S.	P.
McKean, Martin	1	2	1	S.	
McClean, Robert	1	1	7	S.	
McDermott, Daniel	1		2	Mi	
McDermott, Jno	1		1	Mi	D.
McRoberts, Jas	1		1	Mi	D.
McCool, Jno	1		1	S.	
Mantler, Jno	1		2	Mi	D.
Neal, James	2	3	4	Mi	
Neely, Wm	1	2	1	S.	
Neely, Saml	1	2	1	S.	
Neely, Alexr	1		7	Mi	P.
Nye, Andw	1	1	3	S.	P.
Neely, Thos	1		4	S.	P.
Nevill, Jas	1	1	4	S.	P 18
Phillips, Michl	2	1	2	Mi	
Patterson, Robt	2		2	Mi	P.
Powell, Jno	2	2	3	S.	
Phillips, David	2	1	3	Mi	
Pittegrew, Ed	1		2	S.	
Price, Tristram	1			Mi	
Piercall, Sampson	1	2	3	Mi	P/D
Patterson, Thos	2		2	S.	
Phillips, Benja	1	1	1	S.	
Phillips, Benjn	1		2	S.	P/D
Patterson, Jno	1		2	S.	
Powell, Isaac	2		2	S.	
Phillips, Joseph	2	2	6	S.	7 1
Patterson, Bell	2		3	Mi	
Pearceall, Jno	1	1	3	Mi	P.
Plummer, Nathl	1		2	S.	P.
Riser, Daniel	3	3	3	Mi	D.
Riser, Jno	1	3	3	Mi	D.
Reed, Jno	2	2	2	Mi	D. 4
Robinson, Jno	2		2	S.	
Robbins, Daniel	1	2	3	Mi	P.
Robbins, Amos	1		1	Mi	
Rutherford, Jas	1	3	3	S.	P.
Rigdon, Thos	1		3	S.	P.
Ramsay, Thos	1	2	2	S.	P.
Reed, Paul	3		5	Mi	
Richie, Robert	1	1	4	Mi	
Reed, James	1	2	2	Mi	D
Rouse, Geo	1		2	Mi	D
Ross, Jno	2	2	2	S.	P.
Richardson, Jno	3	3	3	S.	P.
Small, Jno	1		1	Mi	
Spray, Jos	1			Mi	
Snodgrass, Alexander	3		4	Mi	D
Shafer, Lewis	3		3	S.	D
Stewart, Jas	1	2		S.	
Shen, Jno	1			S.	D

NAME OF HEAD OF FAMILY.	Free white males of 16 years and upward, including heads of families.	Free white males under 16 years.	Free white females, including heads of families.	1789 Wash TL
MIFFLIN / ST. CLAIR				
Stewart, Wm	1	1	3	S. D
Stewart, Jno	1	2	1	S.S.
Stewart, Thos	1	3	4	Mi
Stewart, Richd	1	2	2	S.S.
Strawbridge, David	1			P.P.
Bickman, Geo	1	4	7	Mi
Stirling, Hugh	1		1	S.S. P.
Stewart, James	1	1	2	S.S.P.
Stewart, James	1	1	6	Mi
Swaswick, Geo	2	3	5	Mi
Stilley, Tobias	2	1	3	Mi
Shields, Jno	1	1	4	Mi D
Sheriff, Jno	2	1	2	Mi
Smith, Robert	3		2	S.S.
Stone, Jno	1	1	3	S.S. P.
Snodgrass, Robert	1	3	3	S.S.P.
Stoops, James	4	2	2	S.S.P.
Shawhen, Robert	1		2	Mi D
Snodgrass, James	4	1	3	D

NAME OF HEAD OF FAMILY.	Free white males of 16 years and upward, including heads of families.	Free white males under 16 years.	Free white females, including heads of families.	1789 Wash TL
MIFFLIN / ST. CLAIR				
Saunderson, James	1	2	2	Mi D
Test, William	1	3	1	Mi
Thatcher, Jos	2	1	3	Mi
Tiddball, Thos	1	4		Mi P.
Tunnehill, Mitzar	1		1	Mi
Torrence, James	3	3	5	Mi D
Trumbo, Jno	2	2	5	Mi D
Thomas, Elem	2		1	S.S.
Tidball, William	3	1	5	Mi P.
Vandergriff, Samuel	1	1	2	Mi
Whitacre, Aron	1	1	3	Mi D
White, Thos	1	1	3	Mi
West, James	1	1	2	Mi D
Whitacre, Isaac	1	1	1	Mi
Warner, Jno	1		1	Mi 3
Wiley, Christopher	1	1	1	Mi
Witeman, William	1	3	3	S.S. D
Wilson, Benjamin	1		1	S.

NAME OF HEAD OF FAMILY.	Free white males of 16 years and upward, including heads of families.	Free white males under 16 years.	Free white females, including heads of families.	1789 Wash TL
MIFFLIN / ST. CLAIR				
Wright, Edwd	1		1	Mi D
Wright, Zadock	2	2	2	Mi
Walker, Samuel	2	3		Mi
Wilson, Andw	1			Mi
West, Jno	1			Mi
Wilson, Abm	1	2	1	Mi P7D
Wilson, Jno	1		1	Mi
Wilson, William	1	2	1	Mi
Wallace, James	1	1	4	S.S.
Warner, Jno	2			S.S.
Whitacre, Jno	1	3	3	Mi
White, Jno	1		2	Mi
White, Robert	1	5	2	S.S. P.D.
Williams, Isaac	1	1	1	S.S.
Williams, Jno	1	1	4	S.S.
Watson, Jeremiah	1		2	S.S.
Williams, Thos	2		3	S.S. P.
Wright, Robert	1	1	3	Mi
Yager, Jno	1	1	2	Mi

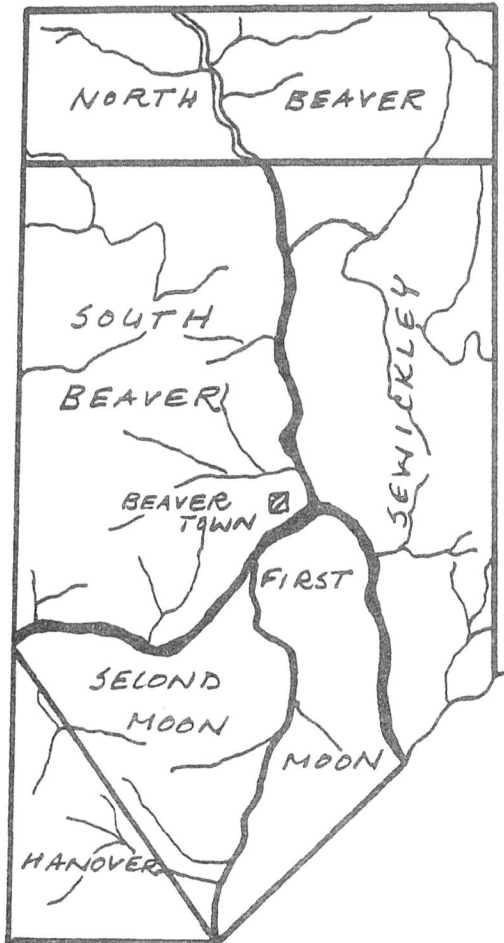

BEAVER COUNTY, PA TOWNSHIPS
IN 1800

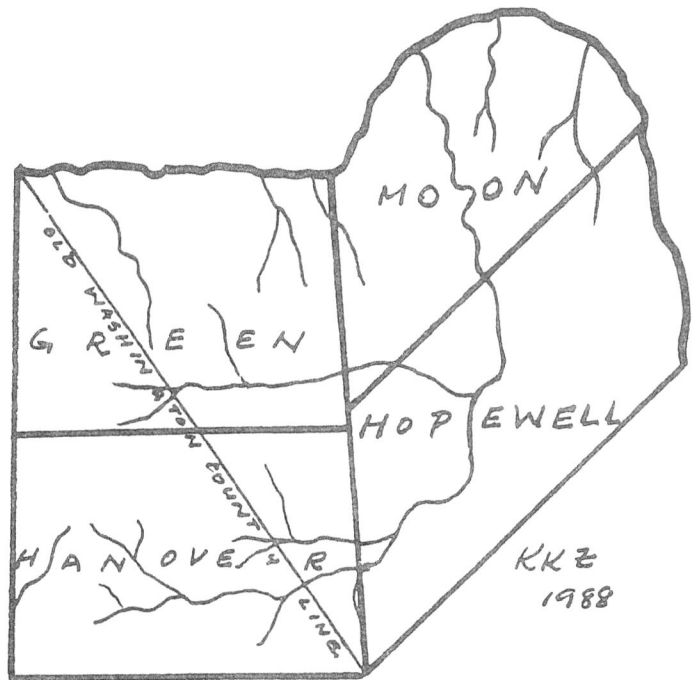

LOWER BEAVER COUNTY, PA TOWNSHIPS
IN 1812

BIBLIOGRAPHY

U.S. Bureau of the Census. Heads of Families at the First Census of the United States Taken in the Year 1790: Pennsylvania. Reprint. Baltimore, MD: Genealogical Publishing Company, 1970. [Originals available on microfilm M637 #9 from National Archives and Record Service, Washington, D.C.]

Pennsylvania Historical and Museum Commission. Tax Lists for Washington County, Pennsylvania 1782-1789, Microfilm RG 4 #340 and 341. Division of Archives and Manuscripts, Box 1026, Harrisburg, PA 17108.

Egle, William Henry, ed. Pennsylvania Archives. Third Series, Vol. XXII. "Effective Supply Tax for the County of Washington, 1781" pp. 699-782. "Return of Taxables in the County of Allegheny, 1791" pp. 643-679. Harrisburg, PA: Wm. Stanley Ray, State Printer, 1897.

Library of Congress. 1794 Allegheny County, Pennsylvania Tax List. MSS 16804, p. 371.

Wall, Elizabeth J. A General List of the Taxables in Allegheny County, Pennsylvania. Pittsburgh, PA: Privately printed, 1987. [author: 310 Scotia St, Pittsburgh, PA 15205]

SOURCES FOR MAPS

Crumrine, Boyd. History of Washington County, Pennsylvania. Philadelphia: L.H. Everts & Co., 1882. p. 476-477 "Facsimile of the Edward Lynch Plan of the Town of Washington, 1784".

Bausman, Rev. Joseph H. History of Beaver County, Pennsylvania. Vol. II. "Draft E. Showing Townships of Beaver County at Date of Its Erection (1800)" p. 864. "Draft H. Draft of Four Townships Situated South of the Ohio River, 1812" p. 880. New York: Knickerbocker Press, 1904.

Hennen, Dorothy T. Cemetery Records of Greene County, Pennsylvania. Vol. 6 "Greene County, Pennsylvania", frontispiece. Parsons, WV: McClain Printing Co., 1976.